FLOWERS OF GREECE
and the Aegean

FLOWERS OF
GREECE

AND THE AEGEAN

by

Anthony Huxley *and* William Taylor

*With 483 colour illustrations
from photographs and 77 line drawings by*
Victoria Gordon

1977
CHATTO & WINDUS
LONDON

Published by
Chatto and Windus Ltd
40 William IV Street
London WC2N 40F

*

Clarke, Irwin & Co Ltd
Toronto

Hardback ISBN 0 7011 2190 4
Paperback ISBN 0 7011 2228 5

PRINTED IN GREAT BRITAIN
BY RICHARD CLAY (THE CHAUCER PRESS) LTD
BUNGAY, SUFFOLK

CONTENTS

Illustration References. Please see note on page 4.

ACKNOWLEDGEMENTS

Many people have helped and encouraged us with this book, and we are indeed grateful to all these.

Mr Desmond Meikle of the Herbarium, Royal Botanic Gardens, Kew, has resolved many botanical points, confirmed identification of certain specimens and photographs, assisted the artist Miss Victoria Gordon, and generally given positive encouragement, and we are particularly grateful for his readily given support. Mr Brian Mathew, also of Kew, gave detailed help on the latest botanical thinking on Monocotyledons, which has been supplemented by his colleague Mr Chris Grey-Wilson, and by Mr C. D. Brickell, Director of the R.H.S. Gardens, Wisley.

Our own photographs have been augmented with those of several friends, to whom warm thanks are due, as follows.

Mr Ivor Barton, 80, 158, 190, 280, 351, 352, 353, 354, 394, 395. Mrs Felicity Baxter, 34, 86, 148, 183, 262, 284, 385, 403, 404. Mr C. D. Brickell, 22, 28, 73, 100, 104, 105, 126, 129, 191, 194, 209, 213, 321, 325, 329, 330, 380, 381. Mr Herbert Crook, 25, 27, 57, 70, 72, 131, 149, 160, 162, 168, 216, 224, 250, 309, 326, 359, 363, 364, 391, 396, 399, 410, 421, 422, 449.

Mr Peter Green, 101, 119. Mr Roy Lancaster, 94, 103, 118, 159, 179, 180, 270, 412. Mr Oleg Polunin, 481. Mr George Sfikas, 33, 85, 132, 152, 163, 207, 336, 337, 338, 339, 348. Mr Allan Smith, 23, 383, 400. Mr Dennis Woodland, 117, 167, 210, 237, 282, 363. In addition I have been able to use four photographs by my late friend Mrs Mimette Wardle.

Margaret Taylor collaborated nobly in typing the initial drafts; Alyson Huxley also did some typing, plotted the weather graphs in 'Geography and Climate', and assisted with the illustration layout. Denys Baker drew the maps.

INTRODUCTION

Over many years both authors have paid numerous visits to Greece and its islands. Between us we have been to most of the botanically interesting areas of the country, at varying seasons, recording and photographing plants.

From our joint experiences developed the desire to produce a book, partly to help others to identify the Greek wild flowers, and also to describe the terrain in which they grow and the plant communities most often to be seen.

Our book therefore falls into three main parts. The first chapters describe Greece in general and different communities in particular, under the headings Sea Shore, Hillsides, Mountains and Islands, and not forgetting flowers of the Ancient Sites.

Following these more or less narrative chapters there are 64 pages of colour plates, the first six showing views of countryside to give some idea of the enormous variety of scenery and interest in this relatively small country. The remaining colour plates contain 471 photographic portraits of some 452 species and forms of plant, occasionally in both flower and fruit or in varying colour forms.

The remainder of the book is taken up with plant descriptions, both of those illustrated in colour and of a number of others which are common or interesting enough to merit inclusion. These latter include a number of trees and other plants difficult to show effectively in colour, as well as some of which no good photograph was available. To aid identification 77 of these are illustrated in line drawings by Miss Victoria Gordon, mostly from specimens in the Herbarium of the Royal Botanic Gardens, Kew.

The descriptions have been written in the simplest possible way, avoiding technical terms almost entirely. They are not full botanical descriptions, but are, we hope, adequate to confirm to the reader that he has made an accurate identification of a given plant compared with one of the illustrations. 660 species, sub-species and forms are described in all.

To many of the descriptions are added notes on the uses and importance of the plants in antiquity and today, and references to mythology where appropriate. These 'postscripts' come largely from the pages of Theophrastus' *Enquiry into Plants* and Dioscorides' *Herbal*, more details of which are given in chapter 8, 'Reference Books'.

Our choice of plants has been based very much on our observations. It seemed to us that, after so many visits to different areas and at different seasons, the plants we had seen reasonably frequently would also be those likely to be seen by the average visitor. Moreover, one of us has escorted several botanical tours to Greece, which provided a good idea of which plants arouse interest, and those that do not. Because of the habitual lack of interest, as well as difficulty of identification, we have therefore omitted almost all grasses, all the sedges, rushes, and ferns.

At the same time, we have included a number of less common or even rare plants, for instance some alpine endemics, which only the fairly adventurous will see. However, none of the localities in which we have seen these plants are difficult of access to the reasonably energetic walker.

The plants described include a number of non-natives which have been grown for long enough to have become naturalised in the wild on occasion. We have followed the views of *Flora Europaea* in this respect. Some other exotic plants often grown for decoration, but never naturalising themselves, are mentioned in chapter 7.

The Botanical Basis

Most of the plants mentioned in this book were initially identified, from specimens collected and pressed by one of us, by one of the major botanical institutions, and the descriptions have been based where possible upon such specimens.

The nomenclature follows in the main that adopted by *Flora Europaea*, in which European botanists have attempted a consensus of opinion (see also page 58). At the time of going to press the first three volumes of this have been published. However, we have been able to see proofs of Volume 4 and have had advice on the probable treatment of groups to be covered in Volume 5 (Monocotyledons).

Where we have, very occasionally, departed from the decisions of *Flora Europaea* this has either been on the advice of botanists following later research, or to simplify taxonomic problems which do not need to concern amateur botanists. Where such simplification has been made this is noted in the descriptive text. In any case, where well-known names have been superseded, for whatever reason, these are always given in the text as synonyms.

The order of families, and genera within them, again follows that of *Flora Europaea* to date. This is the Englerian order, largely used on the Continent but less familiar to the amateur in Britain where floras are usually based on the system of Bentham & Hooker. The sequence of genera of Monocotyledons follows that of Rechinger (*Flora Aegaea*) in the absence of the final volume of *Flora Europaea*.

The order of *Orchidaceae* in our book follows that of Clapham, Tutin & Warburg in *Flora of the British Isles*, while the botanical detail of the genera *Ophrys* and *Serapias* are based on Erich Nelson's monographs of 1962 and 1968.

One might add that a botanical order of families and genera broadly reflects its author's view of evolutionary development, and points up close relationships. However, the evolutionary record of plants is partly a matter of surmise, and taxonomic botanists differ in their views of family relationships, so an order can never be said to be definitive.

Plant families fall into three main groups, the Gymnosperms (literally 'naked-seeded'), which include all the plants broadly known as conifers (pines, junipers, etc.); and the two groups of Angiosperms ('enclosed-seeded' flowering plants), namely the Dicotyledons and Monocotyledons. These words refer to the number of cotyledons or seed-leaves. In very general terms the leaves of dicotyledons have netted veining; the flowers usually have clearly defined, green outer sepals or calyx and coloured inner petals or corolla; and the flower parts are most often in fours, fives, or indefinite numbers. The monocotyledons have parallel leaf veins and flower parts typically in threes or sixes, the sepals usually resembling the petals.

Within genera we have, for ease of reference, placed the species described in alphabetical order except in a very few cases where some subdivision has been made in complicated genera (e.g. *Crocus*).

The names of botanical authorities (normally shown abbreviated after the botanical names in technical floras) have been omitted in this volume except on one or two occasions where required for clarification; our view being that they are not important to the average flower-lover and merely clutter up a simple text. (In this we have had the encouragement of some senior botanists.)

It is perhaps desirable to expand on the categories of plant classification, since these often puzzle amateurs. The *family* is a group of plants in which certain characters – almost always those of the flower – are readily differentiated from those of other families. Within the family there are *genera* (singular *genus*), subsidiary groups (sometimes of only a single plant) which again each have a similar structure and can be considered to have developed from a common ancestor. The members of a genus are called *species* (abbreviated sp. for one species, spp. for more than one), which are basically constant entities which breed true (whereas breeding between two species, if it occurs, results in a *hybrid* which is different from both parents).

Botanists often wish to subdivide species even further where there is much variation, or there are, say, kinds which differ in flower colour, or in habit of growth, but are not sufficiently distinct to merit separate specific rank. The categories include *sub-species* (ssp., sspp.) or *varietates* (varieties, abbreviated var.), and sometimes *formae* (forms). Whether the breakdown is into sub-species or varieties depends largely on the botanist responsible for studying the group; in some cases opinions differ even as to whether plants deserve specific rank or should be classed as sub-species. This is especially marked, among the plants mentioned in this book, in the genus *Ophrys* of the Orchid family. The status given to some of these entities (or *taxa* as the botanist calls them) is our interpretation of modern botanical thinking, which often varies from one authority to another. In such difficult cases some part of the name at least will usually be constant, i.e. *Ophrys sphegodes ssp. attica* is the same as *Ophrys attica*.

The metric system has been used for plant dimensions and altitude measurements, in accordance with modern practice.

The Illustrations and Descriptive Text

The colour pictures, which occupy a 64-page block between pages 58 and 59, are numbered in sequence. 1 to 12 are views of terrain, and 13 to 483 plant portraits.

Further plants are depicted in line drawings numbered from 484 to 560, a total of 77. The first 31 of these are embodied in five full-page plates on pages 59 to 63; the remainder are in the descriptive text.

References to the illustrations are given by bold numerals after the text descriptions. Where the drawing is on one of the five plates mentioned above, the text page number is also given; those in the descriptive text are normally adjacent to the written description.

The views of terrain (plates 1 to 12) are cited in Chapters 2 to 6 by numerals in brackets.

Unfortunately it has been impossible, for technical reasons, to provide a direct reference from plates to text; the names of the plant illustrated should be sought in the index where the text page reference is given.

It must be added that the order of the colour illustrations does not always exactly follow that of the text. This is due to problems of layout, in which the use of illustrations of different shapes and sizes, and at different magnifications from the originals, often made it impossible to follow the order strictly. However, every effort has been made to group close relations together. Approximate scale indications are given on the colour plates.

After each plant description the symbol ✳ is followed by a note of typical habitat, localities, and the months when the plant is normally in flower. Localities are only given when the plant's range in Greece is restricted: no attempt has been made to specify relative rarity nor even endemic species, except in a few cases where the word 'only' implies restriction to the locality cited.

Note on Place Names

Greek place names vary from map to map, guide-book to guide-book, and sometimes from one signpost to the next. In many cases the variations are only in spelling, the Greeks naturally tending to use spellings which approximate closely to the word in Greek characters, and the British those which have become generally accepted in English literature. In our text and on the maps we have had to select a set of spellings which seemed to be in reasonably general English usage, though some are inevitably arbitrary. It may, however, be helpful to list here some important places with alternative names which cannot be easily recognised:

Corfu = Kerkyra	*Lesbos = Mytilene*
Euboea = Evvia	*Salonika = Thessaloniki*
Ida = Psiloriti	*Santorini = Thira*
Ioannina = Janina	*Thebes = Thivai*
Kythnos = Thermia	*Zante = Zakynthos*

1. GEOGRAPHY AND CLIMATE

Greece is a country marvellously rich in flowers: it has a flora of at least 6,000 species, many of them endemic, and many more are certainly still to be found and described. But mere lists of plant names mean little without some understanding of the setting in which each plant grows, including the characteristic plant communities in which each takes its place. So it becomes essential at the outset to look at the geography of their home, the climates in which they live, and some of the factors which have produced the unequalled flora of Greece as we see it today.

Greece lies in the south of the most easterly of the three great peninsulas of southern Europe, with the Italian and Iberian peninsulas lying to the west. All three are bounded to the south by the Mediterranean sea, and all three show important features in common: notably the climate, which will be described later, and which, with the Mediterranean providing the common link, has from the dawn of history provided ideal conditions for human life and civilisation.

The Balkan peninsula, however, of which Greece forms a part, differs from the Italian and the Iberian peninsulas in the absence of a high mountain barrier between it and the rest of Europe. The Balkan peninsula, in fact, can be described as having a broad base, set in the Balkans to the north, which is geographically and climatically part of Central Europe, and shares the Central European flora; while the southern part of the peninsula, including most of Greece, enjoys a Mediterranean climate, and has a Mediterranean type of flora. Parts of northern Greece, including southern Macedonia, Thrace, and parts of Thessaly, show geographical and climatic features intermediate between those of Central Europe and the Mediterranean.

Although most visitors today enter Greece by air, landing at Athens, geographically the ideal way to do so is by the old route from the north – by road or rail through Yugoslavia. During this journey, the physical features of south-east Europe come alive: the Dinaric mountain system continues the geologically young Alps of Austria through southern Yugoslavia; they lie on the far southern horizon as the way crosses the vast Yugoslav plain. Further east this great mountain system passes through Albania to Epirus in Greece, and then across the gulf of Corinth to the Peloponnese, at last reappearing in distant Crete.

The route to the north of Greece, having left the Danube at Belgrade, follows a tortuous way through the high barren limestone country of south-east Yugoslavia to reach the valley of the river Vardar which, together with other rivers rising in the mountains of the geologically ancient Rodope massif of the Balkans, enters the Aegean sea along the coast from Thrace to Thessaly. This old route to Salonika, the northern gate to Greece, is time-consuming, yet rewarding in the understanding it gives of the broad area of bare rugged uplands in the Balkans between Central

Europe and Greece – a great barrier between the Central European and the Mediterranean floras.

From Salonika there is another day's travel to Athens; starting across the flat rich plains of Thessaly where the great cornfields are often scarlet with poppies. There Thessalian Olympos raises its great mass, often cloud-topped, but sometimes showing its snow-capped peak against the blue sky, which gains in intensity as one travels southwards. Mount Ossa lies across the vale of Tempe on the seaward side, and Pelion still further south, before the railway begins its climb into the eastern foothills of the Pindos range, finally descending to the smaller plain of diminished Thebes. Late in the day there is Parnassos to the west, snow-streaked in spring, with its pine forests black against the snow, and we know that Mount Parnes and Athens itself are close.

The other approach to Greece from western Europe is by sea, and this too has its advantages. From Trieste, Venice, or Ancona ships sail down the Adriatic, and soon offer glimpses of the Dinaric Alps. Before long there are the Ionian islands, Corfu, Cephalonia, Zante, their sharp-contoured rocky heights rising from the blue Aegean – they seem what in fact they are, the weathered peaks of almost submerged mountains. For here is manifest the result of the cataclysm during the Tertiary geological epoch when the Mediterranean first penetrated into an ancient Aegean land mass, engulfing it; first up to the line of the Cyclades and the Dodecanese, and later into the Pontic basin up to the coast of Thessaly and Thrace. This vast inundation, resulting in the drowning of much of the old Aegean peninsula, took place gradually, and was not complete until geologically recent times, certainly after the last Ice Age.

So one sails past the high cliffs of these nearly-submerged mountains, brilliantly outlined in the hard clear light of Greece, and approaches the harbour of Patras at the north-western tip of the Peloponnese. Here the Gulf of Corinth opens up – originally a geological fault in the southward line of the Dinaric mountain system, later flooded by the sea, and now, thanks to the short man-made Corinth canal at its eastern end, an important shipping route.

If one follows the main road from Patras to Athens through Corinth, there lies to the north, across the gulf, a noble range of mountains, many of them snow-capped up to late spring, with Parnassos and Helicon outstanding. South of the road rise steeply the mountains of the central Peloponnese, further continuations of the Dinaric system, with Eryman-thos, Chelmos, and Killini among their finest northern peaks. Mount Taygetos lies far to the south, like a backbone to the Peloponnese. The coastal plains of the Peloponnese lie mostly in the north-west and west, with smaller plains on the southern and eastern coasts, where rich vineyards, orange and lemon groves, and farms produce their fruit and vegetables for the easily accessible Athens market.

So, by using one of the older and more leisurely approaches to Greece from the west, it is possible to obtain a clearer picture of the geographical setting of the country and a more coherent picture of what must seem at first acquaintance a confused and intricate geography of mountains, peaks, plains, islands, and gulfs. Once in Greece, travelling by car or the universal, comfortable, and always punctual national bus services, the physical geography of Greece will grow ever more clear and more fascinating.

Something must be said of the soils of Greece, for these of course play a part in determining the local plant life. The limestones and their soil, which is often red (*terra rossa*), are predominant throughout the Balkan peninsula including Greece; in the Mediterranean climatic zone of Greece the slowness of the weathering process is partly due to the seasonal distribution of the rainfall, and partly to the absence or rarity of frost. This accounts for the great areas of exposed limestone which is so striking an element in the classical Greek landscape. The soil in these predominantly limestone areas is alkaline and rich in mineral salts, though often shallow and subject to much loss from the rainfall which, when it occurs, is frequently heavy.

The soils derived from the breakdown of the older crystalline rocks are varied in nature, basic or neutral in reaction, and poor in mineral content. Crystalline schists and sometimes deep sand and conglomerate areas also occur outside the limestone zones.

Although soil reaction is of relatively minor importance in determining the make-up of plant life in Greece, it certainly plays some part. Notable examples are seen in the preference of Ericaceous genera for acid or neutral soils, and one may see very large areas of *Erica arborea*, sometimes growing with *Arbutus* species, covering hill and mountain sides in some non-limestone areas.

Important as are the physical features of the Greek terrain in determining the nature of its plant life, it is the climate which is by far the most important factor. As we have seen, the north of Greece forms part of the base of the Balkan peninsula, and shares to some degree its Central European climate, with severe winters followed by hot summers and a rainfall more evenly distributed through the year than in the Mediterranean zone, although dry periods in summer are common; snow is frequent in winter. Southwards through Greece the climate changes progressively to the Mediterranean type with its warm winters, wet from a succession of low pressure systems which pass through the Mediterranean from west to east; the summers are hot and dry.

It is this climate which has produced the 'Mediterranean' flora, composed of plants adapted to its special features. These adaptations in the plant life include a high proportion of evergreen species, which ensures that photosynthesis continues through the winter; in the Mediterranean domain this is not a period of rest for the plants but of continuous growth. In the long hot dry summers, during which strong winds often blow persistently, the danger to plant life is excessive desiccation. Against this, protective modifications have developed, such as thick leathery leaves, densely felted hairs covering leaves and often stems, or the tendency to produce narrow tough spines and prickles, all of which help to diminish evaporation –

though they may have the incidental effect of making walking neither easy nor comfortable in the 'macchie' of the Grecian hills. These are all familiar features of plant life throughout the Mediterranean countries generally, but are often seen in extreme form in Greece.

While the characteristic flora is basically similar throughout the whole Mediterranean area, both in the broad pattern of its plant communities, and in the genera and many of the species forming these communities, there are marked differences in the details of the flora as one follows the Mediterranean from west to east. These differences are most striking in Greece itself, the most easterly of European Mediterranean countries and therefore the closest to Asia. It is this Greek proximity to Asia, so obvious in the eastern Aegean islands, which has given the Greek flora much of its special character. It must be borne in mind that, before the comparatively recent formation of the Aegean sea, Greece was in fact part of a broad peninsula of Asia Minor, so that the formation of the Greek flora was freely influenced from the east. Another important factor influencing the Greek flora is that much of Greece, by its geographical position, was largely shielded from the effects of the Ice Ages. In consequence much of the pre-glacial flora has survived. Further, the relative isolation of some mountains and many islands in Greece has produced plant enclaves where species threatened with extinction elsewhere have persisted, and these special conditions have also favoured the development of endemic species, and much variation in already existing species.

To illustrate the wide differences at the present day in the temperatures and rainfall levels in the various areas of Greece, graphs are given on pages 10 and 11 for various centres, details of which are as follows.

Crete (Herakleion) exemplifies the Mediterranean climate in its most striking form, with a very dry summer, a rainfall almost restricted to the winter months, with regular winter snowfalls in the mountains and with periods in the summer of very hot dry sand-laden winds (sirocco) from North Africa.

Patras, at the north-west tip of the Peloponnese, shows the higher rainfall of western Greece, this being even more striking in the Ionian islands still further to the west.

Athens represents the temperatures and rainfalls of much of mainland Greece. The Cyclades are not widely different, though sea winds, including the often stormy 'etesian' winds, keep the summer temperature somewhat lower.

Salonika, in southern Macedonia, has a climate intermediate between Mediterranean and Central European, with cold winters, frequent snowfalls, and strong northerly 'Vardar' winds, as well as a heavier, rather more evenly distributed rainfall than Athens.

A simple and very obvious indication of the type of climate prevailing in any particular area is the olive. The presence of this lovely tree is an infallible sign that one is in the Mediterranean vegetational zone. Athene's tree, so much a part of the Greek landscape, is found throughout the whole

9

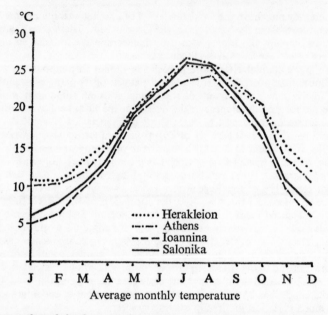

Average monthly temperature

country, though in the central, western, and northern mountainous areas of the Pindos, Epirus, and Macedonia, it is restricted to coastal or lower hill areas.

Man's influence on the flora of Greece is shown most clearly in the scarcity of true forests. Since the earliest human settlement in Greece, deforestation has been taking place by tree felling for the provision of timber for house or boat building, and of wood as fuel or for production of charcoal; and regeneration by natural seeding has been prevented by intensive grazing, since antique times, by sheep and goats, voracious herds of which can be seen today grazing in every lowland area, on every hillside and every mountain in Greece. The result after so many thousand years has been the predominant low-growing brushwood whose composition we will be analysing later.

True forest is rare, and mostly confined to the higher mountains, where the Greek Fir *Abies cephalonica* may cover quite extensive areas, sometimes accompanied by the Black Pine *Pinus nigra*, as on Olympos and elsewhere. The Aleppo Pine *Pinus halepensis*, so characteristic a tree of the Mediterranean area, is both handsome and common, often growing singly or in scattered clumps, but sometimes forming woods at any height from sea level up to about 1,000 m. Sweet Chestnut, *Castanea sativa*, is another characteristic native tree of the south-eastern Mediterranean area, and forms woods here and there in Greece where it may be seen on the slopes of Mount Pelion, in southern Epirus, and elsewhere. The evergreen oaks,

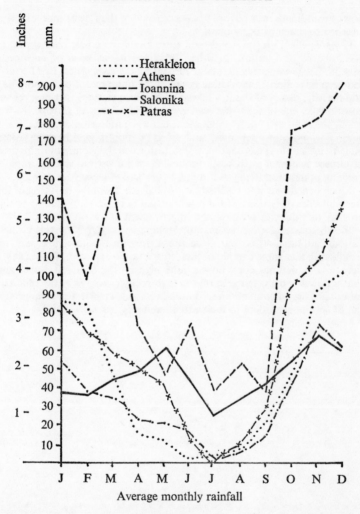

Average monthly rainfall

often growing more as shrubs than trees, are characteristic of the brush-wood on the hill slopes, but deciduous species, of which the Valonia Oak *Quercus aegilops*, sometimes accompanied by *Q. lanuginosa*, are examples, may form true woods on the Grecian hills. Beech woods, so frequent on the limestone of Central Europe, are seen in the north of Greece, but do not extend south of Thessaly. All these woods and forests are of quite limited extent, and it is much to be hoped that the judicious re-afforestation, which is now proceeding, and some control of grazing to allow natural regenera-

11

tion of woodland, may restore to Greece some of the forests that long ago adorned so much of her mountains.

If man's effect on the woods and forests of Greece has, over the ages, been one of devastation, in other directions it has been of enormous benefit. The great low-lying plains formed by the river deltas in Thessaly, southern Macedonia, and Thrace were in the quite recent past undrained and marshy, places of shallow lakes and brackish swamps. It was a region notorious as one of the worst endemic malarial centres of Europe, with a small, sick, and dwindling population; but now, following drainage of the land, anti-mosquito schemes, and effective public health supervision, modern agricultural methods have so transformed the picture that this area of Greece is now a great grain-producing centre with a healthy, rapidly growing population living in thriving towns and villages.

Much benefit has also resulted, as we shall see, from the terracing of the steep hillsides of Greece, with a resulting halt in the natural process of soil erosion, and the conservation and improvement of the precious soil.

In subsequent sections we shall be looking at the Greek flowers in their various habitats and typical associations through the flowering year, remembering that some overlap occurs; thus a flower typical of the sea shore may, and sometimes does, flower quite high on the hillsides above; and that a flower most often seen on the high rocky outcrops of the hills and mountains may also sometimes be found on the sea cliffs. A general grouping of species according to their usual habitat is, however, valid.

2. FLOWERS OF THE SEA SHORE

Sea shore flowers, in whatever country they grow, have a very special charm which is derived in part from their natural setting near the ever-changing sea. Many of the plants show remarkable adaptations to the special conditions in which they live. Furthermore, the effect of the sea has been, through the ages, to provide a relatively stable and equable climate with protection from extremes of temperature, so enabling species to survive eras such as the Ice Ages when plant life over huge areas was severely affected. The distribution of many sea shore plants is therefore very wide, and it may come as a surprise to see, flowering on the shores of Greece, a number of species equally at home on the coasts of northern Europe.

In Greece the sight and sound of the sea are never far away; the coast-line is long and infinitely varied, so that the land may meet the sea along wide sandy beaches, often backed by low cliffs; at the margin of wet marshy plains; along the steep stony or pebbly beaches so painful to the feet of bathers; or, as happens so often, where hills and mountains descend in steep cliffs into the blue depths (12). There are, in fact, nearly 10,000 miles of coast-line in Greece.

Coastal plains, as we have seen, are the exception in Greece and, where they do exist, tend to be narrow and intensively cultivated. Salt marshes are uncommon, though they do occur, and may carry dense thickets of Tamarisk mingled with the Giant Reed *Arundo donax* (11). Extensive sand dunes are rare.

The trees of these zones are characteristic. The Aleppo Pine *Pinus hale-pensis* grows singly, in small groups, or is often planted deliberately in little plantations, and thrives even at sea level. The Stone or Umbrella Pine *P. pinea* is not a common tree in Greece; it suffered greatly in the age-old search for timber, and the only surviving natural woods of this unmistakable pine are seen on the shores of the west coast of the Peloponnese. The tall, gravely handsome Cypress *Cupressus sempervirens* is common on the lower slopes of many hills as they climb from the sea, being often planted in ones or twos, and sometimes seeds itself. This cypress is most probably a true native of Greece in some areas, notably in Crete and in the eastern Aegean islands such as Samos.

Another fine native tree, the Eastern Plane *Platanus orientalis*, forms dense natural woodland along the hill streams of Samos and other eastern islands as they hurry on their way across the little coastal plains to the nearby sea. With the plane grows the White Poplar *Populus alba*, especially beautiful in early spring when its graceful pure white trunks and branches are outlined against the blue sky. On the sea shore itself, often rooting in almost pure sand, and seemingly enjoying the salt spray, grows the Tamarisk in one or more of the six species native in Greece, their bark varying with the species from red-brown to black, slender-branched, pink or white with a profusion of the little flowers which are produced at any time from spring to autumn, though most abundantly in early spring.

It is necessary to emphasise that, in order to see many of the flowers of Greece, and perhaps especially those that grow near the sea, it is desirable to be there in the early part of the year, between March and May. It must be admitted that even the inviting Aegean sea is not at its warmest, but there are many advantages in a spring visit to Greece; not only in the profusion of flowers, unsuspected by those who only see Greece in the heat of summer, but also in the absence of crowds, the ease of obtaining accommodation, and the greater comfort of travel, making a few degrees difference in the sea temperature a small price to pay.

In spring, then, the sand of the average beach will be rosy pink with the gay little flowers of *Silene colorata*, interspersed with the clustered lemon-yellow heads of the dwarf *Medicago marina*, belonging to the pink and pea families respectively. The combination of these two species will be repeated on mile after mile of Grecian beaches. Not so profuse as these two species, but equally charming, and growing with them, is the dwarf white-woolly *Anthemis tomentosa*, with large white orange-centred flowers. On the rocks of the shore, and in the crevices of the sea cliffs, flowers *Malcolmia flexuosa*, unaffected by spray from the waves which in early spring will still be whipped up by storms. Its large lilac and white crucifer flowers, set low among the dark green and fleshy leaves, light up the dark rocks, especially in the eastern Greek islands where it may replace the related Virginian Stock *M. maritima*, so abundant on the sandy shores further west.

From early March onwards these first spring flowers of the sea shore are joined by others in a rapidly growing stream. On low cliffs the first ground orchids are beginning to flower – golden *Ophrys lutea* and dark-lipped *O. fusca*; while little indigo-flowered *Muscari commutatum* is everywhere. Here too are the small brown and green Monk's Cowls of the arum-like *Arisarum vulgare*. Back on the sea shore itself the Sea Stock *Matthiola sinuata* will be producing its first heads of rosy lilac flowers, dwarf at this time of year, sitting on their rosettes of wavy-edged grey leaves. Its larger relation, the Great Sea Stock *M. incana*, is already producing its reddish-purple flowers from woody-based plants on the sea cliffs and on the shore below where it so often seeds itself.

The first of the spring flood of annuals are already in bloom on the edges of the fields and vineyards that back the sea shore, and on every path side. The great golden suns of the Crown Daisy *Chrysanthemum coronarium* are there, as everywhere in Greece from the overgrown building sites of Athens to these remote and lovely sea cliffs. With them will be the various blues and reds of *Echium plantagineum* and the lupins *Lupinus angustifolius*, *L. albus ssp. graecus* and *L. micranthus*; the tall white spikes of the mignonette *Reseda alba*, the purple salsify *Tragopogon porrifolius*, and *Tordylium apulum* with its delicate white umbels. Vetches are there too in profusion, with purple and white *Vicia dasycarpa* climbing, scrambling and colourful on the cliffs, where it is joined by the dwarfer pale yellow *V. hybrida*.

Another handsome pea, *Pisum elatius*, with red and purple flowers, climbs and scrambles in and over low bushes and herbage on the cliffs and up the hillsides. *Malva sylvestris*, the common mallow, with its rosy purple flowers, abounds in every piece of waste land, and the geranium family provides the storksbill *Erodium gruinum*, distinguished not by its pale purple flowers but by the fantastically long-beaked fruits. Another common and attractive annual of Greece, flowering from early March onwards, is the Honeywort *Cerinthe major*, a variable plant whose leafy stems carry large, drooping tubular flowers of a creamy yellow. As the name implies it is a flower much worked by honey bees. One cannot fail to notice also the coarse-growing white henbane *Hyoscyamus albus* with its greenish-white flowers, and the Squirting Cucumber *Ecballium elaterium*, with small yellow flowers to be followed later by explosive fruits. Both plants flourish on cliff tops, in waste places, and on rubbish dumps.

Early in the year, in the rushy, sometimes marshy little plains which here and there lie between sea and hills, there is water still in the stony beds of the streams which rise high in the overlooking hills, and also in the ditches which drain the small fields. There grows the giant reed, *Arundo donax*, both decorative and useful. Also in such places, in the rough grassy waste-land just behind the sandy shore, where no one comes but the shepherds with their shaggy wild-looking and long-horned herds of goats and sheep, watched over by fierce sheep dogs, is one of the loveliest of the narcissus tribe, *Narcissus tazetta*. In such a deserted place, in distant Samos, thousands of this narcissus bearing their heads of heavily perfumed flowers – perianths of palest yellow, cups of a light orange – swayed in the warm light sea breezes of earliest March.

On gravelly spits of land lying between sea and marsh, relics of old stream beds provide well drained scree-like conditions which favour certain plants. Among these are the grey-leaved spreading *Alkanna tinctoria* or Dyer's Alkanet, covered with its heads of sky-blue flowers, and wide mats of the blue form of pimpernel *Anagallis arvensis*, studded with flowers of deepest blue.

The sea cliffs have a flora of their own, and these plants and their flowers are displayed to particular advantage in such a setting where every beauty of flower, leaf, and growth form can be appreciated against their rocky background without the distraction of surrounding and encroaching plants. This cliff flora is wonderfully evident in late March at Nauplia in the Peloponnese, a small port to whose massive stone quays little shipping now comes, where the town is Venetian rather than Greek, where the imposing Italianate building, which in olden days served as warehouse for the Venetian merchants, now houses one of the finest and best displayed of the smaller museums of local antiquities in all Greece. The Venetian fortress, set on the precipitous summit of a vertical hill, guards the town, and looks beyond it across an almost land-locked gulf. In the often unruffled blue of the sea are reflected the surrounding high mountains of the Peloponnese, snow-capped at this early season of the year.

15

To see the cliff flowers, take a path which follows the base of a small promontory east of the harbour. In the rock crevices grows *Campanula rupestris*, whose radiating stems carry small grey-green leaves and handsome bells of a clear lavender blue. Here also is Golden Drop *Onosma frutescens*, a bristly plant forming wide curtains of growth hanging from the vertical rock, and whose ornate yellow tubular flowers are already opening in late March. The related *Alkanna baeotica ssp. graeca* is here too, with bright yellow trumpets, and so is *Euphorbia acanthothamnos*, its prickly, tightly woven cushions moulded to the rock, small yellow flowers scattered over the light green foliage. Higher up the cliff the tree spurge *E. dendroides* carries its yellow inflorescences on tall woody branches. Below the sheer cliff, on sandy banks above the sea, grows the earliest of the Greek verbascums, *Verbascum undulatum*, producing spikes of light yellow flowers from rosettes of wavy-margined leaves.

From Nauplia a bus leaves each morning for the villages along the most easterly peninsula of the Peloponnese. It follows a leisurely and tortuous course through hilly, even mountainous country south of Epidauros, bare, high, and rocky, till there begins the long descent to the coastal plain, with the sea blue in the distance between the hills, and off-shore islands coming into view. On this coastal plain, in late March, is flowering *Tulipa boeotica*, perhaps the most splendidly handsome of all the Greek tulips, carrying its great scarlet purple-throated flowers on tall stems above blue-green wavy-edged leaves. It is here in its thousands, growing in the early cornfields in the heavy wet soil of the plain, and spreading up to the lower slopes of the juniper-covered limestone hills, where nothing else grows but a host of ground orchids.

By the end of March early spring is over, the main flowering of the plants of Greece has already begun, and will continue through April and much of May. The coast of Greece in mid-May provides a magnificent display of flowers. On the sand and the pebble beaches the Sea Stock will still be flowering, but taller and bushier than it was in early March. With it will be an old friend of northern coasts, the Yellow Horned Poppy *Glaucium flavum*, with its large silky yellow flowers. Here too is the scarlet poppy *Papaver rhoeas* which, though it abounds in every situation in Greece, is particularly splendid when it grows among the white stones and sand of the sea shore. With luck one may see the spiny chicory *Cichorium spinosum*, with fleshy stems and pale blue flowers.

On the cliffs above the shore is flowering in full splendour the Spanish Broom *Spartium junceum*, its almost leafless wands closely set with large flowers of deepest gold. With it grows the Greek Sage *Salvia triloba*, tall spikes of purple flowers above lobed grey leaves, aromatic in the heat. Sweet-scented Myrtle grows here often, its white flowers opening in May, and another plant of the sea cliffs, particularly in the eastern islands, is the tall-growing, narrow-leaved *Chamaepeuce mutica* with handsome purple flowers like an aristocratic knapweed. The gaudy Hottentot Fig *Carpobrotus acinaciformis*, a plant introduced from South Africa, is now so much at home on the cliffs of the Mediterranean and the Aegean that its mats of fleshy leaves and its gay magenta flowers form part of the sea coast scene, blooming from March till July.

On the rocks and in the cliffs at the very sea edge flowers the winged Sea Lavender *Limonium sinuatum*, with its delicately branched yet tough stems carrying the striking blue-mauve, yellow-centred everlasting flowers. The common Sea Lavender of all Europe is here too.

By June the hot dry Greek summer has fully arrived, withering leaf and flower, ripening seed, bringing the end of the growing and flowering period for most plants of the sea coast, as of most lowland habitats. But if the coast from June till September is given up to the enjoyment of sea and sun by the swimmers and the refugees from the stifling heat of the cities and towns, there are still flowers to be seen and enjoyed in autumn. In the dry stream gullies above the beaches will be flowering the Chaste Tree *Vitex agnus-castus*, really more a bush than a tree and rather straggling, but with pleasant loose spikes of sweet-scented lilac to purple flowers like some small buddleia. On dry banks and stony places overlooking the sea grows the attractive *Daphne gnidium*, making narrow-leaved bushes covered by small waxy white, sweet-scented flowers, often accompanied by red berries. Growing flat in fields and waste places may still be found the autumn-flowering form of the Mandrake, the short-stalked bell-shaped flowers, purple or blue, rising from rosettes of dark green leaves.

In the burnt-up yellowed grass of dunes and hummocks above the beaches the observant may be lucky enough to find the flowers of the little autumn-flowering *Narcissus serotinus*, single or twin flowered, with white perianth segments, cup of gold, and narrow rush-like leaves following the flowers. In similar places there may be a muscari, a genus usually spring-flowering. *Muscari parviflorum* is uncommon, with little heads of flowers of the usual muscari form and arrangement, but of a charming pale china blue.

A much more common but very striking flower of the Greek autumn is the sea squill *Urginea maritima*, whose tall narrow candle-like spikes of pure white flowers up to 1½ m. high decorate the parched slopes on cliffs and coastal hills. Their large, wide leaves will not be seen till the late autumn when the flowers have died, rising from huge green bulbs.

On the shore itself there are still a few late flowers of the great sea stock on the cliff-sides and the shore below, while the snapdragon *Antirrhinum majus* with its red-purple flowers will still be flowering on the cliffs. In the sand and among the rocks and pebbles are the wide mats of the aromatic Rock Samphire *Crithmum maritimum*, whose blue-grey fleshy leaves and umbels of yellowish flowers flourish as happily here as in the cold sea spray of the north of Europe. The Sea Holly *Eryngium maritimum*, with stiff blue leaves and rounded bluish flowers, is often still flowering in the autumn on Grecian sands.

Finally, frequent in many places, grows one of the loveliest of all the flowers of the southern sea shore, the Sand Lily *Pancratium maritimum*. Its large deliciously fragrant narcissus-like flowers, with white perianth tube and segments, are carried in loose clusters on quite stout stems, and appear from late summer to autumn. It grows in suitable places all along the Mediterranean and Aegean coasts, signalling the close of the flowering year on the sea shores of Greece.

3. PLANTS OF THE HILLSIDES

The first sight and the last sight of Greece, as the traveller arrives or departs, will be of mountains, of hills, of bare rocky slopes climbing from the sea to high ridges and crests. There is nothing here of softness and obvious charm. There is beauty in plenty, but of a stern uncompromising type where weathered rock and stone are set at such an angle that soil has scarce chance to collect, and where it would seem at first sight that there is nothing to offer for human settlement and cultivation. The lucid atmosphere of Greece accentuates this impression, with every rock outcrop and boulder on the hillsides, every pinnacle on the mountain tops, standing out hard and clear in the brilliant light.

On the hillsides there is often evidence of the many generations of resolute toil which has produced soil and crops where only stone and rock existed before. The key to success has been terracing of the hillsides on walls built from the stone and rock so readily available (4). On the terraces thus formed the scanty soil is no longer swept away each winter by the heavy rainfall; it can be manured, and crops raised. Here flourish vine-yards, olive groves, even corn and vegetables, and fruit trees which might have been thought impossible in such positions. Irrigation from springs, streams, or cisterns is used wherever possible.

But only a small proportion of hill and mountain slopes are available for such reclamation. The rocky bones of Greece are too near the surface, and the slopes are often too steep. With less than a quarter of the land of Greece available for cultivation by any method, a vast area remains in which a special plant community has developed, perfectly adapted to its life in these apparently unfavourable conditions, and which forms what may be described as the typical 'Greek flora'. This situation varies from being very stony to almost pure rock, and the winter rain and the occasional summer storms constantly wash away whatever scanty soil and humus may collect. Moreover much of Greece possesses the 'Mediterranean' type of climate, with the eastern regions particularly showing to exaggerated degree its hot dry summers, winter and spring having lower rainfalls than in the more western Mediterranean areas.

These factors combine to encourage a growth of plants whose growing and flowering periods are largely restricted to the relatively mild and wet months of winter and spring. A high proportion of annual and biennial plants occur, which spend the summer as seeds, and perennials include many shrubs which with their leathery or felted leaves are able to cut down water loss by transpiration, and so survive the extreme drought and heat of summer. The name usually used for this specialised type of vegetation found throughout the Mediterranean area, but perhaps most strikingly exemplified in Greece, is that of 'maquis', a name first used for this type of vegetation as it occurs in Provence: in Italy it is 'macchie', and in Spain 'matorra'. Perhaps because of the relative proximity of Italy we should use

19

'macchie' to describe this low, shrubby, often prickly, vegetation which covers so much of the uncultivated areas in Greece.

It is convenient, and perhaps helpful, to examine the macchie of Greece at each season. Yet there are difficulties in such a subdivision, for in Greece seasonal differences may be blurred since the all-important stimulus to plant growth in this land, parched for so long in the year, is rain. Over most of Greece little rain falls between April and October. The resting time for vegetation is basically during the hot dry summer months, and plant life recommences activity with the first autumn rains in October and November. It is then that one sees not only the flowering of the autumn bulbous plants, but the appearance of the next season's young shoots of a great variety of others, annual and perennial: growth which will be only temporarily slowed, but not damaged, by the cooler weather of the winter months, when nothing comparable to the cold of northern Europe is experienced.

Among bulbous plants colchicums and autumn-flowering crocuses begin to bloom with the first autumn rains, continuing and even increasing in glory till December. The last of the autumn-flowering cyclamens still produce a few late flowers till near December, when the snowdrops start to bloom. These are forms of *Galanthus nivalis ssp. reginae-olgae*, the earliest being the Corfu form sometimes called *G. corcyrensis*. These are followed in January by *G. graecus* from further east, and the broad-leafed snowdrops are still later – *G. elwesii* in Samos and *G. ikariae* in Ikaria. All these snowdrops occur locally and are easily missed.

Crocuses abound in Greece, and flowers of the spring-flowering species overlap those of the autumn-flowering species – thus making nonsense of the apparent distinction between the two groups which seems so obvious in northern latitudes. In January, with the white and pale lilac *C. laevigatus* still flowering, the gold of *C. aureus* and *C. chrysanthus* is colouring the stony slopes of mainland Greece and the islands. Little graceful *C. olivieri*, too, has deep orange flowers and a wide distribution, while among the lilac flowered species *C. nubigena* with blackish anthers must be sought in the mountains of Samos in January and February. Strikingly handsome is *C. sieberi atticus*, of a rich purple, with golden coloured throat, flowering very early in the year on the lower hills, but found in full bloom, as we shall see, much later on the mountains.

In January appear the first flowers of the Crown Anemone *Anemone coronaria* in its many colour forms, varying from white through mauve and purple to pink, and the most glorious of all, the scarlet 'poppy' anemone. You will see it in grassy places on stony hillsides, but perhaps most typically in the vineyards and among the olive groves, where the farmers and their families are still completing the winter harvest of the olives. Only distinguishable from *A. coronaria* by minor differences in structure, and flowering at the same time, is its close relation *A. pavonina*. Up in the hills, usually above the upper limit of the olive groves and vineyards, will be found *Anemone blanda*, low growing with soft yet rich blue flowers, often seeking the shelter and shade of pine woods and bushy gullies. It flowers from January onwards, when it is a characteristic and beautiful feature of the Greek hills and mountains.

To the shrubs and low trees of the macchie, winter brings no striking changes, for they are mostly evergreen, and though winter is their growing period, their main flowering time is to come. The only patches of colour on the rocky hillsides in the late winter come from the Spiny Broom *Calicotome villosa*, whose wickedly prickly stems are beginning to produce their golden flowers in January. By mid-February the rain and gales of the winter depressions, chasing each other across the Mediterranean, are giving way to better weather, and by early March the Greek winter is giving way to the Greek spring with bewildering, almost explosive, speed.

One of the most lovely signs that spring has arrived is the flowering of the Judas tree *Cercis siliquastrum*. This tree, so widely grown throughout the Mediterranean area for its decorative qualities, is in fact a native of the eastern Mediterranean, and it finds its proper setting on the dry hills of Greece. Here it is one of the scanty trees of the macchie, sharing this distinction with the Kermes Oak *Quercus coccifera*, the Aleppo Pine *Pinus halepensis*, the wild olive or oleaster *Olea europaea ssp. sylvestris*, the Locust bean *Ceratonia siliqua* and the Fig *Ficus carica*. The Judas tree carries its clusters of handsome rosy-purple flowers on the bare stems from the beginning of March before any signs of leaves appear, making a memorable sight against its rocky background where it may be accompanied by the white blossom of wild pear.

Meanwhile the anemones go on in full splendour, and the first of the ground orchids are coming into bloom – Bee orchid relations like the ubiquitous golden-lipped *Ophrys lutea var. minor*, dark *Ophrys fusca* and its fine sub-species *iricolor* with lip decorated by large iridescent blue patch; and spike-flowered species like delicate carmine *Orchis quadripunctata*.

The white Stars of Bethlehem are plentiful, beautiful, and difficult to identify. *Ornithogalum nanum* is one of the commonest dwarf and large flowered. The greenish-white *O. nutans* is frequent, and so is the taller-spiked *O. narbonense*.

On the limestone outcrops and screes *Iris pumila attica*, with flowers of yellow, purple, or yellow touched with violet, has been flowering since late February but reaches its full flowering in March. *Iris unguicularis ssp. cretensis*, a sub-species of the Algerian Iris of gardens, with long grassy leaves and blue, often heavily patterned flowers, lurks among bushes. A remarkable relation, frequent among the rocks and bushes of the macchie is the Snake's Head or Mourning Iris, *Hermodactylus tuberosus*, with narrow leaves and flowers of green and black. In similar rocky situations in the hills and mountains grows the Greek fritillary *Fritillaria graeca* with widely bell-shaped flowers of brown and green, or sometimes all brown – never very common, but a most attractive flower.

Everywhere, from February onwards, flower the Grape Hyacinths, com-

21

plex in nomenclature but always attractive with their little spikes of pinched bells, blue or purple in a variety of modifications of form and shade. *Muscari commutatum* is the commonest, frequently forming a background for many more striking flowers. *M. comosum*, the tall Tassel Hyacinth with its top-knot of long-stalked violet sterile flowers, and lower fertile flowers of dark olive green, is also common and handsome.

Some bulbs, like *Muscari comosum*, readily turn into weeds of cultivation. The handsome *Tulipa boeotica* (5) and *Gladiolus segetum* (6) often dominate cornfields; they, and other garden-worthy bulbs like leucojums and sternbergias, can sometimes be seen weeded out of fields by the sackful, for though the deep bulbs are out of reach of old-style ploughs they are reached by modern machinery when the fields are large enough. Equally serious as field weeds, though highly decorative to the visitor, are annuals such as larkspurs, legousias, and corn poppies.

In the stoniest places, growing under the hottest and driest conditions where plant life of any sort would seem nearly impossible, flourish the Asphodels. *Asphodelus microcarpus*, the largest, forms tufts of long narrow leaves from which rise branched flowering stems carrying their starry white flowers veined with brown. Similar, but smaller and more graceful in all its parts, with pinkish flowers, is *A. fistulosus*. Both species flower very early in the year, and by March are in full bloom.

Closely related to *Asphodelus*, but distinguished from it by its unbranched stem which bears narrow leaves all the way up to the flower head, is *Asphodeline lutea*, whose golden-yellow stars are tightly packed along the upper part of the stems. It is not as common as the white Asphodels but is most frequent in the higher hills and mountains where it flowers in April and May.

By March, among the shrubs of the macchie, favouring the partial shade of gullies, or in the clumps of trees, flowers *Coronilla emeroides*, producing its tight clusters of rich golden pea flowers on long willowy stems. Other shrubs which are flowering in March are the Mastic tree *Pistacia lentiscus*, only reaching shrub size in the macchie, where its resinous-scented, dark green leathery leaves and tight clusters of reddish flowers are carried in dense, much branched, spreading branches. Among the shrubby labiates flowering from March onwards are Rosemary *Rosmarinus officinalis* and its close relative *Teucrium fruticans*, with its leaves white-felted beneath, and the pale blue flowers large, with long projecting stamens. Both these shrubs are much beloved by honey bees. Yet another labiate with flowers famed for nectar production is Jerusalem Sage, *Phlomis fruticosa*. This shrub, with large oval white-felted leaves, carrying whorls of large deep yellow flowers, is often the predominant plant of steep limestone hillsides, growing between the boulders, and flowering from early March onwards. Its value as a honey producer is evidenced by long rows of flat-topped beehives, roofs anchored by stones against the winds which often blow up in these exposed places.

With *Phlomis fruticosa* is often associated *Euphorbia acanthothamnos*, which makes low dense spreading domes of intertwining tough grey branches, spiny, and carrying bright green leaves and small heads of bright yellow flowers. These decorative domes mould themselves against and over the white limestone rocks.

There are several other striking euphorbias in Greece, lighting up the macchie and its rocks in earliest spring – notably *E. characias*, so familiar all along the Mediterranean coast, with tall leafy stems carrying the heads of dark centred flowers; *E. characias ssp. wulfenii* with large domed heads of yellow flowers; and *E. rigida*, grey-green-leaved, with heads of bright yellow flowers from February onwards.

But for many the flower of flowers in the macchie, giving delicate colour and grace to the sometimes rather forbidding spiny scrub, is the cistus. Shrubs of this genus play a leading role in the year's succession of flowers in the macchie, the first flowers beginning to open in late February in sheltered places, reaching a climax of colour in April. The most frequent pink species is *Cistus incanus* with large rich pink flowers, with crinkled petals and golden central stamen-clusters. *C. parviflorus* is a similar but smaller-flowered pink species, of wide distribution in Greece, as is the common and beautiful white flowered *C. salvifolius* with grey sage-like leaves and long-stalked golden-centred flowers in clusters of one or two, with rusty red calyces which are striking when the flower is in bud.

Nearly related to the sun-roses is a rather inconspicuous dwarf shrub, *Fumana thymifolia*, whose straggling wiry stems have little narrow leaves adpressed to the stems, and terminal clusters of a few disproportionately large yellow flowers. This little plant may be easily missed in the macchie, but is much more striking in the related but botanically distinct plant community known as the 'phrygana'.

'Phrygana' is the Greek term for the botanist's 'garigue' of the western Mediterranean area, such as Provence, and 'tomillares' of Spain. In the phrygana trees are absent; shrubs are present, but scantier than in true macchie, much of the ground being bare of vegetation, and the desiccation is evidenced by the high proportion of prickly, felted, or deep rooted plants. The large number of aromatic herbs and sub-shrubs in the phrygana is striking, and may be the reason by Theophrastes in classical times was interested enough in this type of plant community to describe it, using the term we do today.

The typical phrygana plant community is found only on limestone, whereas the plants of the macchie are generally indifferent to the soil, showing only minor differences on limestone or siliceous formations. An exception to this is shown by two important plants of the macchie – the Strawberry tree *Arbutus unedo*, and the Tree Heath *Erica arborea*, which are usually found on siliceous soil and, in fact, may be the predominant species on such formations, as in the mountain areas of the island Ikaria and in parts of the Peloponnese. In such areas *A. unedo*, with its dark laurel-like leaves and drooping clusters of waxy white bells, followed by the rosy fruits, set off the sweet-scented tall spires of white Tree Heath and with it may form a special type of macchie stretching for mile after mile of the stony hills.

Conversely, .the Junipers, very frequent shrubs of the macchie, are restricted to calcerous formations, where flourish *Juniperus communis* the common juniper, with sharp needle-like leaves and black fruit, and the Phoenician juniper *J. phoenicea* with scale-like leaves adpressed to the stem and red fruits.

The phrygana proper of the limestone is the home of many aromatic shrubs and sub-shrubs. Here grow rosemary, lavenders (of which *Lavandula stoechas* the 'French' lavender is the commonest, flowering in late spring) and a host of small aromatic labiates, including thyme, basil, marjoram, and sage species, several of which have been used since antiquity for flavouring in cooking, or for the extraction of their aromatic oils for perfumes, and all of which are rich sources of nectar for bees, and the reason for the beehives so often seen on these high bare slopes.

Prickly shrubs, too, are typical of the phrygana, such species as *Sarcopoterium spinosum*, gay with its red flowers in spring, *Euphorbia acanthothamnos* and golden *Calicotome villosa*. In eastern Greece and the islands spiny *Lithodora hispidula* forms tough little bushes starred with small dull blue flowers. Thymelaeas are common in the phrygana too; dull little *T. hirsuta*, with scale-like leaves on many wiry branches, and little yellow flowers, is a poor relation of the daphnes, but there is more distinction about *T. tartonraira* with small spreading silvery-haired leaves and clusters of pale yellow flowers. *Globularia alypum* is a woody-stemmed evergreen shrublet with tough spiny leaves and blue pompon flowers. *Hypericum empetrifolium* is a low-growing shrub with bright yellow-green leaves, needle-like and inrolled, and much-branched heads of yellow flowers; it is the typical Grecian St John's Wort, flowering in June in the phrygana or the macchie.

The phrygana has a rich flora of low-growing bulbous plants in early spring – crocuses, romuleas, ornithogalums, muscari, gageas, fritillaries, and, rarely, tulip species. Ground orchids are also common as spring advances: there are many *Ophrys* species, very confusing to the layman, including *O. speculum*, the extraordinary Venus' Mirror orchid with shining blue patch on the hair-edged lip; *O. scolopax*, the Woodcock orchid, with intricate patterns of lines and circles; and the aptly named Horseshoe orchid *O. ferrum-equinum*. The genus *Orchis* includes the Monkey orchid *O. simia*, so rare in Britain, the yellow flowered Provence orchid *O. provincialis* and, in the Aegean islands, *O. anatolica* with rosy-pink flowers and very long thin cylindrical spur. All these and many more will be flowering from early spring to summer.

A rough indication that summer has begun is given by the final, almost explosive flowering of the annual flowers which abound everywhere. As we saw, many of the most brilliant are plants of the sea shore and its immediate hinterland. They are not typical plants of the macchie and phrygana of the hillsides, but where conditions are favourable, as on cultivated land, in vineyards, olive groves, and along the path sides, the coastal annuals may ascend quite high into the hills, so that even the lower mountain slopes may join in this outburst of brilliant colour that heralds summer. On Ikaria in the late spring the terraced hillsides are blue with flowers of *Lupinus albus ssp. graecus*. The delicate white daisy flowers of *Anthemis chia* carpet many a stony hillside, while *Reseda alba* the white-spiked Mignonette, and *Echium lycopsis* the purple Viper's Bugloss, are often there too.

Summer proper brings the heat and the drought which by late June will spell the end of the year for most annuals and biennials. The total of plants flowering in the macchie and the phrygana falls dramatically. Yet there is still plenty of colour and many interesting plants in flower through much of the long hot summer.

Two dominant summer-flowering shrubs of the macchie are handsome golden-flowered leguminous shrubs – the spiny trefoil-leaved *Genista acanthoclados* and the taller, willowy, nearly bare-stemmed Spanish Broom *Spartium junceum*, with spikes of large fragrant flowers of brightest gold. On the hill and mountain sides grows the wild olive, spiny, but handsome in May and June with its profuse clusters of fragrant whitish flowers. Another small tree, much cultivated, but also naturalised and probably truly native in these Greek hills, is the pomegranate *Punica granatum*, whose dark green shiny leaves and splendid scarlet trumpets make a striking sight in June. Admired since ancient times, the Myrtle, *Myrtus communis*, has shining aromatic leaves and sweet-scented long-stalked white flowers which make it one of the loveliest of Greek shrubs.

Summer is the season of the convolvulus, a genus in which Greece is particularly rich, both in climbing and non-climbing species. Among the climbing – or perhaps more accurately scrambling – species the common *Convolvulus althaeoides* with its deeply divided hairy leaves and flowers of a lilac-tinged pink is common throughout the Mediterranean area. More delicately beautiful with deeply segmented silvery leaves and flowers of a pure light pink is its sub-species *C.a. tenuissimus*; while *C. scammonia*, its leaves smooth-surfaced and narrowly arrow-shaped, and its flowers of a lovely primrose yellow, is as uncommon as beautiful. All these scramble and climb around and over the cistus and other low shrubs of the macchie, from May till August. Among the non-climbing convolvulus species are *C. cantabrica* with woody base and erect stems carrying narrow silvery leaves, covered in June and July with white pink-tinged flowers.

Among the cistus bushes one may be fortunate enough to see, at ground level, the bizarre flowers of *Cytinus hypocistis*, a leafless parasite on cistus roots. The flowers are of a brilliant yellow surrounded by the orange-red scales which have taken the place of leaves.

Summer is the peak flowering time for the labiates which, as we have seen, form such an important part of both phrygana and macchie. These tough wiry little herbs and shrublets carry their small-lipped flowers in whorls up the stems, their colours being usually in a wide range of pinks, mauves, and blues; in the heat and brilliance of the Greek summer they distil abundant nectar for the bees, and their individual variety of volatile oil gives each a characteristic aromatic quality.

More spectacular in their obvious floral beauty are the verbascums or mulleins, a family much at home in Greece where a large number of species occur, usually biennials. These plants, often reaching a flowering height of 2 m., are usually densely white or yellow-woolly and their flower stems, single or more spectacularly branched to give pyramidal inflorescence, carry their flowers in lines or clusters. These are usually canary-yellow, or rarely purple. They are to be found on the stoniest, driest slopes, rising from the brown and scorched grass where annuals are all dead and gone.

In such places too, flourish the thistles and their near relatives. Many are perhaps of limited interest, but some are noteworthy for foliage alone like *Notobasis syriaca* with clusters of purple flowers above narrow long-spined multicoloured stem leaves. The whole plant, with its delicate yet stiff-branched formation, and its spines, is most decorative. The biennial *Scolymus hispanicus* is another forbiddingly spiny plant, but handsome with its golden yellow flowers; it is a plant of stony places, walls, and rocks. Species of *Onopordum* like *O. myriacanthum* grow, like the mulleins, on the high desert-like summer slopes of the rockiest hills, where they produce from spiny-based rosettes huge 2 m. flowering stems topped by great purplish flower heads surrounded by palisades of incurved spiny bracts. Another monumental thistle is well-named *Cirsium candelabrum*, forming a gigantic spiny pyramid.

Among this summer spate of prickly and spiny plants, high place must be given to the Caper *Capparis spinosa*, a very spiny shrub with oval fleshy leaves and remarkable flowers, petals of pale lilac surrounding very numerous purple-stalked stamens of extraordinary length. The fat green flower buds are the edible 'capers'.

It is worth leaving the dry parched hillsides of mid-summer to seek one of the rock gullies which plunge steeply down towards the sea below. They too will be dry, of course, at this time of year, but in their rocky and sandy beds there will be flowering in full glory the Oleanders (*Nerium*), tall dense shrubs with leathery grey-green leaves, carrying handsome clusters of scented pink flowers in terminal clusters. On the sides of the same rocky gullies, but also emerging on to the hillsides, the edges of olive groves, or path sides, may be found the lovely eastern Hollyhock *Alcea pallida*. Its tall leafless stems carry large stalkless flowers, of a pure pale pink untinged with purple. More common is the related *Althaea cannabina*, with tall stems up to 2 m. high, deeply lobed leaves, and flowers of a rosy-purple. It is frequent in stony places.

Autumn comes gradually in Greece; there is a certain tempering of the fierce heat of summer, a perceptible shortening of the days, and occasional storms to bring long-awaited rain to the parched ground. Up on the hillsides the flowering season is not over yet. The Locust Bean *Ceratonia siliqua* is a large handsome tree with widely spreading branches and dark

26

green leaves, as welcome for its shade as for its edible beans, now only used as fodder for animals. In autumn it carries its clusters of green and reddish flowers, welcome source of nectar for bees at this time of year; it often bears flowers and fruit-pods at the same time. At a lower level of the macchie among the small shrubs, climbing over rocks and walls, is flowering *Smilax aspera* with its spined branches, dark green heart-shaped leaves and heads of starry white fragrant flowers.

A flower which it is impossible to ignore is the composite *Inula viscosa*. This is a leafy perennial plant, sticky to the feel, and strongly aromatic, with branched flowering stems bearing its little yellow flowers in gay abundance; a somewhat coarse plant, perhaps, but welcome at a time when so few plants are in flower.

Perhaps the most surprising sight in the autumn macchie, among stones and rocks, are the tall flowering stems of the Sea Squill *Urginea maritima* described in the last chapter – not just a coastal plant despite its name. It ushers in the season of the autumn-flowering bulbs. Soon the first of the colchicums appear on the hillsides, their flowering time being spread from September till December. Of the many species *C. autumnale*, whose pale rose-lilac flowers are so well known all over Europe, is frequent in Greece too. *C. sibthorpii*, with very large globular flowers of tessellated lilac, is widespread in mainland Greece and the islands, while *C. variegatum*, another tessellated species, is found in the eastern Aegean islands and is chequered with rust-red and white. All these species produce their flowers before the leaves, but on the high rocky hillslopes *C. cupanii* produces its charming small rosy-lilac flowers at the same time as its leaves, from early October onwards.

With the colchicums flower the autumn crocuses proper. *Crocus cartwrightianus*, the Greek form of the Saffron Crocus, lilac to white in colour with its famous red stigmas, is common, and so is *C. cancellatus* in lilac and white. *C. laevigatus* is white veined with purple, and *C. boryi* very lovely with pure white flowers and scarlet stigmas. The crocuses of autumn, almost without exception, have a colour range varying from pure white to various shades of lilac, with some species showing darker purple feathering or striping. The yellows and oranges are reserved for the spring-flowering species. Yet we can find gold in the glorious Sternbergias, related to the daffodils, though seemingly closer to the crocuses. Both *S. lutea* with wide blunt-tipped petals and *S. sicula* with narrow pointed petals show the same brilliant golden colour of flower. They bloom from September till November in stony places from the coast up to the higher slopes of the hills.

The final glory of these closing months of the year is provided by the cyclamens, *C. hederifolium* (*neapolitanum*) and *C. graecum*, both species having rather similar flowers of varying shades of rosy-pink, with darker blotches at the bases of the reflexed petals. The leaves of both are often beautifully patterned, and are very variable not only in colour but in shape. To see the cyclamens at their best one should take, in October, one of those little paths that mount hillsides, winding up through the vineyards, now quiet and bare after the completed grape harvest. Up above, in terraced olive groves, preparations are being made for the olive harvest: the ground under the trees is tidied, and there may well be women from the village collecting the first windfalls of purple fruit.

In the stone walls of the terraces are the first of the cyclamens' rosy flowers, long-stalked, opening in the dappled sunshine, springing from huge irregular tubers wedged between or under the stones, or even between the roots of the older olive trees. Their main flowering is among the rocks, on the open hillsides, and in pine woods; a suitable flower with which to end this brief look at some of the beauty that decorates the rugged hills of Greece from the earliest days of the year to the close of autumn.

4. THE MOUNTAIN FLORA

Greece, as we have seen, is very much a country of hills and mountains. Hills, a term which includes 'foothills', rise from the lowlands to a height of about 700 m. Above these begins the mountain (montane) area, having a characteristic flora in which woods and forest often persist, usually because their relative inaccessibility has protected them from man's exploitation. In the north of Greece the Beech *Fagus sylvatica*, which is so typical on the limestone mountains of Central Europe, extends southwards into the mountains of Thessaly and the Epirus, but no further. The characteristic conifer of the Greek mountains, usually growing above 1,000 m., is the Greek Fir *Abies cephalonica*, sometimes associated with the Black Pine *Pinus nigra*, as on Thessalian Olympos. *P. nigra* itself forms quite extensive woods in the mountains of Euboea, the Peloponnese, and Crete.

The macchie, that characteristic plant association in which evergreens predominate, climbs into the foothills and the lower mountain zone. In the hills of northern Greece, and sometimes in the lower mountain zones of southern Greece, there appears a plant association which replaces the macchie; this is predominantly deciduous brushwood made up of such species as the fiercely spined Christ's Thorn *Paliurus spina-christi*, lilac *Syringa vulgaris*, common Barberry *Berberis vulgaris*, *Prunus nana* and *P. prostrata*, Wayfaring Tree *Viburnum lantana*, Cornelian Cherry *Cornus mas*, the shrubby jasmine *Jasminum fruticans*, and *Daphne oleoides*.

In the conifer zone of the mountains (about 1,000–1,500 m.) flowering plants are not usually abundant, and the alpine meadows that are such a delightful feature of similar altitudes in the mountains of western Europe are hardly ever seen in Greece, owing to the steep and rocky nature of the high hills and mountains, where plateau formation with lush pasture land cannot develop.

Above 1,500 m. the trees, which are usually conifers at these altitudes, become scarce, and exposed rock increasingly takes over. Here is to be seen the high mountain flora of Greece. It is here, too, that those of us who are familiar with the 'alpines' of western European mountains may recognise old friends, for a proportion of true alpine plants take their place in the Greek flora. It is not a high proportion and it dwindles rapidly as one moves south from the mountains of northern Greece through the Pindos and Epirus to the Peloponnese, until at last, in Crete, the proportion almost reaches vanishing point. The path by which these true alpines have reached the Greek mountains must remain uncertain, though it is thought that it must have been along the Dinaric Alps from the west, and partly from the Carpathians in the north. Apart from the alpine element in the high mountain flora of Greece, there is an important Central European element, and an important and fascinating proportion of endemic species.

The high mountain flora sometimes descends to somewhat lower altitudes when conditions are particularly favourable such as on exposed rock faces and in steep and sometimes shaded ravines.

It is only proper that the first of these brief summaries of the plants found on some of the better known Greek mountains should start with Thessalian Olympos. It is not surprising to anyone who has seen, with awe, the many-peaked Olympos massif rising to its height of nearly 3,000 m. straight from the plains of Thessaly, that it was this mountain that the ancient Greeks considered the appropriate home for their gods. Appropriate it was, too, that Zeus should have been given the titles of 'Cloud-gatherer', 'Thunderer', and 'Earth-shaker', for it was clear to all that up in these mountain solitudes, while the plains below and the blue sea beyond lay in the sunshine and heat of summer, the storm clouds gathered, day after day the thunder raged, and the peaks were hidden. Olympos remains a mountain of sudden moods, unpredictable and even dangerous to the climber, who may well be thankful for the mountain refuges which offer shelter in the summer months. In winter the mountain is deep in snow; the bitter cold of Central European intensity closes down, and the tiny permanent remnants of glaciers are preserved.

To see the mountain flora of Olympos, July or August are probably the best months. The lower slopes of the massif carry typical shrubby macchie of the classical Mediterranean type which we have seen elsewhere. The lower and middle mountain zones are clothed by fine woods and forests; beech forms woods over extensive areas, and the conifer forests consist of the Greek Fir *Abies cephalonica* with *Pinus nigra*, and *P. leucodermis* appearing at higher levels (10). There are many good woodland flowers to be seen on the way up; old friends from the Alps such as the Willow Gentian *Gentiana asclepiadea* are here, and so is the Wintergreen *Pyrola rotundifolia*; flowering in the full sun, as it does over so much of southern Europe, is lily-like *Anthericum liliago* with its spikes of delicate white flowers. Standing out brilliantly in the broken shade of the woodland are the sealing-wax scarlet Turk's Cap flowers of *Lilium heldreichii*. This local variation of *L. chalcedonicum* is to be seen not only here, but on other mountains of mainland Greece and the Peloponnese. Less exotic, but interesting in these surroundings in the far south-east of Europe, are the two daphnes, *D. mezereum* and *D. laureola*, with woodland orchids also familiar in western Europe, *Neottia nidus-avis* the Bird's-nest, and *Cephalanthera rubra* the Red Helleborine.

For plant lovers there is one plant above all others to be seen on Olympos – *Jankaea heldreichii*. This rare and most beautiful member of the family that includes *Ramonda* and *Haberlea* is the most famous of the endemics of Mount Olympos, with rosettes of oval silvery-felted leaves and heads of delicate lavender bells of waxy brilliance. It grows on limestone boulders and outcrops in the partial shade of the beech or conifer woods. Even on Olympos it is not a common plant, and when found should be admired and photographed, but never collected.

In similar places are found the delicate *Viola gracilis*, a mountain pansy with different colours and shapes, together with the prickly leaved Kabschia saxifrages, white *Saxifraga scardica* and reddish *S. sempervivum*, with flowering stem that uncurls from a crook shape.

After seeing *Jankaea* in its home in the middle and upper mountain zones, Olympos has not shown all its wonders, for there is still much to be admired at the highest altitudes. As the last of the pines is passed, the steep bare slopes showing the last of the snow fields, the rocky outcrops, boulders, and ravines, all hold some very characteristic high altitude plants. Here grows *V. delphinantha*, shrubby, with narrow heath-like leaves and long-spurred flowers of a pinkish lilac; it is a close relation of fabled *V. cazorlensis* from the sierras of far-off south-west Spain. The fine crevice-growing *Campanula oreadum* has little leathery leaves and great purple bells, and *Omphalodes luciliae* grows on the highest screes, its trailing stems carrying glaucous leaves and sprays of porcelain blue flowers. *Saxifraga sempervivum* turns up again on these rocks, as does *Globularia meridionalis*, with a lovely blue and white columbine, *Aquilegia amaliae*, a little reminiscent of *A. alpina* of the Alps.

Still outstanding among such a galaxy of Central European, endemic, and Alpine species, there flowers *Gentiana verna*, the spring gentian, that king of all the highest places from North Africa through to Afghanistan. Here it bears the varietal name of *pontica*, though this is perhaps more of a courtesy title for a regional form than a distinction made on definite morphological differences from the type species.

Not far away to the west from Olympos rise the Pindos mountains, the backbone of Greece, a wide and rugged mountainous area much of which is difficult to reach, with poor communications, but boasting many fine peaks. As might be expected, there is a magnificent mountain flora here, but until quite recently much of it was almost unexplored botanical territory.

In the western Pindos, north of Ioannina the hill town capital of Epirus, lies the rugged massif of Mount Gamila, much of which is a flat rocky table-land deeply cut by river gorges, with much mountain meadow on its flanks (9). From it can be seen the more triangular peak of Mount Smolikas to the north, a giant ranking second only to Olympos. East of these is Mount Vourinon, of special interest because its serpentine rock provides a change from the normal limestones.

These high mountains of Epirus have high rainfall, with severe winters, so that the Mediterranean flora and its macchie scarcely rise above the lower foothills. Beech forests are extensive on these wet mountains with their cold winters, and the conifer forests include *Pinus leucodermis* as well as *P. nigra* and the Greek Fir. It is wild, beautiful, and little visited country, where wild boar is common, and the brown bear and the wild cat were seen within the recent past. The heavy rainfall favours such plants as the Poet's Narcissus *Narcissus poeticus* in its Grecian form *var. hellenicus* and, on the shady rocks, *Ramonda serbica* and *R. nathaliae*.

The yellow Albanian lily *Lilium albanicum* grows in a few localities near the Albanian border, while the Martagon lily *L. martagon* is not uncommon. Here and there too, one may stumble on *L. candidum* in its wild state, on rock faces and in scrub. In the shade of woodland and among the boulders flower familiar western European beauties such as *Gentiana asclepiadea, Ranunculus aconitifolius, Geranium sylvaticum, Globularia cordifolia*, and *Cephalanthera rubra*.

On the higher rocks and screes there is a mixture of such alpines as *Dianthus sylvestris* with its long-stalked scentless flowers of bright pink, *Globularia meridionalis, Campanula rotundifolia, Saxifraga paniculata, Gentiana verna var. pontica, Myosotis alpestris*, and even *Soldanella alpina*, growing with such southern and Central European species as *Doronicum caucasicum* with its big yellow daisies, pink *Corydalis solida*, copper-coloured *Hypericum apollinis*, red or more commonly pale pink *Geranium macrorrhizum* and magenta *G. subcaulescens*, slender lilac *Crocus veluchensis*, and *Thalictrum olympicum*. It is a fascinating blend of west and east, with a strong element of the south, and many Greek endemics. It epitomises the wonderful floral picture to be seen on so many of the high mountains of Greece, where phytogeography becomes a fascinating reality and not a rather dull term.

Towering above Delphi, north of the Corinth Gulf, stands Parnassos, 2,457 m. in height. It is more accessible than many Greek mountains: there is an excellent motor road from Athens to Delphi and a passable road climbs further up the mountain. Thence the various peaks can be reached on foot or by mule. Quite extensive snowfields persist near the summits until late May.

In April, on the lower and middle slopes of the mountain in the conifer zone, snow patches still linger in the shade of the Greek Firs, and in the wake of the melting snow are the flowers of the softly purple *Crocus sieberi atticus*, with bright yellow *C. chrysanthus* shining here and there, and white *Colchicum catacuzenium*, one of the spring-flowering species. At the edge of the woods *Anemone blanda* and *Scilla bifolia* produce their lovely flowers in different shades of blue.

Much higher up, where the fir trees thin out, the slopes are steeper and the limestone outcrops more noticeable. Here the high mountain plants take over. The pretty pink-flowered *Corydalis solida* is flowering, and so is little *Draba parnassica* with large golden flowers, safely rooted in the rock crevices, where also grows pink *Potentilla nitida*, apparently as happy here as on the limestones of the far-off Dolomites. Another far-ranging wanderer on these rock faces is *Prunus prostrata* with its lattice-work of woody stems carrying the small leaves and pale pink blooms.

At these heights *Crocus veluchensis* tends to take over from *C. sieberi var. atticus*, being distinguished from it by its more slender flowers which lack yellow in the throat.

From the heights of Parnassos, if the weather is kind, there are distant views of the high mountains of the Pindos away to the north, while to the south, across the Corinth Gulf far below, the peaks of the northern Peloponnese tower up, snow-capped as late as June.

These high Peloponnese mountains include such giants as Mount Killini (Xiria), 2,474 m., and Mount Chelmos, 2,355 m. There are mountain flowers on these peaks, but differing in interesting respects from those we have seen in the mountains north of the Corinth Gulf. Those having their main centre in the Alps of western Europe have almost vanished; so have the Central European high mountain plants; even the high mountain endemics have dwindled. The general flora of these Peloponnese mountains is, in fact, predominantly Southern Hellenic, a flora closely allied to that of Asia Minor.

On Killini and Chelmos in June, when the snow is melting, even near the summits, will be found many of the lovely mountain flowers of Greece. The large *Crocus sieberi var. tricolor* will be flowering near the snow patches, sometimes replaced by *C. veluchensis*. Pink corydalis, blue muscari and snow-white ornithogalums will be there, with small golden gageas, the deeper yellow of *Tulipa australis* opening wide in the strong sun, and the soft blue of *Anemone blanda* sheltering in a shady gully under dwarfed bushes. Shrubby *Daphne oleoides* with creamy flowers, and pink *Prunus prostrata* hug the boulders, and among these stones grows the gay long-stemmed Grecian Pink, *Dianthus haematocalyx* with its flowers of red backed by yellow, with red calyces. Deeply rooted in the rock crevices grow saxifrages and sempervivums; red and white *Saxifraga taygetea*, tight-packed *S. marginata*, white *S. scardica*, with *Sempervivum reginae-amaliae* raising stems of white-edged crimson flowers above rosettes of a bronze-purple.

There are more excitements, too, on these Peloponnese heights: *Gentiana verna var. pontica* with its incomparable blue stars still persists in a few small stations, and here is the rare and beautiful Peloponnese endemic *Asperula arcadiensis* among the rocks, where its low mats of grey-woolly stems carry the narrow leaves and the little waxy trumpets of pale pink.

Where the Styx rises, high on the steep slopes of Mount Chelmos, grows *Aquilegia othonis* around a shady cave entrance where its flower heads of blue and white are damp in the falling spray.

In autumn, on the high rocky slopes of Taygetos grows one of the finest of the Greek colchicums, *C. boissieri*, producing its large flowers of clear pink. It grows elsewhere in the mountains of Greece, but was first described from Mount Taygetus.

There is one spring flower to be found here and there in high places of the Peloponnese which, perhaps more than any other, proclaims the easterly quality of this mountain flora. This is *Cyclamen persicum*, common in many countries of the south-eastern Mediterranean such as the Lebanon and Israel, and also to be seen in the Greek islands of the far south. This, perhaps the most lovely of all cyclamens, carries its highly scented pink and white flowers with their twisted petals, on tall stems, and it graces with its delicately beautiful flowers some of the barest and stoniest high mountain slopes in May and June.

Some of the high mountains of Greece can be reached without too much difficulty, but others, it must be admitted, need a good deal of time and trouble both to reach and to climb. For those whose time in Greece is limited, and who must therefore be most selective, there are mountains which can be fitted into even the most packed itinerary. These are the mountains of Attica, and in particular the three famous mountains which encircle Athens herself – Mounts Hymettos, Pentelicon, and Parnes. They are not of great height, Hymettos being 1,037 m., Pentelicon 1,100 m., and Parnes 1,313 m.; but they are superbly situated at the very centre of Attica, where they have formed the backcloth to the great happenings in Athens herself from the earliest days. Furthermore, they carry a charming flora, and have the inestimable advantage that a bus or taxi can transport the traveller, however hard pressed for time, to the modest heights within an hour or so.

All three mountains carry very similar flowers, though Parnes, the highest of the three, is crowned at its highest zone by woods of the Greek Fir, with which are found elements of a high mountain flora.

Hymettos, so near to Athens that it is almost touched by the spreading suburbs of the city, will serve as the type. It has always had a very special place in the affections of the Athenians.

Here, in the old days, were altars to Demeter, the Earth Mother, and her daughter Persephone; on the lower slopes the famous Hymettos Spring and its ever-verdant surroundings, so striking on the rocky slopes, was always loved by the citizens of Athens, including Socrates. Ovid knew it, and in a poem spoke of 'the purple heights of flowery Hymettos where lies a sacred spring enclosed by soft green turf. Low growing pine trees, mixed with thick foliaged Box trees and fragile Tamarisk adorn the spot. Most fragrant breathe the aromatic tribes, arbutus, rosemary, dark myrtle, and bay, that dapple the green earth.'

The marble ram's head of the sixth century B.C. carried the spring water then, as it does today, to the stone basin below; and much later, when the pagan world had crumbled, and the Byzantine monastery of Kaisariani had been built by the Hymettos spring, the spring water supplied the monastery and its baths. Early records of the monastery show how different was the Hymettos of those days. It was then by no means treeless, for its trees provided roofing timbers and, with extensive olive groves and vineyards, flourished on and around the mountain, while honey from the apiaries of the monks was famed as far as Constantinople.

At the beginning of the nineteenth century an English traveller, Edward Dodwell, broke into the temporarily empty Kaisariani monastery and, with the characteristic arrogance of western travellers in those days, spent a night there feasting on the honey, olives, figs, grapes, and pomegranates stored so carefully by the rightful owners. He wrote lyrically of the surroundings: the rocks were 'adorned with scattered pine, the general verdure forming such a contrast with the parched and yellow hue of the Athenian plain', the 'clear and copious fountain of perennial water' above the monastery was clearly responsible for 'the surrounding grass of the lively green speckled with Cyclamen, the starry Hyacinth, the Amarillis lutea, and the purple crocus'.

By the beginning of this century the last monk had abandoned the dilapidated monastery, and its carefully tended olive groves and vineyards were deserted. The hardships of wars and foreign occupations took their toll, and by the end of the last world war Hymettos was treeless (the invaders burnt the forest), arid, and scarred by quarries.

But the wounds of savage wars are being healed, thanks to the devoted enthusiasm of a small group of Greeks who have spent many years in the rehabilitation of Hymettos and its monastery. On the mountain the tree-plundered slopes are again growing olives, almonds, carobs, and pines, as they used to; the monastery has been repaired with scrupulous care, so that, though no monks live there now, Kaisariani still provides, as it did in the past, a haven of quite extraordinary beauty and peace for Athenians.

We can still see, too, the same flowers that gave Edward Dodwell delight on his autumn visit – *Cyclamen graecum* and *C. hederifolium*, *Scilla autumnalis*, *Sternbergia sicula*, and *Crocus laevigatus* are still there, and as we climb the bare rocky slopes above they are joined by *Crocus boryi*, snow-white with scarlet stigmata, *C. cartwrightianus* the Greek saffron crocus, and little *Colchicum cupanii* with small bright purple flowers opening as the leaves appear, in defiance of the usual colchicum sequence.

There is a motor road to the summit of Hymettos, or one can make a rough steep climb to the ridge, which is generally treeless save for the occasional wild olive bearing its crop of hard sour little purple fruits, and a few acorn-covered Kermes Oaks. But the view from the Hymettos heights is worth the climb in itself. All Athens is below, the Acropolis miniature at its centre, with Piraeus and the blue of the sea beyond, and in the distance Mount Pentelicon, source of the Parthenon marble; while to the north is the long high wall of Parnes, topped with its fir forests.

The further side of Hymettos is of very steep, sharp limestone cliffs, but the adventurous can descend it and make an interesting circuit of the eastern end of the mountain.

On Mount Pentelicon, and on the lower and middle slopes of Parnes, the flora of Hymettos repeats itself. On both mountains the lower slopes carry the typical flora of the macchie; the cistus, brooms, rosemary, and sages are all here, with the colours and the aromatic fragrance that repeats itself in infinite variations on every Greek mountain, and an abundance of low-growing bulbous flowers and ground orchids.

As the road to the heights of Parnes zig-zags its way up at last to the fir zone, the air becomes cool and fresh and the hot dusty plains of Attica become blurred in the heat haze below. The flowers, too, are changing. The path that winds up has, in late March, a little snow still lying here and there in shady hollows and gullies, and here are the soft purple flowers of *Crocus sieberi var. atticus*, with the dark blue flowers of *Scilla bifolia* among them. In the crevices of rocks, and wedged between spreading roots of the firs, are the corms and handsome leaves, patterned in infinite variety, of the autumn-flowering cyclamens *C. hederifolium* and *C. graecum*. Among the firs and by the pathsides flowers *Anemone blanda*, the loveliest and most typical of woodland flowers on the Greek mountains, with white centred flowers of clearest blue. It is often accompanied by a little mountain viola, *V. hymettia*, dwarf and creeping, with small leaves and little flat flowers of yellow and purple.

In the clearings, and approaching the summits where the limestone rises white and dazzling above the tree level, grow other mountain flowers. *Doronicum caucasicum* is here with its fine golden yellow flowers above the rather coarse leaves; bright yellow starry-flowered *Gagea reticulata*, pink *Corydalis solida*, and the large and handsome red deadnettle *Lamium garganicum*, all provide their gay colours. Among the rocks, in the hottest sun, grows *Tulipa orphanidea*, and its flowers, though sparingly produced, are gracefully slender and copper tinged. In rock crevices flowers purple *Aubrieta deltoidea* and so does *Aethionema saxatile* var. *graecum* with delicate pink flowers and tight tufts of bluish-green leaves. Frequent on the steep summit slopes of limestone is *Orchis quadripunctata* with long-spurred pink flowers spotted with purple. The fine red-flowered *Paeonia mascula* used to grace these mountain slopes but, sadly, it has been collected to the point of extinction.

Anywhere on Parnes, from the lower slopes to the highest levels above the firs, may be found, early in spring, the flowers of *Hermodactylus tuberosus*, the Snake's-head Iris. It is a beautiful and graceful flower of green and near-black purple, not deserving its ugly name. Its dwarfer relation, *Iris pumila attica*, also grows plentifully, making clumps in many different colours.

So, if the traveller to Greece lacks the time and the opportunity to reach the heights of Olympos, or even of more accessible Parnassos, he or she should not despair of seeing mountain flowers in Greece. Many of them are on these easily reached mountains that surround the Athenian plain.

5. FLOWERS OF THE ISLANDS

Take any of the blue and white steamers from the quays at Piraeus; and, clearing the point at Sounion with Poseidon's temple white and high on the summit, you will, whichever course your boat follows, pass island after island, steep and rocky, shouldering their way out of the sea. Each island of the Aegean has its individuality, but most of the smaller ones have the same characteristic of apparent harshness so that it comes as a surprise, as one approaches by ship, to see signs of human habitation in these collections of white houses perched at unlikely heights; sometimes, even, signs of cultivation. What sort of a living could human beings wrest from these rocky mountainsides?

The islands were not always barren. According to Homer, the goddess Athene, disguised as a shepherd, explained to Odysseus that his island, Ithaca, had 'a name known to all peoples of the dawn and sunrise, and that people live on the other side towards the Western gloom. I grant that it is rugged and unfit for driving horses, yet narrow though it may be, it is very far from poor. It grows abundant corn and wine in plenty. The rains and fresh dews are never lacking; and it has excellent pasturage for goats and cattle, timber of all kinds, and watering places that never fail.' Since Homer's time much of the 'timber of all kinds' has been felled, but Greeks of today show the same pride in their native island, and the same perseverance in wresting a living from a soil which to a stranger seems so unpromising.

The islands of Greece were formed in the remote past when the present limits of the Mediterranean and Aegean seas were being established. Before this series of vast inundations they formed part of the southern tip of the Balkan peninsula, and as such shared its flora. Their resulting isolation provided refuges where have been preserved many species of flowers which, for various reasons, failed to persist on the Greek mainland; at the same time it encouraged the emergence of new varieties and even species.

For convenience the Greek islands have always been divided into geographical groups. Thus the Sporades are the islands of the north-west Aegean, including Thasos, Skiathos, Skopelos, and Skiros. The Ionian islands, including Corfu, Ithaca, Cephalonia, and Zakinthos, lie to the west of the Peloponnese. The Saronic islands, the nearest to Athens and Attica, include Hydra, Aegina, and Salamis. South-east lie the Cyclades, with Andros, Syros, Mykonos, Paros, Ios, Serifos, Santorini, and Milos as some of the most famous of the group. Away to the east, often with Asia Minor in sight, lie the eastern Aegean islands, with Lesbos, Chios, and Samos as examples. South of these there lie the Dodecanese, from Patmos in the north of the group to Kalymnos, Kos, Tilos, and Rhodes. Finally, in the far south lie Crete and Karpathos. Altogether there are around 1,500 islands large and small.

Climatically the islands have milder winters than the Greek mainland, with cooler summers, thanks to the sea winds. Frosts very seldom occur, and snow, though it sometimes falls in the mountains (notably in Crete), is very rarely seen at sea level.

Rainfall in the southern and eastern islands is low, averaging about 400 mm. in the year, thus resembling the southern areas of the Greek mainland, with most of the rain falling during the winter months. In the western islands, however, the annual rainfall is considerably higher, averaging 700 mm. in Corfu, for example.

The general picture of vegetation is one of luxuriance in the moister western islands, in striking contrast to the bare and rocky Cyclades with a flora poor both in quantity and variety. The eastern Aegean islands tend on the whole to be green, blessed with many springs and permanent streams, and the quality and variety of their vegetation benefits accordingly. The flora of the large islands of the far south, Rhodes and especially Crete, show strong Asiatic affinities; and Crete especially, presumably because of its large size and its isolated position, half-way to Africa, has a remarkably large number of endemic species.

In general the Greek islands have hills rather than mountains. The most important exception is Crete, where the White Mountains reach 2,400 m. Karpathos in the Dodecanese has Mount Profitis Elias (1,140 m.); Lesbos has Mount Olympos (930 m.); Samos has Mount Kerketeus (1,436 m.), and Mount Ampelos (1,140 m.); Rhodes in the Dodecanese has another Mount Profitis Elias (750 m.).

Woods are rare in the islands except for groves of Aleppo Pine, and the higher slopes of the mountains where the Greek Fir may occur at altitudes above the 1,000 m. level.

The islands of the Saronic gulf, the Saronic group, so quickly reached by boat from Piraeus, share in general the vegetation of the hills of Attica. Their hills are too low for any true forest formation, and in any case their proximity to the mainland has resulted over the centuries in high populations, with intensive tree felling and the replacement of woodland by macchie and phrygana; present-day woodland is usually formed by Aleppo Pine. The few special features in the flora of the Saronic group include an endemic Fritillary, *F. rhodokanakis*, on Hydra, and a small form of *Cyclamen persicum* on Aegina.

The group of the Cyclades, south-east of the Saronic islands, also lack any true mountains. They are rocky, with only low hills, and have a scantier vegetation than any of the other island groups. In summer their sun-baked ochre-coloured hills are only redeemed by verdant green where cultivation in the valleys and the narrow plains at the foot of the hill slopes allows the production of fruit and vegetables. Olive groves often extend their grey-green patterns up the lower hill slopes, and vineyards grow where irrigation can be carried out. But much of these near-barren Cyclades remain impossible to cultivate, and carries only the scantiest of phrygana made up of the usual dwarf aromatic herbs with, in spring, a good deal of golden flowered *Calicotome villosa*. However, in some of the southern

Cycladean islands there grow the rare woody-stemmed Dianthus species *D. fruticosus* and *D. arboreus,* and two islands of the Cyclades, Kythnos and Syros, are graced by their own fritillaries – *F. tuntasia* and *F. ehrhartii.*

There are two notable exceptions to this picture of the Cyclades and their vegetation. South of the main group lies Santorini or Thira, linked by ancient legend and dim history with the lost Atlantis and the volcanic disaster in which the glorious Minoan civilisation died. Santorini remains a volcano and is devoid of natural vegetation, though vineyards produce a wine of outstanding quality.

At the other end of the Cyclades, away to the north, lies Andros, as different from the southern Cyclades in its vegetation as Santorini is in its extraordinary fashion in the far south of the group. Andros is a large island, with hills almost worthy to be called mountains. Woods of chestnut and plane trees grow on the hills, watered by numerous springs, while shady ravines carry a rock flora, and in boggy places white and yellow primroses flower in early spring.

The Sporades lie north of the Cyclades, and form a pleasant group of islands, with sandy beaches, pine woods, olive groves, and fruit orchards. They are not mountainous and their flora is akin to that of the nearby mainland, consisting mostly of macchie of the usual type, giving way on the upper hill slopes to the aromatic phrygana. Aleppo Pines sometimes form extensive woods. Only in Skyros, the most easterly island of the group, does one find bare rocky conditions resembling those seen in the Cyclades.

Far away to the east, off the coast of Asia Minor, lie the eastern Aegean islands in a long string, from Samothrace and Limnos in the north to Samos and Ikaria in the south, south again of which begin the Dodecanese. Lesbos has special interest for the botanist. It possesses in Mount Olympos a mountain of 950 m., and in the pine forests of its upper slopes grow the broad-leafed snowdrop *Galanthus elwesii, Fritillaria pontica,* and *Tulipa hageri.* In autumn ancient and huge corms of *Cyclamen hederifolium* and *Cyclamen graecum* flower in the cool moss under the pine trees, and here too are the flowers of *Colchicum variegatum* with their lovely pink tessellation. Down at the coast vast olive groves border the wide bays and ascend the hill sides, and here in the spring the Anemones *A. pavonina* and *A. coronaria* flower in a magnificence of scarlet, white, and purple. At sea level, too, there grows in stony stream beds *Rhododendron luteum* with sweet-scented yellow flowers in May. Here in Lesbos this Asiatic shrub finds its only European home. Where the rushes grow in the coastal swamps one will find the great yellow and white Iris, *Iris ochroleuca,* on its metre-high stems.

South of Lesbos and Chios lies green and verdant Samos, its twin mountains of Kerketus (1,436 m.) and Ampelos (1,140 m.), visible from afar in their splendid height. Samos has a long and glorious history and is famed for its outstanding natural beauty, both of landscape and of flowers. The island's spring-fed streams run steeply down the mountain sides, shaded by woods of sweet chestnut, Oriental Plane *Platanus orientalis*, and White Poplar *Populus alba*, where nightingales sing, and golden Leopard's Bane *Doronicum pardalianches* flowers in the shade. Dense thickets of rose-coloured Oleander, *Nerium oleander*, replace the woods as the streams approach the sea. The lower mountain slopes are terraced for vines and olives, and in spring are coloured by the pink of almonds and the white of Wild Pear. Higher up still the Tree Heath *Erica arborea* takes over, and the Pine woods of *Pinus halepensis* are succeeded at the highest levels by the Greek Fir *Abies cephalonica*. A striking feature of the Samos mountain sides from near sea level up to the Fir tree zone is the handsome Funeral Cypress *Cupressus sempervirens*, growing singly or in small clumps. Although sometimes planted, *C. sempervirens* is a true native of Samos as of other Greek islands.

In spring the conifer woods are carpeted with that lovely harbinger of the Grecian spring, blue *Anemone blanda*, often growing with crocuses, golden *C. balansae* and lilac *C. nubigena*. Later on there flowers in these woods the little yellow fritillary *F. pineticola*. In spring too blooms one of Samos's endemics, the yellow *Muscari macrocarpum*. There is still some mystery about this species, as it has been, and still is, confused with the more spectacular and very heavily scented *M. moschatum* which is often placed in bunches on hotel tables and which is widely cultivated in gardens on the island, but in fact is a native of Asia Minor. Another flower of Asia Minor, but also a native of Samos, is the sweetly scented *Hyacinthus orientalis*, the parent of our garden hyacinths, which flowers in the olive groves and on the hillsides in March.

Orchids abound in Samos: *Ophrys speculum* and *O. lutea var. minor* flower in profusion, with the heavily patterned Woodcock orchid *Ophrys scolopax*, and little *Orchis anatolica* with delicate stems, carrying pink long-spurred, purple-spotted flowers.

June in Samos brings a glory of golden *Spartium junceum* on the sea cliffs, with the bushy, centaurea-like *Chamaepeuce mutica* and the small pink *Cistus parviflorus*, often growing with sweet-scented myrtle, *Myrtus communis*. On the hillsides flowers the tall graceful hollyhock, *Alcea cretica*, tall mulleins such as *Verbascum sinuatum* with its great branched inflorescence, and the enormous thistle *Onopordum myriacanthum*, whose large flowers, surrounded by incurved purple bracts, are carried on stems nearly 2 m. high.

In autumn the golden flowers of *Sternbergia lutea* appear among the dead herbage and even between the stones of walls, while higher in the mountains *S. colchiciflora*, with lemon yellow starry flowers, shares the autumn scene with the typical colchicum of these eastern islands, *C. variegatum* with tessellated pink flowers. Here and there can be found the powder-blue flowers of *Muscari parviflorum*, often growing at sea level, but spreading quite high into the hills. *Scilla autumnalis* is everywhere, and so is the Sea Squill *Urginea maritima*, whose tall spires of tightly packed white flowers decorate the driest, rockiest places on the coast, where they are sometimes accompanied by pink-flowered *Erica manipuliflora*, especially where the predominant limestone is replaced by a less alkaline soil.

South-west of Samos lies Ikaria, a high steep island whose main claim to botanical fame is that of being the only home of a very lovely broad-leafed snowdrop, *Galanthus ikariae*. Other interesting botanical features of this island are the great areas of the mountain crests which are covered by the ericaceous *Arbutus unedo*, so loved by bees, a source of the famous local honey, is accompanied by the tree heath *Erica arborea*. Lower down the hillsides the dark blue and white annual lupin, *Lupinus albus ssp. graecus*, colours miles of the hillsides in March.

Southwards again are the Dodecanese, stretching from Patmos in the north to Rhodes in the south, and including many more islands than the name implies. Rhodes is the largest and the most botanically interesting of the group, in that here the strong botanical influence of nearby Asia is evidenced by the occurrence of such striking plants as the scarlet form of *Ranunculus asiaticus*, and a few individuals of *Liquidambar orientalis*, a handsome tree with its main range in Asia Minor. It also possesses such plants as *Cyclamen persicum*, the distinct, large-leaved Rhodes form of *Cyclamen repandum*, and its own white peony, *P. rhodia*.

Karpathos, lying between Rhodes and Crete, shares some of the striking flowers of both.

Crete itself is unique among the Greek islands; it is both the largest, 257 km. long and up to 57 km. wide, and the most southerly, only 322 km. from the coast of Africa. It is also the most mountainous, consisting almost entirely of a chain of mountains, only partially interrupted by the large Messara plain which lies in the south of mid-Crete. The White Mountains in the west of the island, Mount Ida in the centre, and, further east, Mount Dikti all rise to over 2,000 m. The easternmost Sitia range is lower, with peaks up to 1,476 m. Coastal plains are narrow or non-existent, but a striking feature of the Cretan geography is the formation of small isolated plains high in the mountains, notably the Omalos plateau in the White Mountains, the Nibha plain in the Mount Ida massif, and the Lassithi plain under Mount Dikti (7).

Such is the background for Crete's famous flora, which includes 130 species endemic to the island, a mountain flora of quite extraordinary interest and beauty, and a unique display of 'chasmophytes', plants adapted and often restricted to the cliffs and the shady depths of the gorges which are so striking a feature, especially of the White Mountains (8).

The geographical relationships are of equal interest; the eastern affinities of the flora of all southern Greece and its islands have already been stressed, and this relationship is seen in extreme form in Crete. It is noteworthy that its mountain flora has lost the last remaining examples of 'alpine' species, which had persisted even as far as Mount Taygetos in the southern Peloponnese; instead, the high mountain species of Crete show many Asiatic relationships. There is even a hint of Africa in such a species as little *Viola scorpiuroides* of North Africa which scrambles among the low cistus bushes in the far east of the island, beyond Sitia, opening its small brown-blotched yellow flowers in earliest March.

The sea shore of Crete shows many of the plants to be seen elsewhere in Greece, but there are a few special features. *Cichorium spinosum*, much branched and spiny, with pale blue flowers, is here quite a common plant. Low-growing *Anthemis cretica* is common on and near the shore, often growing in pure sand, with much-dissected leaves and bright yellow button flowers lacking ray florets. On the rocks and cliffs of the coast grows, though very locally, the shrubby *Dianthus arboreus*, forming quite large bushes with narrow and curved blue-green fleshy leaves and short-stalked scented pink flowers. On the sea shore of the far eastern tip of Crete, at Vai, grows the only indigenous palm of Greece in a grove which has appeared in so many of the travel brochures of Greece and its islands. It is a Cretan form of the Date Palm *Phoenix dactylifera*, sometimes called *P. theophrasti*, and is another link with North Africa. It originally occurred in several places in Crete and in 1968 a new grove was discovered in a very inaccessible spot on the south coast.

The macchie of Crete contains a higher proportion of spiny, prickly, and fleshy-rooted species than elsewhere in Greece, reflecting the need for plants living in this very dry, hot climate to reduce water loss. Spiny *Berberis cretica* and *Euphorbia acanthothamnos* are often dominant. In the phrygana there is a high proportion of white-felted species, some spiny, some tap-rooted. These include several species of *Sideritis*, with whorls of pink, yellow, or white flowers. *Teucrium polium*, also white-felted, carries dense rounded heads of whitish flowers; and these are joined by such common constituents of the phrygana as pink-flowered *Satureia thymbra* and *Micromeria graeca*, both of them hairy and bristly plants, and by all the thymes and other aromatic herbs that we have seen in the same plant association all over Greece.

The anemone of early spring in Crete is *A. coronaria* and is most usually seen in colours ranging from white to pale or dark purple. The dark purple colour form often predominates, and sometimes reaches a very large size; the scarlet colour form which is so often the commonest plant in many parts of Greece is rare in Crete, but a very beautiful clear pink form is outstanding. One of the most beautiful of the endemic flowers of Crete is *Anemone heldreichii*, a small delicate species with numerous narrow petals backed with blue and with purple centres, sometimes low on the ground, or quite long-stemmed among shrubs. This anemone is never very abundant, growing in small groups or singly, and is most often seen in the western half of the island. At the time of the anemone's flowering there also flowers throughout Crete that link with Asia Minor *Ranunculus asiaticus*, usually in white, pink, or yellow colour forms.

Many of the bulbous plants which can be seen elsewhere in Greece grow also on Crete, but *Tulipa saxatilis* (including *T. bakeri*) and *T. cretica* are unique to the island. *T. cretica* is a delicate, small tulip, white touched with pink, while the other species is of varying shades of pink with yellow at the base of the flower; the botanical status of its different forms is at present under discussion.

Fritillaries in Crete are only represented by *F. messanensis* in a variety of forms, and cyclamens by the island's own species, small white-flowered, sweet-scented *C. creticum*, for long regarded as a geographical variety of *C. repandum*. Pink-flowered varieties of *C. creticum* have been reported, but are rare. *Cyclamen persicum* has been reported on several occasions from Crete but there seems to be some doubt about these records. In autumn *C. graecum* comes into flower.

In the mountains, where the winter snows may lie until late June, grow many of Crete's rarest and most beautiful flowers. At the edge of the melting snow appears *Crocus sieberi var. sieberi*, a form local to Crete, and perhaps supreme among all the crocuses, white or palest purple in colour with darker featherings and with rich golden yellow at the flower's base. Also flowering at the edge of the snow is *Corydalis uniflora*: it carries one or two long-spurred white flowers veined with purple on delicate stems. *Chionodoxa nana* is one of the two Cretan species which represent an otherwise completely Asian genus; its small light blue flowers often accompany the corydalis. In the steep stone screes of the upper mountain slopes flowers *Asperula incana*, even more densely white-woolly than *A. arcadiensis* of Mount Taygetos in the Peloponnese, but with the same charming pink flowers. But the undisputed king of these high, bare, and rocky places is *Anchusa caespitosa* whose brilliant dark blue flowers sit low in the centres of their rosettes of narrow bristly dark green leaves, and will not be seen until late May or June.

In the crevices of the steepest rock faces flowers *Linum arboreum*, covering its tough woody-based little shrubs with such a profusion of widely open golden flowers that the leaves can hardly be seen. Three mountain St John's Worts (hypericums) also inhabit crevices, making small prostrate mats on the rock face, with spreading branches carrying tightly packed little blue green leaves and bright yellow flowers, reddish in bud. *Gagea* (*Lloydia*) *graeca* grows in these same rock crevices, with narrow grass-like leaves and small sprays of white flowers streaked with purple, like miniature lilies.

Among the mountain boulders flower bushes of sweet-scented purple to yellow *Daphne sericea*, and pink-flowered *Prunus prostrata* moulds its woody much-branched stems around the rock surfaces. In the shade of larger rocks and in small damp gullies you may be fortunate to find *Arum creticum*, loveliest of arums, with small creamy white to yellow slender spathe up to 12 cm. long around the purple spadix; the leaves are arrow-shaped and unspotted. Happy in the crevices of shady cliffs, even at quite high altitudes, flowers the striking yellow, long-spurred *Orchis provincialis*, often accompanied by *Cyclamen creticum*. In the hottest, sunniest and stoniest places, where the golden spikes of *Asphodeline lutea* relieve the dazzling white of this limestone wilderness, you may come across tightly-growing tufts of *Onosma erecta* with its lemon-yellow flowers.

43

The lovely golden-centred white flowers of *Paeonia clusii* may be seen here and there in the high mountains of Crete, striking in April and May among the boulders and in the thin woods of cypress; you may sometimes see shepherds, bringing their flocks back from their far-ranging search for scanty pasturage in the hills, carrying great bunches of this glorious peony.

In the famous Cretan gorges, through which the mountain torrents make their steep way to the sea, grows and flowers a rich assemblage of plants adapted to life on the cliffs in these narrow, damp, and shady places. They include many endemic species. Here *Paeonia clusii* grows, and shrubby *Ebenus cretica* hangs in wide festoons which flower in May in cascades of pink and silver. *Verbascum spinosum* makes dense, low silvery bushes where the short-stemmed yellow flowers appear in summer among the spines. Another species, *Verbascum* (*Celsia*) *arcturus*, has its softly hairy grey rosettes of wavy-edged leaves in the cliffs, sprouting long, wiry flowering stems of long-stalked violet-centred yellow flowers in loose sprays.

The campanula family is well represented: *Petromarula pinnata* is the Cretan Rock Lettuce, a cliff and gorge plant with long tap roots in the rock crevices, basal tufts of large deeply cut leaves, and flowering stems up to half a metre high carrying spikes of widely open starry flowers of a pale purple. In the deepest darkest depths of the Cretan gorges, where little sunlight ever penetrates, flowers its relation *Symphyandra cretica*, with unbranched stems up to 60 cm. high rising from basal clusters of light-green hairless leaves, carrying large white or palest purple bells.

So the long rough and stony walks down the Samaria (8), the Nimbros, or other smaller and less famous Cretan gorges will be well worth the effort, taking one through a unique habitat where grow beautiful and rare plants which can be seen nowhere else in the world.

In Crete, as we have here seen, there are many endemic species, enriching its flora and of the greatest botanical interest; but it must always be borne in mind that the basic flora here, as in all the islands, is that wonderfully rich and varied collection of species to be seen throughout Greece.

6. WILD FLOWERS ON THE ANCIENT SITES

Visitors to the famous sites of Greek antiquity can hardly fail to be impressed by the great wealth of flowers on and around most of them. This is common to all, and has nothing to do with their physical or geological features, whether they are set in the mountains, on the lower hills, on the plains, or by the sea shore. It is a common experience among leaders of groups visiting the sites to have difficulty in holding the interest of the party in Greece's antiquities, in face of the counter-attraction of the colourful and exciting wild flowers displaying their living charms all around. Why should these ancient places be so favoured? The answer is usually that these sites and their wild flowers are protected by fences or other means from grazing by herds of sheep and goats.

The ancient Greeks with their innate perception often set their religious centres in places of great natural beauty, sometimes quiet and peaceful as at Epidauros, sometimes majestic and awe-inspiring as at Delphi, and it is to these perfect settings that the wild flowers, which were there before man, have returned, persist, and now decorate these sites with their beauty. Naturally the flowers on the old sites will flower, here as elsewhere, at their normal times, so that one must be there in spring to see their finest display.

Greece is so well endowed with famous sites of antiquity that it would be absurd to try to deal with them all, so here we will mention but a few of the better known and most easily accessible of these places. What better site to begin with than the 'Navel of the Earth', Delphi, regarded with awe throughout the old world of Greece. Delphi remains today supreme among the sites of antiquity, in a setting where awe-inspiring mountain scenery – the lower slopes of Parnassos itself – is set above the vast chasm of the Pleistos gorge. Far below, stretching away to the gulf of Corinth, lie limitless stretches of olive groves, silvery grey on the plains and the lower slopes Ancient Delphi, even the shattered ruins that remain, relics of so many years of human aspiration, demands to be seen (1). Much beauty remains, and this beauty is enhanced by the wild flowers that bloom so brilliantly among the broken walls, the grass-grown Stadium, and the Theatre.

In April *Campanula rupestris* flowers purple in the crevices of ancient marble blocks; golden *Alkanna graeca* hangs down the faces of the walls, with tubular-flowered Golden Drop *Onosma frutescens*. Along the path which winds steeply up above Apollo's temple towards the Stadium, in broken shade from the trees where the grass grows long and lush, there flowers the Grecian Honesty *Lunaria annua ssp. pachyrhiza*, purple flowered and distinguished by its sweet scent. Here too, is handsome yellow-flowered *Euphorbia characias ssp. wulfenii*. In and around the Stadium grow ground orchids in abundance. Many of the common species are here, including the handsome Sawfly orchid *Ophrys tenthredinifera*, the Venus's Looking Glass orchid *Ophrys speculum*, and the tall fleshy-stemmed Giant

45

Orchid *Barlia robertiana* with tight-packed reddish-purple or greenish flowers and long bracts.

Above the Stadium itself, on the steep grassy and stony banks which lead up to the cliffs, are opening the first starry flowers of the yellow asphodel *Asphodeline lutea*. Still further above the Stadium, growing low and inconspicuous in the grass below walls and around boulders, flower small bulbous plants; among them a very beautiful grape hyacinth relation of a striking turquoise blue, *Bellevalia dubia*, and a small light blue 'hyacinth', *Strangweia spicata*. Here and there flowers *Tulipa australis*, its small golden stars backed by orange-red, and wherever the limestone pushes out of the hillside in low outcrops *Iris attica* can be seen flowering in its varied colour forms from grey and yellow through violet and gold to dark purple.

Far below, past the Castalian spring, on the terraces below the road where lie the ruins of the Gymnasium and the lovely Doric Tholos, the olive groves begin, and they are well worth attention, for at their edges and between the trees grows a most handsome form of the Honeywort, *Cerinthe retorta*, its smooth blue-green leaves and flowers of purple and gold standing out in the dark shade of the olives.

Probably the approach to Delphi has been the usual one by car or coach up the fast motor road from Athens, perhaps with a pause to visit one of the most lovely of the Byzantine monasteries of Greece, Osios Loukas in the foothills of Mount Helicon. There is much to be said for a return to Athens by a different route from Delphi, which starts down the steep mountainside towards Itea, the little port on the north shore of the Corinth Gulf. This road offers a wonderful impression of the sea of olive trees which back the shore of the Gulf and climb far up the hillsides as far as eye can see. By the roadside and in the olive groves flower anemones, scarlet, blue, and purple. From the small harbour of Itea there are frequent ferry boats that chug their noisy way across the blue Gulf to Egion on the southern shore; from there it is a couple of hour's bus journey to the heart of Athens.

Not so far away, to the south of Corinth, lie two of the most famous of the old sites, Mycenae and Epidauros, each so significant in the history and legends of ancient Greece. They represent dramatically two aspects of the old world. Mycenae, with its fierce warrior traditions of the north, squats impregnable behind great fortifications in its mountain setting; Epidauros, low-lying among quiet olive groves, still breathes healing and recreation, even though the old inns where the sick came for lodging are now jumbled ruins of broken walls and columns. In March or April the grass-grown site of Epidauros with its immense area of pathetic ruins is gay with scarlet *Anemone pavonina* and *A. coronaria* flowering among the broken marble. Wild almond trees are flowering pink against the blue sky, their trunks often growing out of the stone or marble of the old walls.

There is a sandy path to the great amphitheatre, which is usually quiet and empty early in the season, so different from July and August when the happy Athenian crowds flock here to participate in the great Greek plays that were first performed so long ago. On the little hills behind the theatre the silvery olives grow, and among them the ground is white with the delicate daisies of the Grecian Chamomile *Anthemis chia*. Between the stone seats of the theatre itself is flowering the indigo blue *Muscari commutatum*, handsome in this setting against the white stone. In the grassy banks below are the sky-blue flowers of the narrow leaved annual *Lupinus angustifolius*, and the dwarf Star of Bethlehem *Ornithogalum nanum* with its snow-white stars.

North-east from quiet Epidauros lies Mycenae, and a greater contrast could hardly be imagined. No peace was here in these bare rocky hills where the immensely thick stone walls seem to have grown out of the underlying rock, and where the great lioness-crowned portal still seems a living threat. Yet, as one walks up in the brilliant sunshine of an early spring morning from the village down below, the savage old tales of war and death are softened by the beauty of the scene. The Judas trees on the hillside are in full glory of rosy-purple flowers on the still leafless branches. Tall white mignonette and purple viper's bugloss flower by the roadside, and the approach to the grim walls of the old city is lightened by trees of the wild pear *Pyrus pyraster* foaming with white blossom.

In the Citadel itself the wild flowers have taken possession again. *Sarcopoterium spinosum* the Spiny Burnet, low growing and densely spiny, shows the buds of its red flowers among the ruins, and here are the asphodels *A. microcarpus* and *A. fistulosus*, gay vetches and many annuals. On the hillsides behind the Citadel golden *Ophrys lutea* is in particularly fine form, while between boulders, preferring their shady side, are the fascinating green and brown bells of *Fritillaria graeca*. Their slightly mysterious, even sinister air seems appropriate in this setting with the legend-haunted Citadel of Mycenae immediately below.

From this vantage point the plain of Argos, now so rich with olive groves and orange orchards, stretches away in the distance to the sea, and the road to Nauplia passes another grim Mycenaean fortress in Tiryns, now in the inappropriate setting of fruit orchards and tidy farmsteads (and the local prison!). Brilliant scarlet corn poppies sprout among the huge stones.

From Nauplia a short bus ride takes one to Asine, yet another Mycenaean citadel, but this time in a lovely setting on a small rocky headland with sea on three sides. Inland lie the orange groves in a wide plain ending at the sea shore in quiet sand dunes. The remains of the citadel have to be looked for, but still look out to sea from the cliff edge, and some of the rich finds from the site can be seen in the museum at Nauplia. The approach to the headland from the landward side is well guarded by cliffs, and on their steeply angled slabs flowers the tree Spurge *Euphorbia dendroides* in dense rounded thickets. With it blooms the Red Valerian *Centranthus ruber*, so gay on this steep rock face. Below there are orchids, *Ophrys fusca* with its sub-species *iricolor* growing in the rough grass. High on the headland, overlooking the sea, are the tall spikes of the sage *Salvia triloba*, grey-leaved and purple flowered. It is a small, little-visited site, this Mycenaean Asine, but of the greatest charm.

In the Peloponnese still, Olympia must be visited (3), and here there are flowers in plenty: a rich abundance of annuals, biennials, and bulbous plants. It is a low-lying site, tending to be wet in the winter, and is much favoured by graceful *Gladiolus segetum* with its rosy purple flowers, and innumerable anemones. There are many orchids in the low heathy hills around, notably the Monkey orchid *Orchis simia*.

The Peloponnese also holds Mistra, a magnificent abandoned Byzantine city on a steep hillside packed with flowers including a remarkable assemblage of orchids (2). It adjoins Sparta, where nothing is left of that stern warrior state but a rocky hillside. In steep ravines in the foothills of near-by Mount Taygetos there are many flowers including carpets of bright pink *Cyclamen repandum* above marbled leaves.

In the far south old Nestor's palace at 'sandy Pylos' is well worth seeing, and so is the extraordinary peninsula of Monemvasia, reached only by causeway. Pylos especially is rich in orchids.

Now, as in classical times, Athens is the focal point of Greece. It is a modern city, full of noisy traffic; but constantly, at the end of some un-exciting street, one sees high up the Acropolis crowned by the Parthenon, honey coloured against the blue sky. The wise traveller, timing his visit early in the year to enjoy the wild flowers to the full, will also have the advantage of seeing such wonders as the Acropolis, in the heart of Athens, without the distraction of the inevitable crowds during the tourist season.

Below the Propylaea are gay flowering shrubs; planted certainly, but native nevertheless, to be found wild on many a country hillside, and most suitable here. There is the Tree Medick *Medicago arborea*, with trefoil leaves and clusters of orange-yellow flowers. Here too is *Teucrium fruticans*, relation of rosemary, lacking its aromatic fragrance but striking in its long-lipped pale blue flowers and narrow inrolled leaves of darkest shining green with silvery-felt below.

On the summit of the Acropolis, even between the marble slabs, grow the wild flowers that have doubtless always persisted here: *Asphodelus fistulosus* with its delicate pinkish flowering spikes, *Erodium gruinum*, *Echium plantagineum*, *Reseda alba*, and many others.

The cliffs of the southern face of the Acropolis have been widely colonised by the Prickly Pear *Opuntia ficus-indica*, which is not a true native plant, but was introduced in the sixteenth century. It is a handsome cactus, with large yellow flowers from May onwards, followed by squashy purple and yellow fruits. On the cliffs, and around their base, between the theatres of Herodius Atticus and of Dionysos, grows the handsome onion *Allium sphaerocephalum*, whose large spherical flower heads of a sombre red-purple are at their best in May and June.

Below the Acropolis are the ancient Greek Agora and the reconstructed east Stoa of Attalus. In front of the building is a delightfully planted wild garden containing many wild Greek shrubs and other plants. They include splendid bushes of *Teucrium fruticans*, cistuses of several species, and fine specimens of *Jasminum fruticans* with its clusters of unscented golden-yellow flowers and dark green shining leaves.

Opposite the Stoa is the beautifully preserved Doric temple called the Hephaisteion (though traditionally known as the Theseum), erected about 474 B.C. Around it myrtle, pomegranate, and other bushes grow in rows. In fact, they are thriving in the original planting pits, a metre square and deep, cut from the solid rock, in the bottom of which were found remains of earthenware pots.

In Attica, within easy reach of Athens, lies Cape Sounion, with its beautiful headland temple to Poseidon, dazzling white above the blue sea. Around it there is a display of wild flowers which can hardly be matched in all Greece.

Shun the tourist coaches, for they go late in the day, believing that visitors only wish to see sunset over the sea beyond the temple, and then to return hurriedly to Athens for dinner. There are frequent ordinary buses, and if one leaves early enough, the day is before one at the headland. The 70 km. drive, after passing through rather terrible seaside resorts, becomes increasingly beautiful along the rocky coast with occasional sandy beaches, finally rounding glorious steep headlands before, suddenly, the white pillars of Poseidon's temple appear, surprisingly high above the sea, and small in the distance.

In spring these rocky cliffs and headlands are golden-yellow with the Spring Broom *Calicotome villosa* and the softer yellow of the large-flowered Jerusalem Sage *Phlomis fruticosa*. The first cistus flowers will be opening, and over the boulders are massed low densely woven cushions of *Euphorbia acanthothamnos*, brightly green with yellow flowers. In autumn can be seen the large purple cups of colchicums flowering among these same rocks.

On the path leading up to the temple you will find in March an almost bewildering variety of flowers. On the limestone outcrops is *Iris attica* in every variety of colour and shade, with perhaps the yellow and grey colour forms outstanding. In the grass are vetches in great variety: yellow *Vicia hybrida*, *Lathyrus cicera* with striking solitary brick red flowers, and at the bases of the marbled pillars and walls of the temple the low growing *Trifolium uniflorum* with trefoil leaves and close-packed solitary flowers of a soft flesh pink. The grassy slopes leading down to the cliffs and the sea are a blaze of scarlet Poppy Anemones, *A. coronarium*, rising from sheets of pink *Silene colorata* and starry white *Ornithogalum nanum*. Bushes of white-flowered *Cistus salvifolius* and soft pink *C. incanus* are already in bloom, and so is the aromatic Mastic Bush *Pistacia lentiscus* with its tightly packed small red flowers in the leaf axils. Around the shrubs, enjoying the partial shade, are the beautiful little miniature lily flowers of *Gagea* (*Lloydia*) *graeca* with upturned trumpets of white streaked with purple.

On the cliffs themselves, in March and April, there flowers the huge 2 m. high Giant Fennel *Ferula chiliantha*, its thick, hollow, branching stems clasped by inflated sheaths, and carrying great orange, rounded umbels. It is safe here, on these rock cliffs high above the breaking waves, for it is an uncommon plant of Greece, seen only in the east of the mainland and in the eastern islands. Its slimmer relation *F. communis* is much more widespread.

Only a little way from the headland and Poseidon's great temple are the remains of a smaller temple dedicated to Athene. This site is little visited and somewhat overgrown, but has its beauty too, with a small rocky bay down below, very enticing for swimming on a warm day. In the cistus macchie around the temple site grows a rich assortment of orchids, including many examples of the Horseshoe orchid *Ophrys ferrum-equinum*, its lip carrying the characteristic blue horseshoe marking.

Between the stones of Athene's temple grows *Anchusa hybrida* with wavy-edged leaves and dark purple flowers, and here too are the small heath-like bushes of *Hypericum empetrifolium*, not yet in flower. Growing by the pathside, on the way down to the bay, are plenty of the pretty lace-like white flowers of little *Tordylium apulum*, with handsome Tassel Hyacinth *Muscari comosum*, and the Naples Garlic *Allium neapolitanum*.

In June, when all the early flowers have withered, the headland carries dwarf woody bushes of *Convolvulus oleaefolius* with narrow silvery leaves, covered now with its white trumpets, sometimes tinged with pink, and touched with yellow in the throat. The commoner scrambling *C. althaeoides* is everywhere, carrying its large flowers of purplish pink. In and around the temple the white marble is edged with scarlet poppies, while all around the tall graceful stems of mallow-like *Althaea cannabina* carry their narrow-petalled flowers of pale lilac-pink. On the headland are still flowering bushes of rosemary and rosemary-like *Teucrium fruticans*, while the wild olive will be covered with its sprays of creamy flowers.

Even in October there are wonderful flowers to be seen at Sounion. Where the poppy anemones carried their scarlet flowers in spring there is now the bright gold of crocus-like *Sternbergia sicula*, spreading down to the cliff edge, while all along the cliffs the autumn cyclamens *C. hederifolium* and *C. graecum* open their rosy flowers among the rocks, and so does the Autumn Lady's Tresses orchid *Spiranthes spiralis*. In the withered grass, rising from the dust of the long and hot summer, one may be fortunate enough to see the little pure white flowers of *Narcissus serotinus*; the gold of sternbergia and the white fragility of the narcissus form an epilogue to the changing display of flowers that has graced Sounion's headland through the year.

On Samos in the eastern Aegean, far from mainland Greece and the Peloponnese, lies the temple of Hera, once so magnificent in size and famed throughout the ancient Grecian world. It is now reduced to a single tall stone column still standing on the great site by the sea's edge, the drums of the rest lying in chaos. The site is decorated by wild gladioli and pale pink *Allium roseum* growing in the grass between the ruins, and is surrounded by rushy low lying swamps where the tall white and yellow *Iris ochroleuca* grows, as it does in near-by Lesbos, and also immense pink spikes of *Orchis laxiflora*.

Away to the south, with North Africa not so very distant, Crete is adorned by ancient sites where historical fact is encrusted with legend. What we do know is that these magnificent remains of Minoan royal or princely palaces were built in situations which must surely have been chosen for their outstanding beauty; for the people who inhabited them were not, apparently, warriors who owed their dominance in the ancient world to military success. The Minoan civilisation of Crete and of nearby Santorini has left us a glorious legacy of works of art in its architecture, frescoes, paintings, sculpture, decorated pottery, and jewellery, which testifies to a love of beauty, a flair for colour and design, and a superb technical mastery.

They must have been flower lovers too, these Minoans, for the flowers that surrounded their cities, palaces, and villas are repeated in their arts: frescoes, paintings, and pottery show such flowers as *Gynandriris sisyrinchium*, *Ranunculus asiaticus*, crocuses, sternbergias, the sea daffodil, with lilies, rushes, and olives, most delicately drawn and painted; and as you visit the sites you will find the same flowers blooming still.

In contrast Gournia, in mid-Crete, set on a low hill looking out seawards to the Gulf of Mirabello, is no royal palace, but a small town where the foundations and lower walls of little houses lie along narrow steep paved streets, radiating from central courts and halls. Among these, in March and April, the paved floors are ablaze with anemones, blue, purple, pink, or white; with an especially fine form of a large and deep golden *Ranunculus asiaticus*. Here and there are large patches of bright yellow gageas, snowy-white dwarf *Ornithogalum nanum* and taller growing clumps of *Hermodactylus tuberosus*. On the grassy hillock outside the town wall grow orchids, including *Barlia robertiana*, and great masses of the bi-coloured form of Crown Daisy, *Chrysanthemum coronarium var. discolor* – as good as any garden hybrid.

Phaestos in the south is perhaps supreme in its setting. From its small hill one looks northwards across foothills carrying terraced olive groves which succeed the oranges in the valleys, and lead the eye up to snow-capped Mount Ida. From the main part of the site the view is downwards and southwards on to the Messara plain. There are wild flowers here in plenty, with anemones in early spring and the mandrake, whose low-growing rosettes of dark green leaves hold central clusters of almost stalk-less purple flowers, flowering between the steps of the broad terraced stairways and on the palace floors. The hillsides around are thick with flowers, notably white and pink forms of *Ranunculus asiaticus* and the large pink heads of *Orchis italica*.

From Phaestos it is an easy walk to Aghia Triada, a smaller site commanding yet another outstanding view, this time to the blue southern sea beyond the coastal plain below. On and around the site flower a rich selection of orchids in March and April: pink and green *Orchis collina*

51

blooming in February is soon followed by dark-lipped *Ophrys fusca*, the pink Butterfly orchid *Orchis papilionacea*, and by later ophrys species including the endemic *Ophrys cretica* with white patterns on dark maroon lip. *Anemone heldreichii*, another Cretan endemic with narrow-petalled white flowers touched with blue on the reverse, is frequent here, with *Anemone coronaria* in an unusually fine large-flowered purple form. Around Aghia Triada may be seen another famous Cretan endemic, the silvery leaved, pink flowered *Ebenus cretica*; here this leguminous shrub does not grow in its classical habitat in gorges or on cliffs, but in the sandy soil of the hillside along the path to the site.

On the north coast of the island lies the ancient site of Mallia on a narrow coastal strip between coast and steeply rising mountains. The site itself is not especially noteworthy for plants; but very near, on the shore where in early spring the waves thunder in on the rocks, and up the deep and often sandy little bays, there is all the habitual colour of the Grecian sea shore flowers.

In the west, near Ayios Nikolaos, the originally Doric site of Lato should not be missed. Its remains rise in tiers up two small parallel rocky ridges. From their summits there is a wide view across huge groves of olives and almonds to the sea. Among Lato's many floral attractions are splendid specimens of the bright yellow form of *Ranunculus asiaticus*, and on the rocky heights the Cretan endemics *Petromarula pinnata*, a tall campanula relation, and *Alyssoides cretica*, a crucifer with bright gold flowers and spherical bluish seed capsules.

The ancient sites of Crete, Minoan, Mycenaean, Hellenistic, and even Roman, are many; some unexcavated, others relatively unimportant and virtually unknown. An example of such a site, well known to the expert, but little visited and rather difficult of access, is Polyrrhenia in the far west of Crete, a few miles north of Kastelli. It is a site bearing remains from the Minoan era to Byzantine times, finely situated in the hills behind the coast, perched on the summit of one of these hills, and commanding splendid views over rolling hilly country to the coastal plain and the sea beyond. From the road below, a maze of narrow stony mule tracks zig-zags up between the little white houses of the village; and if you guess right your path will emerge above, and continue up the hillside through as fine a display of yellow-flowered Tree Spurge, *Euphorbia dendroides*, as can be seen anywhere in Crete. The crest of the hill is littered with old walls, foundations of old houses, circular threshing floors surrounded by great stone slabs, and a small Byzantine church. Towering higher still on the neighbouring acropolis stand ancient fortifications and ruined towers. The Tree Spurge continues to dominate the scene while, here and there, little miniature fields cleared of stones produce their scanty crops of barley and oats, ripening to gold in early May, gay with poppies, crown daisies, scabious, gladioli, the bright purple of Venus' Looking-glass *Legousia speculum*, and the lilac coloured wild leek *Allium ampeloprasum*. Here and there grow the aromatic shrubby Rue, *Ruta graveolens*, with branching clusters of yellow flowers, and the little yellow flowered feathery-leaved Pheasant's Eye *Adonis microcarpa*.

Little-known Polyrrhenia, gloriously situated and rich in flowers, is an example of many more antique sites which the enquiring traveller can seek out and enjoy.

One sad comment must finally be added. Some ancient sites have, within the last two or three years, apparently been treated with weedkiller, at least immediately around antique stonework. The official explanation would presumably be that this is to prevent plants obscuring the remains and damaging them by deep-penetrating roots. It is clear that such damage can occur through the agency of strong-growing shrubs, notably figs which seed themselves freely; but the presence of bright-flowered annuals, bulbs, and plants like *Campanula rupestris* can only enhance the appeal of the sites to the great majority of visitors. It is greatly to be hoped that the Greek authorities will apply weedkiller, if at all, with more discrimination; otherwise the sites will have an unnatural aridity, while many plants will be eradicated entirely. Orchids are especially sensitive to weedkillers and regenerate very slowly, since there is a very long period between germination and flowering.

7. CULTIVATED PLANTS

The Greeks are not notable as gardeners, but they grow a number of trees for shade and decoration in squares, streets, and along country roads, as well as some for their fruits. A few plants are grown for decoration in gardens or on house walls. (The main agricultural crops are cereals and tobacco.)

This short chapter may help visitors to identify the most common decorative plants, many of which will be familiar from elsewhere in the Mediterranean region, and indeed many other places with that type of climate. Some have become more or less naturalised, and these – indicated by an asterisk below – will be found described and often illustrated in the relevant sections of this book.

The most widely cultivated tree is, of course, the Olive, *Olea europaea*,* whose fruits and their resultant oil form a major commodity and export. Its wild ancestor, *ssp. sylvestris*,* forms spiny bushes in the macchie. The Fig, *Ficus carica*,* Quince, *Cydonia oblonga*, Almond, *Prunus dulcis*,* and Pomegranate, *Punica granatum*,* are all grown, usually in small numbers. In some areas there are large groves of citrus fruits, notably lemons and sweet oranges; Crete even boasts banana plantations. The Loquat, *Eriobotrya japonica*, is regularly cultivated in gardens, where its handsome foliage is valued as much as the large-seeded orange fruits. Vines are of course widely planted – for wine-making, for currants, and over arbours as a summer shade plant. The Mastic Bush, *Pistacia lentiscus*,* is grown for mastic especially in Chios.

The American Prickly Pear, *Opuntia ficus-indica** and other species, and Century Plant, *Agave americana*,* are often used to form impenetrable hedges, and the Giant Reed, *Arundo donax*,* is sometimes grown as a wind-break, or its dry stems used to form them.

The most impressive shade tree is the Oriental Plane, *Platanus orientalis*,* old specimens of which grace many a village square and monastery terrace. Mulberries, *Morus* spp., are often grown in streets, but – like the Montpellier Maple, *Acer monspessulanus** – they are cut back drastically every spring to make vigorous heads of large, shade-producing foliage. Several species of *Eucalyptus* will be seen, mainly lining country roads; they grow fast in the congenial climate.

Another frequent street tree is the Bead Tree or Chinaberry, *Melia azederach*,* whose attractive sprays of blue and white flowers are followed by clustered brownish-yellow fruits. The Pepper Tree, *Schinus molle*, is so called because its small whitish flower sprays are followed by small reddish berries in long 'strigs', which can be used as a kind of inferior pepper; it has long fern-like leaves on pendulous branches.

The columnar Italian cypress, *Cupressus sempervirens*,* has been very widely planted, especially in and around monasteries. Frequent in towns are *Araucaria excelsa*, the Norfolk Island Pine, and *A. bidwillii*, related to

54

the Monkey Puzzle but making very tall conical trees with thin, horizontally tiered branches. Several palms are also often grown. The Tree of Heaven, *Ailanthus altissima*,* seems favoured in country villages.

Flowering trees occasionally planted include the evergreen *Magnolia grandiflora*, the Judas Tree *Cercis siliquastrum*,* *Jacaranda mimosaeflora* with its spectacular blue blooms, and *Catalpa bignonioides* the Indian Bean Tree.

Many kinds of 'mimosa' are planted for ornament; the most frequent species is probably *A. longifolia*, with willow-like leaves and flowers in spikes. Once in a while the white or pink powder-puff flowers of another leguminous tree, *Albizzia julibrissin*, will be seen. *Lagerstroemia indica* makes a bush or small tree with tightly massed pink or red flowers, whose crinkly petals give it the name Crape Myrtle. True Myrtle, *Myrtus communis*,* is sometimes seen in gardens with its small white flowers and aromatic evergreen foliage. Bay, *Laurus nobilis*,* is also cultivated.

Brightly coloured flowering shrubs include the Oleander, *Nerium oleander*,* not just in its wild red-flowered form but in pink, white, and even yellow. The brilliant red form of *Hibiscus rosa-sinensis*, with big trumpet flowers and projecting stamens, is much more often seen than its other varieties in pink, orange, etc.; there is also *H. syriacus* which is grown outside in Britain. *Pittosporum tobira* is an evergreen looking a little like a citrus especially when it produces its strongly scented white flower clusters. *Medicago arborea*,* the Tree Medick, makes a bush with orange pea flowers; *Colutea arborescens*,* the Bladder Senna, and some kinds of *Cassia* are other leguminous shrubs sometimes cultivated. The shrubby acanthus relation *Adhatoda vasica* has rather unattractive two-lipped white flowers in spikes, and leaves whose bitterness gives rise to the Latin name, which means, broadly, 'goats do not touch'.

Several climbers are often spectacular on houses. These include the familiar *Bougainvillea glabra*, almost always in its basic magenta form; trumpet vines, usually *Campsis (Bignonia) grandiflora*, and the smaller Cape Honeysuckle, *Tecomaria capensis*, with narrow trumpets in large clusters; occasionally the pale blue *Plumbago capensis*, and frequently wisteria, often allowed to grow up tall cypresses with spectacular results.

Roses are often grown, and especially in the mild climate of the eastern Aegean islands are often spectacular in size both of blooms and bushes.

Herbaceous plants are less evident, although the usual pelargoniums, asparagus ferns, and miscellaneous succulents, notably the Tree Houseleek, *Aeonium arboreum*, appear in pots. Cannas or Indian Shot are often grown in parks; monasteries seem to go in for aspidistras, and we once saw a fine display of the pink *Zephyranthes grandiflora* in pots at St Stephen in the Meteora.

Garden plots often contain Hollyhocks, *Alcea rosea*, and in Kosani, in the north-east Pindus, every one is massed with Madonna Lily, *Lilium candidum*,* which is to be found wild in the scrub near the town and was probably brought thence. Snow-in-the-Mountain, *Euphorbia marginata*, with wide white-edged bracts to the flowers, is an annual sometimes grown in gardens, to be seen as an escape, and this must also be the case with Shoofly Plant, *Nicandra physalodes*, blue-flowered and bladdery-seeded, although we have only seen it 'escaped'.

Many sandy areas of the coast are colonised with Hottentot Figs, *Carpobrotus spp.*,* and their not-so-fleshy relations the *Lampranthus**; these are South African succulents which find the climate as congenial as their own, and which are thoroughly naturalised after being grown in seaside gardens.

Signs of Turkish occupation in the past exist in old mosques, especially in the north of Greece and the Aegean Islands. A living sign is *Iris florentina*,* a handsome white 'flag' often well established, which the Moslems used to plant in their cemeteries.

Finally, there are several areas where the Arum Lily, *Zantedeschia aethiopica*, is cultivated as a florist flower, especially around Marathon.

8. REFERENCE BOOKS

It is impossible to describe and illustrate in a single reasonably small book the whole flora of mainland Greece and its islands. What we have attempted to do here is to select as representative a selection of the flora as possible, as explained in the Introduction.

Of the larger and more comprehensive Greek floras which may be used to take identification further, the standard works are *Conspectus Florae Graecae* by E. von Halácsy (1901–4); *Prodromus Florae Peninsulae Balcanicae* by A. von Hayek (1924–33); and *Flora Aegaea* by K. H. Rechinger (1949). All three books are in Latin, without illustrations, and bulky. Facsimile reprints of the first two are obtainable, but still expensive.

Of the illustrated books on the Greek flora, by far the most impressive ever produced is the *Flora Graeca* by John Sibthorp, a magnificent work produced in folio form in ten volumes between 1806 and 1840. John Sibthorp, who was Regius Professor of Botany at Oxford, travelled widely in Greece, Asia Minor, and Cyprus between 1776 and 1795, making extensive collections of botanical material, and laying the foundation of our modern knowledge of Greek wild flowers. *Flora Graeca*, which was produced after his death from an illness contracted during his travels, has an introduction by Sibthorp, and is illustrated by 966 outstandingly accurate and beautiful drawings by Ferdinard Bauer. Curiously enough they are mostly of distinctly weedy plants; there is not a monocotyledon among them! The text is in Latin. It is possible to study and enjoy Sibthorp's *Flora Graeca* only in the larger botanical libraries – the original edition was limited to 30 copies and a few more copies were collated later.

Flowers of Attica by S. C. Atchley (1938) is long out of print, though well worth looking for. It has 79 illustrations, mainly of commoner plants, and interesting comments on each. A handsome but expensive folio production, *Wild Flowers of Greece* (1968), by the late Dr C. N. Goulimis, is illustrated by paintings by Niki Goulandris of the Goulandris Botanical Museum; it gives a selection of 120 flowers, some rare, some common, and has an introduction interesting especially for the localities it gives. Dr Goulimis, whose knowledge of the Greek flora was unequalled, discovered a number of new species of Greek wild flowers. A smaller book of the same title, by K. A. Argyropoulou, is a recent Greek production, available in Athens. The text is attractive, and the 60-odd excellent colour photographs show the selected flowers in typical habitats. A series of articles by Anthony Huxley, originally published in the Journal of the Royal Horticultural Society, has been republished in revised form as an illustrated booklet by the R.H.S. under the title *Flowers in Greece*.

Of books dealing with the flora of the Mediterranean, and including many common Greek flowers, mention must be made of the excellent *Flowering Plants of the Riviera* by H. Stuart Thompson, published in 1914 and long out of print; it has a quantity of coloured illustrations. *Flowers of the Mediterranean* by Oleg Polunin and Anthony Huxley, was published in 1965, revised in 1972, and is generously illustrated by both colour photographs and line drawings. This book in particular includes many plants found in Greece.

The ultimate court of appeal in all questions of identification, terminology, and distribution of the flowers of Europe (even if one does not always agree with them) is now becoming available in *Flora Europaea*. In this herculean labour, sponsored by the Linnean Society of London, an editorial committee under the chairmanship of Prof. T. G. Tutin, with an advisory panel of Editors and regional advisers representing botanists in all European countries, has already produced the first three volumes of what is expected to be a five-volume work. It is a technical text with botanical keys and no illustrations.

The ecological aspects of the flora of Greece are fully dealt with in *The Plant Life of the Balkan Peninsula* by W. B. Turrill (1929), a long and detailed ecological study of the flora not only of Greece, but of the whole peninsula.

The works mainly used for the 'postscripts' to descriptions, mentioned in the Introduction, are those of Theophrastus and Dioscorides. Theophrastus lived from 370 to 285 B.C. and his *Enquiry into Plants* would at any period have been a very remarkable compilation about their habits, uses, and cultivation. The translation, by Sir Arthur Hort, was published in 1916 (Loeb Classical Library: Heinemann).

Dioscorides' *Herbal*, compiled in the first century A.D., is often referred to by its Latin name *De materia medica libri quinque*. It was the first comprehensive, systematic publication of its kind and greatly influenced medicine and especially herbalism ever since its first Byzantine translation in A.D. 512. It was 'Englished' by the botanist John Goodyer between 1652 and 1655, for his own use; his translation was not published until 1934, edited by Robert J. Gunther (Oxford University Press).

We have quoted freely from these authors, retaining Goodyer's original spelling and style which give an antique flavour, if not a very Greek one. One may add that Dioscorides was very free in his attribution of virtues to many plants, and we have often had to restrict ourselves to the more amusing or unexpected remedies quoted.

Information on the uses of plants has also been derived from Atchley's *Flowers of Greece* already mentioned, and L. Marret's *Fleurs de la Côte d'Azur* (1926), a useful little book sometimes available second-hand.

1. The Temple of Apollo at Delphi, with the cliff face of the Phaedriades Rocks behind. Delphi is at around 570m altitude, and the cliffs are up to 300m high.

2. Part of the Byzantine hillside town of Mistra (14th–15th centuries), overlooking the plain of Sparta. The yellow flowers are *Euphorbia characias ssp. wulfenii*.

3. An old olive and *Phlomis fruticosa* overlooking the alluvial plain of the River Alpheus and the Olympia site in the N.W. Peloponnese.

4. Stone-walled terraces on the Palaiokhora hill on the island of Aegina, south-east of Athens. This was originally the site of the island's main township.

5. *Tulipa boeotica* grows in large numbers in cornfields in the Peloponnese, where this photograph was taken, as well as in central Greece.

6. Further cornfield weeds – beautiful but harmful to crop yields – include *Gladiolus segetum* and *Chrysanthemum coronarium*. This view was taken in central Crete.

7. The Lassithi plain in eastern Crete, a flat, very fertile alluvial plateau at 830–850m altitude, with Mount Dikti (2148m) beyond it to the west.

8. A view in the Samaria Gorge in south-western Crete, which cuts down from the Omalos plain at 1100m to sea level, its cliffs up to 300m high.

9. Looking N.W. from the Astraka peak of the Gamila massif in the Pindus, across the plateau (about 2000m altitude) bisected in the distance by the Vikos gorge.

10. A dried-up river bed at about 1000m altitude on Mount Olympus in late April. Beeches just coming into leaf are giving way to *Pinus leucodermis*.

11. A coastal salt marsh with groves of Tamarisk and Giant Reed behind sandy beaches, near Gytheion in the southern Peloponnese.

12. Near the monastery of Palaiocastritsa in Corfu the cliffs plunge into the sea. Despite their steepness they are clothed in low shrubs wherever a roothold offers.

13. Ficus carica ×1/10

14. Viscum album ssp. abietis ×1/10

15. Aristolochia
clematitis ×1/3

16. Aristolochia
cretica ×1/2

17. Aristolochia hirta
×1/2

18. Aristolochia longa ×1

19. Cytinus hypocistis ×1/2

20. Carpobrotus acinaciformis ×1/12

21. Carpobrotus edulis ×1/2

22. Mesembryanthemum
    nodiflorum ×1/4

23. Aptenia cordifolia ×2/3

24. Paronychia
    argentea ×1/4

25. Paronychia
    capitata ×1/5

26. Agrostemma
    githago ×1/2

27. Silene behen ×1/6

28. Silene colorata ×1/8

29. Saponaria calabrica ×1/4

30. Dianthus sylvestris ×1/5

31. Consolida orientalis ×1/10

32. Delphinium halteratum ×2/5

33. Aquilegia amaliae
×1/3

34. Aquilegia ottonis
×1/2

35. Clematis cirrhosa
×1/3

36. Helleborus cyclophyllus ×1/3

37. Clematis flammula ×1/10

38. Anemone coronaria ×1/5

39. Anemone coronaria ×1/3

40. Anemone
coronaria ×2/5

41. Anemone
pavonina ×1/5

42. Anemone
pavonina ×1/5

43. Anemone blanda ×1/3

44. Anemone heldreichii ×1/3

45. Adonis annua ×2

46. Adonis microcarpa ×2/3

47. Adonis cupaniana ×2/3

48. Ranunculus asiaticus ×1/2

49. Ranunculus asiaticus ×1/2

50. Ranunculus asiaticus ×1/2

51. Ranunculus ficaria
ssp. ficariiformis ×1/4

52. Ranunculus ficarioides ×1/3

53. Paeonia clusii ×3/8

54. Paeonia mascula ×1/10

55. Berberis vulgaris (flower) ×1/8

56. Berberis vulgaris (fruit) ×1/8

57. Leontice leontopetalum
(flower) ×1/7

58. Leontice leontopetalum
(fruit) ×1/7

59. Corydalis solida
×1/4

60. Fumaria capreolata
×1/3

61. Hypecoum imberbe
×1/2

62. Glaucium
    corniculatum ×3/8

63. Glaucium flavum
    ×1/4

64. Papaver rhoeas
    ×1/4

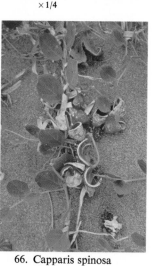

65. Capparis spinosa
    (flower) ×1/2

66. Capparis spinosa
    (fruit) ×1/4

67. Erysimum raulinii
    ×1/7

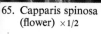
68. Malcolmia chia ×1/2

69. Malcolmia flexuosa ×1/3

70. **Malcolmia maritima** ×1/5

71. **Matthiola incana** ×1/6

72. **Matthiola sinuata** ×1/4

73. **Matthiola tricuspidata** ×1/8

74. **Aubrieta deltoidea** ×1/4

75. **Alyssoides cretica** ×1/4

76. **Draba scardica** ×1/2

77. **Aethionema saxatile** ×1/2

78. **Lunaria annua ssp. pachyrhiza** ×1/4

79. **Umbilicus horizontalis** ×1/7

80. **Jovibarba heuffelii** ×1/6

81. Saxifraga rotundifolia ×1/3

82. Saxifraga scardica ×1/5

83. Saxifraga marginata ×1/3

84. Saxifraga sempervivum ×1/4

85. Rosa pendulina ×1/4

86. Rosa sempervirens ×1/7

87. Sarcopoterium spinosum ×1/7

88. Prunus dulcis ×1/60

89. Prunus prostrata ×2/5

90. Cercis siliquastrum ×1/6

91. Calicotome villosa ×1/4

92. Genista
    acanthoclada ×1/5

93. Spartium junceum
    ×1/7

94. Colutea
    arborescens ×1/6

95. Lupinus
    angustifolius ×1/3

96. Lupinus
    micranthus ×1/3

97. Psoralea
    bituminosa ×1/4

98. Lathyrus aphaca ×1/2

99. Lathyrus grandiflorus ×2/3

100. Lathyrus cicera ×1/4

101. Astragalus lusitanicus ×1/9

102. Astragalus
hamosus ×1/4

103. Astragalus
parnassi ×1/3

104. Vicia dasycarpa
×1/5

105. Trigonella balansae ×1/4

106. Trigonella coerulescens ×1/3

107. Vicia hybrida ×1/2

108. Pisum elatius ×1/3

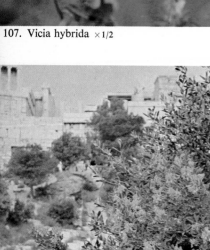

109. Medicago arborea ×1/12

110. Medicago marina ×1/2

111. Trifolium stellatum ×3/4

112. Trifolium uniflorum ×1/2

113. Coronilla varia ×1/2

114. Tetragonolobus purpureus ×1/2

115. Anthyllis tetraphylla ×1/2

116. Anthyllis vulneraria
ssp. praepropera ×1/2

117. Anthyllis
hermanniae ×1/5

118. Ononis viscosa
×1/2

119. Ebenus cretica
×1/7

120. Oxalis pes-caprae ×1/5

121. Oxalis pes-caprae fl. pl. ×1/2

122. Geranium cinereum ssp.
    subcaulescens ×1/2

123. Geranium macrorrhizum ×1/2

124. Geranium sanguineum ×1/2

125. Geranium tuberosum ×1/2

126. Euphorbia characias
ssp. wulfenii ×1/10

127. Euphorbia rigida
×1/12

128. Euphorbia
dendroides ×1/50

129. Euphorbia characias
ssp. characias ×1/20

130. Euphorbia myrsinites ×1/6

131. Erodium
chrysanthum ×1/3

132. Linum arboreum
×1/2

133. Linum leucanthum
×1/6

134. Erodium gruinum ×1/12

135. Linum pubescens ×1/3

136. Euphorbia
acanththamnos ×1/8

137. Ruta chalepensis
×1/2

138. Dictamnus albus
×1/8

139. Melia azederach (flower) ×1/2

140. Melia azederach (fruit) ×1/10

141. Cotinus
coggygria ×1/16

142. Pistacia lentiscus
×1/3

143. Pistacia
terebinthus ×1/6

144. Paliurus spina-
     christi (flower) ×1/10

145. Paliurus spina-
     christi (fruit) ×1/5

146. Malva sylvestris
     ×1/6

147. Althaea hirsuta
     ×2/3

148. Malope
     malacoides ×1/4

149. Lavatera arborea
     ×1/5

150. Althaea
     cannabina ×1/10

151. Alcea pallida
     ssp. cretica ×1/12

152. Alcea rosea ×1/12

153. Daphne gnidium ×2/3

154. Daphne oleoides ×1/2

155. Daphne sericea ×1/2

156. Thymelaea tartonraira ×1

157. Daphne jasminea
×1/2

158. Thymelaea
hirsuta ×3/4

159. Rhamnus
alaternus ×1/6

160. Hypericum
apollinis ×1/3

161. Hypericum
empetrifolium ×1/4

162. Hypericum
olympicum ×1/7

163. Viola
delphinantha ×1/2

164. Viola gracilis ×1/2

165. Viola hymettia
×1/3

166. Tuberaria
guttata ×1/4

167. Helianthemum
oelandicum ×1/5

168. Fumana
procumbens ×2/3

169. Cistus incanus ssp. creticus ×1/5

170. Cistus monspeliensis ×1/2

171. Cistus parviflorus ×1/3

172. Cistus salvifolius ×3/8

173. Tamarix parviflora ×1/40

174. Ecballium elaterium ×1/4

175. Opuntia ficus-indica (flower) ×1/8

176. Opuntia ficus-indica (fruit) ×1/10

177. Myrtus communis ×1/2

178. Punica granatum ×1/3

179. Cornus mas
(flower) ×1/4

180. Cornus mas
(autumn leaf) ×1/10

181. Eryngium
creticum ×1/3

182. Crithmum
maritimum ×1/3

183. Ferula communis
×1/30

184. Ferula chiliantha
×1/30

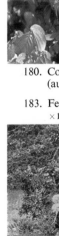

185. Tordylium
apulum (flower) ×1/2

186. Tordylium
apulum (fruit) ×3/4

187. Smyrnium
perfoliatum ×1/6

188. Arbutus andrachne ×1/16

189. Arbutus unedo ×1/7

190. Lysimachia
atropurpurea ×1/4

192. Primula vulgaris
var. alba ×1/4

191. Anagallis
arvensis ×1/3

193. Cyclamen creticum ×1/2

194. Cyclamen graecum ×1/4

195. Cyclamen hederifolium ×2/5

196. Cyclamen persicum ×1/5

197. Cyclamen repandum ×1/6

198. Cyclamen repandum var. rhodense ×1/5

199. Limonium sinuatum ×1/5

200. Styrax officinale ×1/3

201. Jasminum fruticans ×1/2

202. Fraxinus ornus ×1/10

203. Vinca herbacea ×1/3

204. Cionura erecta ×1/4

205. Nerium oleander
×1/10

206. Putoria calabrica
×2/3

207. Asperula
arcadiensis ×1/4

208. Convolvulus althaeoides
ssp. althaeoides ×1/5

209. Convolvulus althaeoides
ssp. tenuissimus ×1/5

210. Convolvulus cantabrica ×1/8

211. Convolvulus oleifolius ×1/7

212. Convolvulus tricolor ×1/2

213. Cuscuta sp. (on Euphorbia
acanthothamnos) ×1/5

214. Heliotropium europaeum ×1/2

215. Buglossoides purpurocaerulea ×1/3

216. Lithodora hispidula ×1/6

217. Onosma montana ×1/8

218. Onosma erecta
×3/5

219. Onosma frutescens
×1/8

220. Onosma graeca
×1/6

221. Cerinthe major ×1/3

222. Cerinthe retorta ×1/8

223. Alkanna graeca ssp. boeotica ×1/2

224. Echium italicum ×1/25

225. Echium
angustifolium ×1/3

226. Echium
plantagineum ×1/3

227. Echium
plantagineum ×1/3

228. Anchusa azurea
×1/7

229. Anchusa undulata
ssp. hybrida ×1/3

230. Borago officinalis
×1/2

231. Cynoglossum
creticum (flower) ×1/3

232. Cynoglossum
creticum (fruit) ×2/3

233. Cynoglossum
columnae (fruit) ×2/3

234. Vitex agnus-castus ×1/5

235. Ajuga chamaepitys ssp. chia ×1/2

236. Teucrium fruticans ×1/2

237. Prasium majus ×1/3

238. Phlomis fruticosa ×1/10

239. Phlomis herba-venti ×1/10

240. Lamium
garganicum ×1/6

241. Ballota
acetabulosa ×1/12

242. Melittis
melissophyllum ×1/4

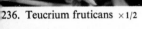

243. **Stachys candida** ×1/3

244. **Thymus capitatus** ×1/3

245. **Rosmarinus officinalis** ×1/4

246. **Lavandula stoechas** ×1/3

247. **Salvia glutinosa** ×1/10

248. **Salvia pomifera** ×1/6

249. **Salvia sclarea** ×1/8

251. **Salvia triloba** ×1/8

250. **Salvia verbenaca ssp. clandestina** ×3/5

252. Hyoscyamus albus ×1/3

253. Hyoscyamus aureus ×1/4

254. Mandragora offici-
narum (flower) ×1/5

255. Mandragora offici-
narum (flower) ×1/5

256. Mandragora offici-
narum (fruit) ×1/5

257. Datura metel ×1/8

258. Nicotiana glauca ×1/4

259. Verbascum
     arcturus ×1/5

260. Verbascum
     graecum ×1/20

261. Verbascum
     sinuatum ×1/15

262. Verbascum
     speciosum ×1/25

263. Verbascum undu-
     latum (rosette) ×1/7

264. Verbascum undu-
     latum (flower) ×1/15

265. Linaria
     chalepensis ×1

266. Digitalis lanata
     ×1/10

267. Bellardia
     trixago ×1/2

268. Globularia
alypum ×1/10

269. Acanthus
spinosus ×1/7

270. Orobanche
amethystea ×1/8

271. Orobanche
caryophyllacea ×1/4

272. Orobanche
crenata ×1/12

273. Orobanche minor
×1/6

274. Orobanche ramosa
×1/2

275. Fedia cornucopiae
×1/3

276. Pterocephalus
parnassi ×1/3

277. Michauxia
campanuloides ×2/3

278. Petromarula
pinnata ×1/5

279. Campanula
versicolor ×1/3

280. Campanula rupestris ×1/8

281. Campanula rupestris
ssp. anchusaeflora ×1/5

282. Campanula drabifolia ×1/3

283. Campanula spathulata ×1/2

284. Campanula
ramosissima ×1/2

285. Legousia
pentagonia ×1/4

286. Legousia speculum-
veneris ×1/2

287. Tolpis barbata ×1/2

288. Crepis incana ×1/3

289. Scolymus hispanicus ×1/4

290. Cichorium spinosum ×1/2

291. Scorzonera lanata ×1/3

292. Scorzonera purpurea ×1/3

293. Tragopogon porrifolius ×5/8

294. Carthamus lanatus ×1/2

295. Echinops graecus ×1/10

296. Echinops ritro ×1/5

297. Centaurea mixta ×2/3

298. Centaurea solstitialis ×1/3

299. Onopordum
myriacanthum ×1/10

300. Cardopatium
corymbosum ×1/3

301. Silybum
marianum ×1/2

302. Galactites
    tomentosa ×1/10

303. Notobasis syriaca
    ×2/5

304. Xeranthemum
    annuum ×2/3

305. Anthemis chia ×1/8

306. Anthemis cretica ×1/2

307. Anthemis tomentosa ×1/3

308. Cirsium candelabrum ×1/25

309. Cirsium acarna ×1/15

310. Chaemaepeuce mutica ×1/20

311. Otanthus maritimus ×1/4

312. Evax pygmaea ×1

313. Phagnalon rupestre ×1/5

314. Helichrysum siculum ×1/4

315. Pallenis spinosa ×1/3

316. Calendula arvensis ×1/4

317. Doronicum
    caucasicum ×1/5

318. Doronicum
    columnae ×1/8

319. Inula viscosa
    ×1/10

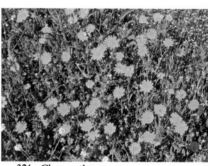

320. Inula candida ×1/4

321. Chrysanthemum segetum ×1/10

322. Chrysanthemum coronarium ×1/7

323. Chrysanthemum coronarium
    var. discolor ×1/3

324. Colchicum
autumnale ×1/5

325. Colchicum
boissieri ×1/5

326. Colchicum
cupanii ×1/4

327. Colchicum macrophyllum
(flower) ×1/4

328. Colchicum macrophyllum
(leaves) ×1/15

329. Colchicum
sibthorpii ×1/6

330. Colchicum
catacuzenium ×1/3

331. Colchicum
variegatum ×1/3

332. Asphodelus albus ×1/4

333. Asphodelus
fistulosus ×1/6

334. Asphodelus
microcarpus ×1/20

335. Asphodeline
    lutea ×1/15

336. Lilium candidum
    ×1/15

337. Lilium martagon
    ×1/5

338. Lilium
    chalcedonicum ×1/4

339. Lilium heldreichii
    ×1/4

340. Urginea maritima
    ×1/15

341. Gagea arvensis
    ×2/3

342. Gagea fistulosa
    ×1/3

343. Gagea graeca ×1/2

344. Tulipa saxatilis (form) ×1/3

345. Tulipa boeotica ×1/4

346. Tulipa saxatilis
(form) ×1/4

347. Tulipa australis
×2/5

348. Tulipa hageri ×1/3

349. Fritillaria graeca
×2/3

350. Fritillaria graeca
×2/3

351. Fritillaria
messanensis ×1/3

352. Fritillaria
bithynica ×2/5

353. Fritillaria pinardii
×1/2

354. Fritillaria obliqua
×2/3

355. Allium ampeloprasum ×1/3

356. Allium subhirsutum ×1

357. Allium roseum ×1/5

358. Allium sphaerocephalon ×1/4

359. **Strangweia**
    spicata ×1/2

360. **Ornithogalum**
    montanum (form) ×3/5

361. **Ornithogalum**
    nutans ×1/3

362. **Ornithogalum**
    montanum (form) ×1/6

363. **Ornithogalum**
    nanum ×1/3

364. **Ornithogalum**
    narbonense ×1/3

365. **Hyacinthus orientalis** ×1/2

366. **Scilla bifolia** ×1/2

367. Scilla
hyacinthoides ×1/4

368. Bellevalia ciliata
×1/4

369. Bellevalia dubia
×1/3

370. Muscari commutatum ×1/4

371. Muscari neglectum ×2

372. Muscari parviflorum ×1/3

373. Polygonatum odoratum ×1/3

374. Muscari comosum ×1/4

375. Muscari comosum var. plumosum ×1/2

376. Smilax aspera (flower) ×1/2

377. Smilax aspera (fruit) ×1/2

378. Asparagus acutifolius ×1/8

379. Ruscus aculeatus ×1/3

380. Galanthus
     ikariae ×1/6

381. Galanthus nivalis
     ssp. reginae-olgae ×1/3

382. Sternbergia lutea
     ×1/3

383. Pancratium maritimum ×1/2

384. Sternbergia sicula ×1/3

385. Narcissus poeticus
     var. hellenicus ×1/3

386. Narcissus tazetta
     ×1/4

387. Narcissus
     serotinus ×1/2

388. Romulea
     bulbocodium ×1/2

389. Romulea bulbocodium
     var. leichtliniana ×2/3

390. Romulea linaresii
     ssp. graeca ×1

391. Crocus boryi ×1/3

392. Crocus cancellatus ×1/3

393. Crocus flavus ×1/3

394. Crocus goulimyi ×1/4

395. Crocus laevigatus ×1/3

396. Crocus olivieri ×1/3

397. Crocus nubigenus ×1/3

398. Crocus sieberi var. atticus ×1/3

399. Crocus sieberi var. tricolor ×1/4

400. Crocus tournefortii ×1/2

401. Crocus veluchensis ×1/2

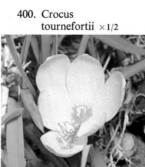

402. Gynandriris
sisyrinchium ×1/4

403. Iris florentina ×1/3

404. Iris graminea ×3/8

405. Iris ochroleuca ×1/2

406. Iris pumila ssp. attica ×1/3

407. Iris pumila ssp. attica ×1/3

408. Iris pumila ssp. attica ×1/3

409. Iris unguicularis ssp.
cretensis (Crete) ×2/5

410. Iris unguicularis ssp.
cretensis (mainland) ×1/4

411. Hermodactylus
tuberosus ×1/3

412. Gladiolus
byzantinus ×1/7

413. Gladiolus
communis ×1/7

414. Gladiolus
segetum ×1/6

415. Arundo donax
×1/60

416. Briza maxima
×1/2

417. Lagurus ovatus
×1/2

418. Arum creticum
×1/4

419. Arum dioscorides
×1/5

420. Arum italicum
×1/5

421. Arum orientale ×1/8

422. Biarum
tenuifolium ×1/4

423. Arisarum vulgare
×1/3

424. Dracunculus vulgaris ×1/6

425. Agave americana ×1/150

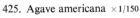

426. Cephalanthera rubra ×1/4

427. Limodorum abortivum ×3/4

428. Anacamptis pyramidalis ssp. brachystachys ×1/4

429. Loroglossum hircinum ×1

430. Barlia robertiana ×1/4

431. Barlia robertiana ×1/10

432. Ophrys apifera ×2 1/2

433. Ophrys bombyliflora ×2 1/2

434. Ophrys argolica (form) ×1 1/3

435. Ophrys argolica (form) ×1 1/3

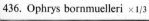

436. Ophrys bornmuelleri ×1/3

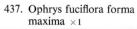

437. Ophrys fuciflora forma
maxima ×1

438. Ophrys cretica ×1 2/3

439. Ophrys fusca ssp. fusca ×2

440. Ophrys fusca ssp. iricolor ×3/4

441. Ophrys fusca ssp. omegaifera ×2/3

442. Ophrys lutea var. lutea ×2

443. Ophrys lutea var. minor ×2

444. Ophrys scolopax ssp.
heldreichii ×1

445. Ophrys scolopax ssp. attica ×3

446. Ophrys scolopax ssp. cornuta ×2

447. Ophrys ferrum-equinum ×1/2

449. Ophrys speculum var. regis-
ferdinandi-coburgi ×1

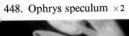

448. Ophrys speculum ×2

50. Ophrys sphegodes
    ssp. mammosa ×3/5

451. Ophrys sphegodes
     ssp. mammosa ×1 1/3

452. Ophrys sphegodes
     ssp. helenae ×1 1/2

53. Ophrys sphegodes
    (form) ×2

454. Ophrys sphegodes
     (form) ×2

455. Ophrys sphegodes
     ssp. spruneri ×1 1/3

56. Ophrys sphegodes
    ssp. aesculapii ×2

457. Ophrys reinholdii
     ×3/4

458. Ophrys
     tenthredinifera ×1/3

459. Orchis italica ×2/3

460. Orchis purpurea ×2/3

461. Orchis quadripunctata ×1/2

462. Orchis simia ×2/3

463. Orchis papilonacea ×1/3

464. Orchis papilionacea forma grandiflora ×1/3

465. Orchis ana-
tolica ×2/3

466. Orchis
collina ×2/3

467. O. coriophora
fragrans ×2/3

468. Orchis
sancta ×1/2

469. Orchis laxi-
flora ×1/3

470. Orchis tri-
dentata ×1/2

471. Orchis
lactea ×2/3

472. Dactylorhiza
romana ×1/3

473. Orchis
pallens ×1

474. Orchis pro-
vincialis ×1

475. Orchis p. ssp.
pauciflora ×2/3

476. Dactylorhiza
romana ×1/3

477. Serapias parviflora ×1/2

478. Serapias parviflora ssp. laxiflora ×1/2

479. Serapias lingua ×1/2

480. Serapias vomeracea ×1/3

481. Serapias neglecta ×1/3

482. Serapias orientalis ×5/8

483. Serapias cordigera ×3/4

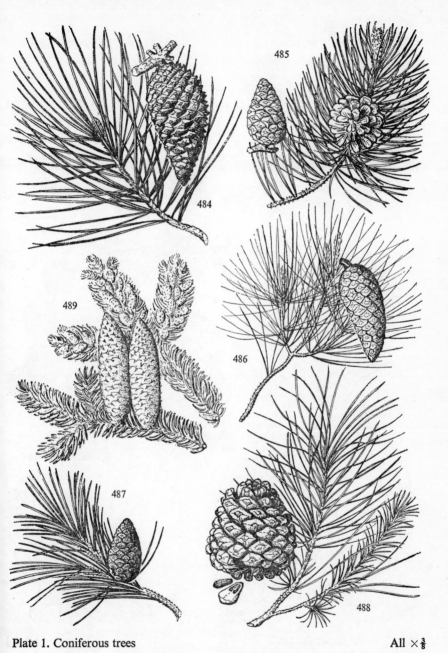

Plate 1. Coniferous trees   All ×⅜

484 Pinus pinaster.   485 P. nigra.   486 P. halepensis.   487 P. leucodermis.
            488 P. pinea.   489 Abies cephalonica.

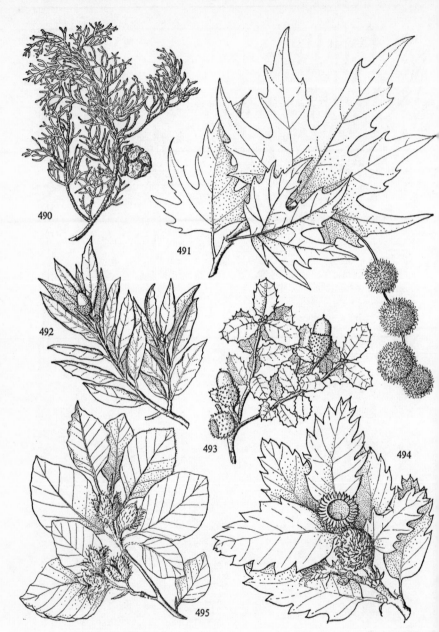

Plate 2. Some important trees

All ×⅜

490 Cupressus sempervirens.   491 Platanus orientalis.   492 Quercus ilex.
493 Q. coccifera. 494 Q. macrolepis. 495 Fagus sylvatica.

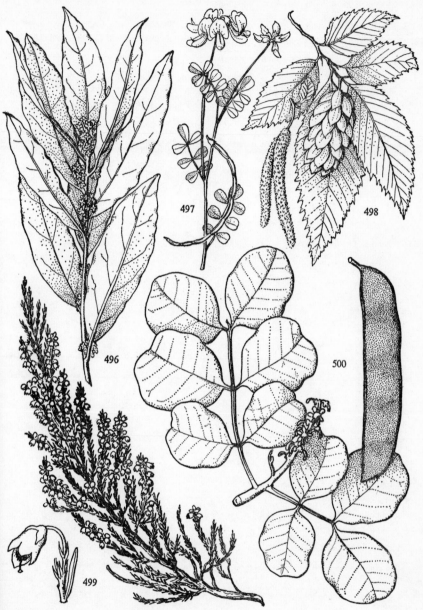

Plate 3. Plants of stony hillsides   All ×½

496 Laurus nobilis.   **497** Coronilla emerus ssp. emeroides.   **498** Ostrya
carpinifolia.   **499** Erica arborea (with floret enlarged).   **500** Ceratonia siliqua
(pod at right).

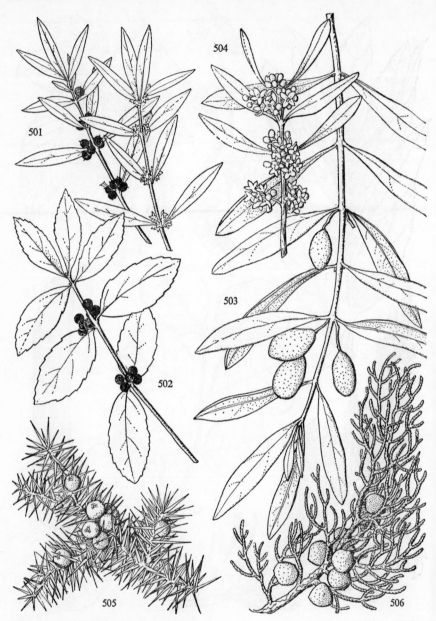

Plate 4. Fruit-bearing trees and shrubs   All ×¾

501 Phillyrea angustifolia.   502 P. latifolia.   503 Olea europaea (in fruit).
504 O.e.ssp. sylvestris (in flower).   505 Juniperus communis.   506 J.phoenicea.

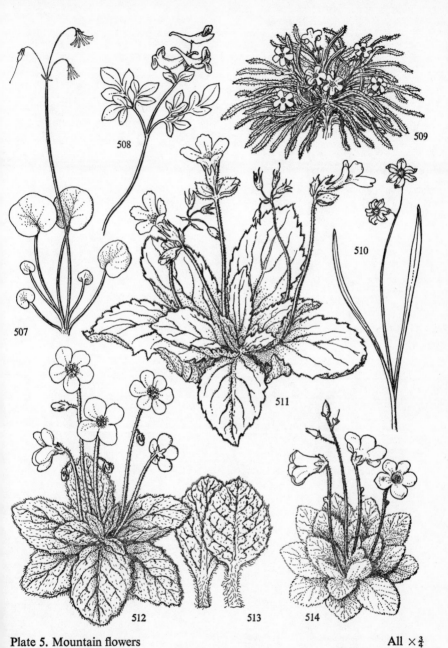

Plate 5. Mountain flowers   All × ¾

507 Soldanella pindicola.   508 Corydalis uniflora.   509 Anchusa caespitosa.
510 Chionodoxa nana.   511 Haberlea rhodopensis.   512 Ramonda nathaliae.
          513 R. serbica (leaf only).   514 Jankaea heldreichii.

PLANT DESCRIPTIONS

Conifers and Relations

PINACEAE – Pine Family

Evergreen resinous trees with spirally arranged needle-like leaves, and persistent woody female cones.

PINUS. Leaves in bunches of 2, 3, or 5 (2 in all species described). Cones with many scales, becoming woody in the second year.

ABIES. Leaves single. Cones erect, with thin scales.

PINUS. *P. halepensis.* ALEPPO PINE. A tree up to 20 m. tall, with silvery-grey bark, bright green leaves, and bluntly conical cones. ❊ Stony hills near the coast. March–May. **486**, p. 59

Like many Greek pines, often tapped for resin and to flavour the wine retsina, a practice originally carried out to prevent wine going sour. The resin, when thickened, was made into pitch, used for preserving wood, an ingredient of sheepwash, and to smear on corks of winejars. The ancient Greeks used the wood widely for ship-building, especially the curved pieces; also for house-building and for fuel. Theophrastus mentions that it was used for making large mallets and, indeed, 'is of use for almost more purposes than any other wood, for it is even used for painters' tablets'. Dioscorides refers to numerous medical uses of the bark, leaves, cones, and seeds of pines in general, including relief of toothache. The resinous pitch also had its uses: 'it doth circumscarificate carbuncles and rotten ulcers', and cured boils and scabs on cattle. As one of the first timbers to be used for ship-building, the pine was sacred to the sea god, and also to Cybele, Attis and Pan.

P. leucodermis. WHITE OR BOSNIAN PINE. Reaching 30–50 m. The trunk is grey, and the habit of growth compact; the leaves are short and erect, and the cones start blue and mature black. Sometimes regarded as a greyish-barked variety of *P. nigra*. ❊ High mountains on dry limestone formations. Northern Greece. May–June. **487**, p. 59

P. nigra. BLACK PINE. A variable species with grey-green trunk, growing up to 50 m. Young shoots brownish, cones rich yellow becoming brown. ❊ Mountains. Also extensively planted. May. **485**, p. 59

P. pinaster. MARITIME PINE. A pyramidal tree 20–30 m. tall, with reddish trunk, long whitish green leaves, and conical cones of a shining light brown in clusters, often long-persisting. ❊ Coasts and lowlands on acid and siliceous soils. April–May.

Often used for the stabilisation of sanddunes; a valuable timber tree and source of turpentine. **484**, p. 59

P. pinea. STONE PINE, UMBRELLA PINE. Easily recognisable with its flat or umbrella-shaped crown, grey bark flaking away to expose reddish patches, and large shining dark brown globular cones. Seldom exceeds 30 m. ❊ Coastal; formerly probably widespread, but now restricted to small areas in the W. Peloponnese and Aegean Islands. April–May. **488**, p. 59

P. sylvestris. SCOTS PINE. An upright tree 30–50 m. tall with reddish branches and trunk, bluish leaves, and pointed dull brown cones. ❊ Widely scattered. May–June.

ABIES. *A. alba.* EUROPEAN SILVER FIR. A pyramidal tree 50–70 m. tall, with smooth whitish bark. The thick flexible leaves are notched at the tip and carried in 2 double ranks. Cones cylindrical, brown. ❊ Mountains of N. Greece. April–May.

A. cephalonica. GREEK FIR. A rounded to pyramidal tree 30 m. or more tall, with widely spreading branches and greyish-brown bark. The narrow leaves are sharply pointed, the buds very resinous, and the brownish cones cylindrical. The male flowers are bright pink, their large clusters being very prominent. ❊ Mountains, forming extensive forests over 800 m. May–June. **489**, p. 59

Silver Firs are mentioned by Theo-phrastus as providing the best timber for ships, being light and durable, and giving 'timber of the greatest length and of the straightest growth; wherefore yard-arms and masts are made from it'. It was also used for houses, and was the favoured wood where glueing was necessary. The columns of the Palace of Knossos were almost certainly of Greek Fir, the smoothed trunks being placed upside down.

CUPRESSACEAE – Cypress Family

Evergreen resinous trees or shrubs, with leaves either narrow and needle-like, or short and scale-like.
CUPRESSUS. Usually trees, with whorls of scale-like leaves covering the branches. Cones of 5–6 adpressed scales, becoming woody.
JUNIPERUS. Shrubs or small trees, leaves either needle-like and spreading, or in whorls of 3 scales adpressed to the branches. Cones of 3–8 tough, fleshy scales fused in berry-like fruit.

CUPRESSUS. *C. sempervirens.* FUN-ERAL CYPRESS. This tree is best known in its densely columnar form with erect branches, exceptionally reaching 50 m., widely planted and naturalised in the whole Mediterranean area, but the wild form, a true Greek native, is typically a spreading tree. The small leaves are dark green and scale-like and the greyish cones are globular. ❧ Hill-sides. March–April.   **490**, p. 60
Cypress wood has long been renowned for hardness and durability. Theo-phrastus mentions how 'the cypress-wood at Ephesus, of which the doors of the modern temple were made, lay stored up for four generations. And this is the only wood which takes a fine polish, wherefore they make of it valuable articles.' It was used in building ships and houses, and for idols. Dios-corides gives many remedies based on cypress, among them the curing of dysentery, drawing off 'rotten nayles', driving away lice, staunching blood, and curing erysipelas.

JUNIPERUS. *J. communis.* COMMON JUNIPER. A dense shrub, up to 4 m., grey-green, with needle-like pointed leaves. The small rounded fruit, green in early stages, ripen to blue-black. ❧ Forms colonies and dense thickets on limestone hills. March–May.
505, p. 62
The oil distilled from the green fruits is the flavouring agent in gin. A strong diuretic, a decoction was recommended by Dioscorides for many ailments, stomach trouble, leprosy, and snake-bite. An ancient good-luck plant: its smoke was believed to drive off demons.
J. oxycedrus. PRICKLY JUNIPER. A sil-very juniper, forming dense shrubs or low trees of up to 6 m. high. The nar-row sharp-pointed leaves have 2 white bands on their upper surface, and the rounded fruits are a reddish-brown. ❧ Dry hills, often on limestone, among rocks, and on sea cliffs. April–May.
A timber very slow to decay, used in classical times for statues; nowadays in cabinet making and for pencils. It also made good charcoal. Oil of Cade, used in veterinary surgery and for toothache, is distilled from the wood.
J. phoenicea. PHOENICEAN JUNIPER. A shrub or small tree, dark green, 4–9 m. tall. The overlapping leaves are scale-like. The fruit is first blackish, changing to greenish yellow and, in its second year, to red. ❧ Dry stony hills. Feb.–April.   **506**, p. 62
Another very durable timber provider, used for house building in antiquity. It also provided pitch.

TAXACEAE – Yew Family

Evergreen trees or shrubs lacking resin, with narrow flattened leaves; fruit: fleshy.

TAXUS. *T. baccata.* YEW. This dark green tree, common in all Europe, grows 5–20 m. tall, with red-brown scaly bark. Leaves spirally arranged. Fruit hard, within a pink or scarlet fleshy cup. ⚜ Woods on the mountains. April.

Among the hardest and most durable timbers: a palaeolithic spear of yew from Britain is the oldest wooden artifact known. An emblem of death and burial since classical times; equally early arose the belief that to sleep or even sit below a yew could easily be fatal.

Dicotyledons

SALICACEAE – Willow Family

Deciduous trees or shrubs, unisexual, with clustered flowers in catkins.

POPULUS. *P. alba.* WHITE POPLAR. A tree reaching 30 m. Leaves dark green above and white below. Trunk smooth and grey, and young twigs and buds white-woolly. ❧ In woods and by water. March–April.
According to Dioscorides, juice from the leaves cures ear-ache; a decoction of the bark 'is reported to take away Conception, it being dranck with a mules kidney'; and pieces of the bark will, if scattered on soil, 'bring foorth edible mushrumps at any tyme of ye yeare'.

BETULACEAE – Birch Family

Deciduous trees or shrubs with alternate leaves and unisexual catkins; seeds winged.

ALNUS. *A. glutinosa.* ALDER. A medium-sized tree, with dark bark and rounded bright green leaves. Male and female catkins on the same tree, appearing with the leaves; females developing into cone-like woody structures. ❧ Damp mountainsides and by streams and rivers. Feb.–April.

CORYLACEAE – Hazel Family

Deciduous trees or shrubs; male flowers in catkins, females solitary. Fruit: a nut.

OSTRYA. *O. carpinifolia.* HOP-HORNBEAM. A small tree with oval, pointed, and doubly toothed leaves. Bark rough and brown. Catkins appear with leaves, up to 10 cm. long; the fruit resembles that of the hop, with overlapping papery bracts. ❧ Woods. April–May.
498, p. 61
Theophrastus remarks, 'It is said to be unlucky to bring it into the house, since, wherever it is, it is supposed to cause a painful death or painful labour in giving birth.'

FAGACEAE – Beech Family

Trees with unisexual flowers in clusters or in catkins. Fruit a nut, surrounded by scaly or woody cup.
FAGUS. Deciduous. Male flowers in hanging catkins; females in pairs. Nut surrounded by spiny or scaly cup.
CASTANEA. Deciduous. Catkins erect, male and female flowers in one catkin; nuts enclosed in spiny cup.
QUERCUS. Male catkins hanging; females very short. Nut half encircled in spiny or scaly cup.

FAGUS. *F. sylvatica.* COMMON BEECH. A deciduous tree growing to 30 m., with smooth grey trunk and oval bright green leaves. ❧ Usually on limestone; Northern mountains only. April–May. **495,** p. 60
The wood was used in ancient times especially for bowls, cups and carpenters' tools. Virgil recommended it for the staff of the plough. Beech bark was sometimes used for writing on.

CASTANEA. *C. sativa.* SWEET CHESTNUT. Deciduous tree up to 30 m. high, with spirally fissured bark, toothed leaves, and erect catkins composed of both male and female flowers. ❧ Lime-free soil on lower mountain slopes. May–July.

QUERCUS. *Q. ilex.* HOLM OAK. Up to 25 m. tall with grey scaly bark. The thick lance-shaped evergreen leaves are

dark green above and grey below. The pointed acorns are held in grey cups. ❧ On dry hills, on limestone. April–May. **492, p. 60**
Used since ancient times as a very hard, durable timber, in house and ship-building, and for underground construction because of its resistance to decay; also for high-quality charcoal. The acorns, as of other oaks, were valuable pig-food.

Q. macrolepis (Q. aegilops). VALONIA OAK. A rather low-growing thick-trunked tree, up to 15 m. high, with leathery leaves shining green above and grey below, deeply divided into unequal toothed lobes. Although deciduous, the dead leaves often persist throughout winter and into spring. Acorns large. ❧ In open woods, or solitary. April. **494, p. 60**
The acorn cups are important in tanning, making a black dye. The acorns were sometimes eaten by humans in times of privation. Dioscorides recommends it for dysentery and 'blood-spitting'.

Q. coccifera. KERMES OAK. A shrub or small tree reaching up to 2 m. The leathery leaves are dark green and spiny edged, making the plant resemble a holly. Acorns 3–6 cm. long, in spiny cups. ❧ Stony hillsides. March–May. **493, p. 60**
The most important use of this tree derives from the scale insect, Chermes or Coccus ilicis, from which it derives its specific name. The female scale, dried, produces a red dye, the 'scarlet' of the Scriptures and the 'Grain of Portugal' of Chaucer. Three sprigs of Kermes Oak are still the crest of the Dyers Company. From the bark a black dye was obtained which Dioscorides recommends for the hair. Theophrastus describes the use of the wood for the stationary pieces of fire-sticks and 'for the axles of wheel-barrows and the cross-bars of lyres and psalteries'. The bark has also been used as a source of tannin.

MORACEAE –
Mulberry Family

Deciduous or evergreen trees or shrubs with milky sap. Very small tightly clustered unisexual flowers; fruit formed by collections of fleshy or dry carpels.
MORUS. Fruit of several fleshy carpels, resembling a raspberry.
FICUS. Fruit pear-like, fleshy, containing dry carpels.

MORUS. *M. nigra.* BLACK MULBERRY. A small tree, up to 20 m., with rough spreading branches. Leaves oval or heart-shaped, toothed or lobed, downy below. Fruit dark red. ❧ Native of Iran, grown for its fruit, and locally naturalised. May.
Despite its origin this tree was known to the ancient Greeks. Theophrastus mentions its 'hot' wood suitable for fire-sticks, its durability – 'strong and easily worked', and its use, like fig (q.v. below) for objects needing readily bent wood. Dioscorides remarks how the fruit 'makes the belly soluble', but recommends various preparations from the tree as remedies, including the expulsion of flat-worms and cure of toothache.
M. alba. WHITE MULBERRY. Like *M. nigra*, but with smooth leaves. Fruit white, pinkish, or purplish. ❧ Native of China; grown as food for silkworms, planted as a street tree, and locally naturalised.

FICUS. *F. carica.* FIG. A small tree or rambling shrub, reaching 4 m., with smooth grey trunk and branches and large deeply lobed dark green leaves. The flowers are concealed within the characteristic pear-shaped fruit, at first green, ripening purple. ❧ Widely cultivated and frequently naturalised, though doubtfully native. Rocks, garigue, woods, often on poor stony soil. June–July. **13**
Figs are a very important food in Mediterranean areas, either fresh or dried. The antiquity of the fig as food is shown by its being mentioned more often in the Bible than any other fruit or food plant. Further east the fruit is used medicinally to cure boils and other skin infections; its milky juice is used to destroy warts. Its laxative properties are well known, though syrup of figs has gone out of fashion. The half-ripe fruit is considered to be poisonous. Theophrastus explains how easily fig wood can be bent and used for 'theatre-seats, the hoops of garlands,

and, in general, things for ornament'. Many peculiar remedies derived from the tree are mentioned by Dioscorides, including curing 'ye noyse and ringing' of the ears, scorpion and dog bites, and toothache.

URTICACEAE – Nettle Family

Herbs with small flowers in spikes or clusters, and leaves which often carry stinging hairs.

URTICA. ***U. pilulifera.*** ROMAN NETTLE. A strong growing nettle up to 1 m. high, with long stalked oval and toothed leaves, distinguished by its remarkable spherical fruits 1 cm. across. ⚘ Rubbish dumps and waste ground. April–Oct. **515**
At Easter, in Greece, young women used to beat themselves with this vicious nettle as a reminder of Christ's sufferings. Nettle-beating has also been used to relieve rheumatism. Dioscorides finds many medical uses for the plant, including the healing of dog-bites, gangrene, ulcers, and tumours.

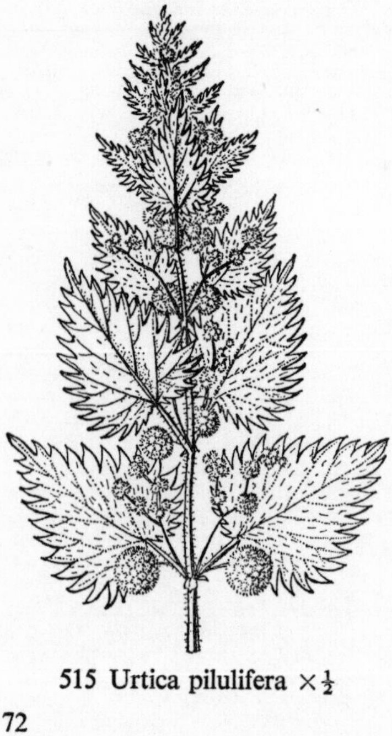

515 Urtica pilulifera ×½

LORANTHACEAE – Mistletoe Family

Parasitic shrubs, growing on trees. Leaves opposite or whorled; fruit usually a berry.
LORANTHUS. Flowers in elongated clusters: leaves deciduous.
VISCUM. Flowers densely clustered; leaves evergreen.

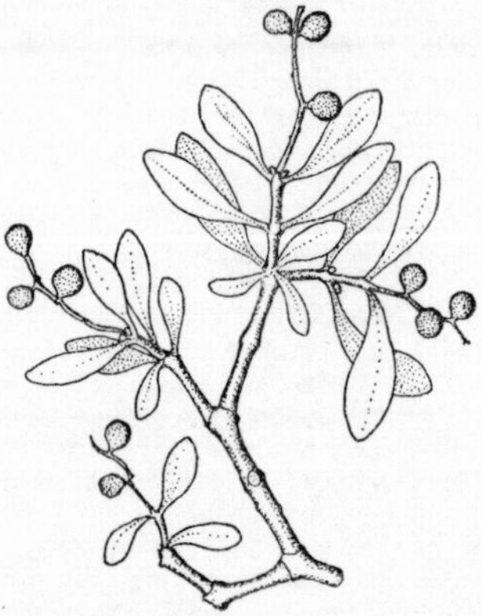

516 Loranthus europaeus ×½

LORANTHUS. ***L. europaeus.*** Forming loose clumps up to 1 m. in diameter, with oval deciduous leathery leaves of a dull green; the clusters of greenish-yellow flowers are followed by rounded yellow fruits. ⚘ On oaks, sweet chestnut, and beech. May–June. **516**

VISCUM. ***V. album.*** MISTLETOE. The greenish-yellow drooping branches form a rounded bushy growth up to 1 m. across. The opposite leaves are greenish-yellow, narrowly ovate, and the stalkless flowers are carried in clusters in the leaf axils, to be followed by white berries. ⚘ On a large variety of trees, usually deciduous spp. (***ssp. album***) and also on *Abies* (***ssp. abietis***). **14**
The magical powers of mistletoe, the

*'Golden Bough' of Frazer's famous
book, often associated with the Druids
and important in early Latin tribal cus-
toms, seem not to have been important
to the Greeks. Theophrastus only mentions it briefly as growing upon oaks.*

ARISTOLOCHIACEAE –
Birthwort or Dutchman's Pipe Family

Herbs or climbing plants with alternate roughly heart-shaped leaves
and bell or trumpet-shaped flowers.
Ovary inferior; fruit a capsule or
berry.

ARISTOLOCHIA. *A. clematitis.* Non-
climbing, stems up to 1 m., with stalked
leaves, and clusters of erect pale yellow
2–3 cm. trumpet-shaped flowers in the
axils of the upper leaves. ✤ Bushy and
shady places. May–June.   **15**
*This and other species are known as
Birthwort. They were used to aid birth
and to remove obstructions after it. Besides this they had a reputation for relieving wounds and bruises, against
snake-bite, and for inducing sleep.
Theophrastus writes 'This plant seems
to have a surpassing variety of useful-
ness.' Dioscorides expands the list to
include antidote to poison, the relief of
asthma, rickets, ruptures, convulsions,
and for driving out splinters.*
A. cretica. Non-climbing, semi-prostrate or scrambling up to 60 cm., with
kidney-shaped or triangular leaves and
large (5–12 cm.) dark maroon pipe-
shaped flowers, lightly hairy on exterior and with white hairs in the wide
mouth. ✤ Stony and among shrubs.
Crete and Karpathos. May–July.   **16**
A. hirta. Similar to *A. cretica* but
flowers rather smaller and less open-
mouthed, very hairy on exterior,
brownish-purple with yellowish mouth;
leaves: triangular with blunt-pointed
lobes. ✤ Stony places among shrubs.
S. Aegean Islands, Cyclades.   **17**
A. longa. Non-climbing, usually
branched, 20–80 cm. Leaves egg-
shaped or triangular. Flowers 3–5 cm.,
brownish or yellowish-green; upper lip
short. ✤ Stony places, scrub. April–
June.   **18**

A. pallida. Non-climbing, sometimes
branched, 15–50 cm. Leaves egg-
shaped to kidney-shaped; flowers 3–6
cm., green, brownish, or yellow with
brown or purple stripe. ✤ Stony
places, scrub. April–June.
A. rotunda. Non-climbing, often
branched, to 60 cm., with rounded
stem-clasping leaves and solitary yellowish 3–5 cm. flowers with brown
upper lip. ✤ Hedges and stony places.
April–June.
A. sempervirens (A. altissima). Climbing (sometimes procumbent) up to 5
m., leaves large (up to 10 by 6 cm.),
dark shining green, heart-shaped.
Flowers solitary, long stalked, 2–5 cm.,
of a sharply curved funnel-shape, yellowish, striped with brownish purple.
✤ Bushes in semi-shade. May–June.

RAFFLESIACEAE –
Rafflesia Family

Parasitic plants growing on the
roots of other plants; leaves replaced by fleshy scales.

CYTINUS. *C. hypocistis.* A leafless
parasite with a globular fleshy head up
to 6 cm. tall of bright yellow flowers,
clothed in brilliant red scales which
take the places of leaves. ✤ On *Cistus*
roots, mainly *C. parviflorus.* Crete,
Karpathos, Aegean Islands (***ssp. orientale***). April–June.   **19**
C. ruber. Similar to *C. hypocistis* but
stems sometimes up to 12 cm. long,
and flowers white or pink. ✤ On roots
of pink-flowered *Cistus.* April–June.
*According to Dioscorides, a preparation
of cytinus was 'good for such as are
troubled with ye Collick, with ye
Dysenterie, spitters of bloud, womanish
flux'.*

CHENOPODIACEAE –
Goosefoot Family

Usually annuals or perennials, occasionally shrubs, with leaves typically fleshy and often mealy. Flowers
small, often greenish, either unisexual or bisexual, often without
petals or sepals; stamens 1–5, stig-

mas 2–3; fruit: usually a 1-seeded nut.

This family includes the Glassworts (*Salicornia*), Seablites (*Suaeda*), and Saltwort (*Salsola*), to be seen in a few Greek salt-marshes.

ATRIPLEX. *A. halimus.* SHRUBBY ORACHE. An erect sub-shrub with woody base, to 2½ m., with silvery-

517 Atriplex halimus × ½ (floret enlarged)

white, rather leathery, oval, or pointed alternate 3–4 cm. leaves. Flowers yellowish, in small clusters in long branched spikes at the stem ends. ❄ Coastal sands and salt-marshes. Aug.–Sept. **517**

AIZOACEAE –
Mesembryanthemum Family

Fleshy herbs with succulent undivided opposite leaves and large solitary daisy-like flowers.
CARPOBROTUS. Stigmas 8–20. Leaves triangular in section.
MESEMBRYANTHEMUM. Annuals. Stigmas 5. Leaves rounded or flattened in section, covered with small projections.
APTENIA. Stigmas 4. Leaves heart-shaped, glistening with tiny glands.

74

LAMPRANTHUS. Stigmas 5, large. Like *Carpobrotus*, but smaller: leaves rounded or triangular in section.

CARPOBROTUS. *C. acinaciformis.* A creeping plant with numerous thick fleshy leaves, thickest near the middle. Arising in pairs from the prostrate woody stems, the very large (12 cm.) many-petalled flowers are magenta or carmine with purple stamens. ❄ A South African plant long naturalised on the rocks and sands of the Mediterranean and Aegean coasts. March–July. **20**
C. edulis. HOTTENTOT FIG. Resembles *C. acinaciformis* but with 9 cm. flowers of a pale lilac, yellow, or purple. Leaves not becoming thicker above the base. ❄ Also a native of South Africa, naturalised on the Mediterranean coast; less common than *C. acinaciformis.* March–July. **21**

MESEMBRYANTHEMUM. *M. nodiflorum* (*Gasoul nodiflorum*). An annual plant, with narrow cylindrical bluish leaves, and small white or yellowish stalkless flowers in the leaf axils. Petals shorter than the sepals. ❄ Sandy or rocky places on the coast, salt-marshes. April–July. **22**
M. crystallinum. ICE PLANT. An annual succulent with oval to spoon-shaped

518 Mesembryanthemum
crystallinum × ½

leaves, the whole plant densely covered with transparent crystalline swellings. Flowers with whitish petals longer than the sepals. ✲ Coastal sands, salt-marshes. April–June.   **518**

APTENIA. *A. cordifolia.* A sprawling perennial with opposite spade-shaped green leaves, covered with small glands; flowers purple. ✲ A South African native, naturalised on coastal sands and rocks. April–July.   **23**

LAMPRANTHUS. *L. roseus.* A woody-stemmed plant, erect or low growing, with large pink flowers. ✲ A South African plant, one of several species much used in gardens and sometimes naturalised on the coast. Flowers for much of the year.

CARYOPHYLLACEAE – Pink Family

Herbs, usually with paired opposite leaves; flowers in branched clusters or solitary. Sepals and petals 4 or 5; sepals either separated or fused to form a tube.

PARONYCHIA. Leaves with papery stipules; flowers very small with silvery bracts.

AGROSTEMMA. Flowers large; sepals fused in long 10-ribbed tube with long teeth; styles 5.

SILENE. Calyx tubular with 5 short lobes and 10–30 veins; petals 5; styles 3–5.

SAPONARIA. Sepals fused in smooth green tube; petals with scale in corolla throat; styles 2–3.

VACCARIA. Sepals fused in 5-angled tube; styles 2.

PETRORHAGIA. With sepal-like segments (epicalyx) of 2 or more membranous scales at base of a single flower, or several bracts at base of a dense flower head; calyx 5–15-veined with papery seams; petals without scales.

DIANTHUS. Leaves paired, from swollen joints, narrow and bluish-grey; flowers with epicalyx of 1–3 pairs of segments beneath each flower; sepals joined in smooth tube; styles 2.

VELEZIA. Resembling *Dianthus*, but usually small annual plants; calyx a long narrow tube without epicalyx.

PARONYCHIA. *P. argentea.* A small semi-prostrate perennial with much-branched stems forming low mats. The very small leaves are paired and oval, with papery stipules, and the clusters of flowers are almost hidden by thin silvery bracts, not longer than calyx. ✲ Dry stony places. April–June.   **24**

P. capitata. Very similar to *P. argentea* but with more conspicuous flower clusters and with larger bracts much exceeding the calyx. ✲ Dry places. April–June.   **25**

P. echinulata (*P. echinata*). Annual, growing up to 20 cm., with reddish leaves and greenish flowers with short bracts. ✲ Dry places. April–June.

AGROSTEMMA. *A. githago.* CORN COCKLE. A softly hairy annual up to 100 cm. high, with narrow leaves and large long-stalked solitary flowers of reddish-purple. ✲ A cornfield weed. April–June.   **26**
The seeds of corn cockle used to get into flour when it was a more widespread weed than today, and could cause severe pain since they are poisonous, as well as spoiling the flour itself. At one time a decoction was used for jaundice and dropsy. Dioscorides states that it 'doth expell by ye belly colerick matter and helpeth ye Scorpion-smitten'.

SILENE. *S. behen.* A branched annual to 40 cm. with oval paired hairless grey-green leaves, and rounded heads of pink flowers. Calyx much smaller, base thicker than flower stalk; with 10

75

branching veins. ⚘ Fields and stony places. March–May. **27**

S. colorata. Annual, 10–25 cm. tall, hairy, with rather narrow leaves; the branched stems carry bright carmine flowers. Calyx cylindrical, with 10 unbranched veins. ⚘ Coasts, often in pure sand on the dunes, often making sheets of colour. March–April. **28**

S. succulenta. 20 cm. high, woody-based, with fleshy stems and leaves, which are oblong or spoon-shaped, hairy and sticky. The large white campion flowers are carried singly or in pairs in the axils of leafy bracts. ⚘ Coastal sands. Crete. April–June.

SAPONARIA. *S. calabrica (S. graeca).* A low growing, much branched annual, with narrowly oblong leaves, and branched stems carrying rose-pink flowers. ⚘ Stony places. April–June. **29**

VACCARIA. *V. pyramidata.* A branched hairless annual up to 60 cm., with lance-shaped grey-green leaves, and much branched clusters of pink flowers with winged calyces. ⚘ A common cornfield weed. May–July. **519**

PETRORHAGIA. *P. velutina (Kohrauschia velutina).* A slender annual, up to 50 cm. high, with narrow grass-like leaves and tightly clustered heads of bright pink flowers surrounded by shining brown bracts. Middle part of stem glandular-hairy. ⚘ Fields and sandy places. March–April. **521**

The very similar *P. prolifera* has hairless stems, while *P. glumacea* has blunter ends to the bracts surrounding the flowers, which themselves are purple.

DIANTHUS. *D. arboreus.* A woody-stemmed pink forming a straggling bush to 50 cm., with tortuous branches. Leaves narrow, grey-blue, fleshy; flowers large, bright pink, fragrant. ⚘ Stony and rocky places. Crete and Cyclades. April–June. **522**

D. fruticosus. Similar to *D. arboreus* but more compact, to 80 cm., with broader (4–8 mm.) leaves; flowers not fragrant. ⚘ Stony and rocky places. Crete. April–June.

D. haematocalyx. With thick tufts of pointed grey leaves, from which rise 30 cm. stems carrying branching clusters of red-purple flowers backed with yellow. The swollen calyces are blood red. ⚘ Rocky slopes, often at the edges of woodland. Near the summits of Olympos and some other C. and N. Greek mountains. June–Aug. **523**

D. petraeus. Forms loose clumps of

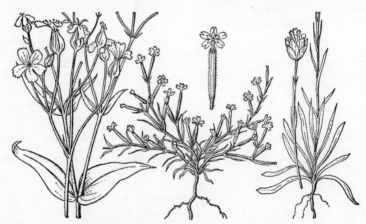

Left to right: 519 Vaccaria pyramidata.   520 Velezia rigida (flower enlarged).   521 Petrorhagia velutina. All × ½

long narrow green or bluish-green leaves. The solitary flowers, of varying shades of pink, are often spotted with darker red. Calyx long and narrow. ❧ Dry rocky places. N. Greece. May–July.

D. sylvestris. WOOD PINK. A very variable species, grossly misnamed since it is a plant not of woods but of the driest, sunniest, and rockiest places. In its best form it makes tight clumps, with very narrow, stiff leaves, and the flowers, carried singly or in pairs on 15–30 cm. stems, are of a bright pink and almost scentless. ❧ Rock crevices, cliffs, stony places. May–June.   **30**

VELEZIA. *V. rigida.* A stiff, branched annual to 15 cm. tall with sticky-hairy stems bearing stalkless pink flowers 5 mm. across, the petals deeply lobed. Calyx tube 10–14 mm. long, very narrow, sticky-hairy. ❧ Dry, stony places. May–July.   **520**

Left: 522 Dianthus arboreus $\times \frac{1}{2}$
Right: 523 D. haematocalyx $\times \frac{2}{3}$ (petal enlarged)

RANUNCULACEAE – Buttercup Family

Herbaceous plants with alternate, dissected leaves (woody and opposite-leaved in *Clematis*). Flowers with numerous stamens; petals may be absent and replaced by enlarged and coloured sepals. Fruit typically of many separate carpels, sometimes of many-seeded pods.

HELLEBORUS. Leaves large, with toothed segments; flowers often greenish; fruits of 3–8 pods.

NIGELLA. Flowers blue, white, or yellowish, with petal-like sepals, the true petals greatly reduced; leaves finely cut; fruits of pods more or less fused together.

DELPHINIUM. Flowers symmetrical in one plane only, blue, with backward-projecting spurs, in spikes; fruits of 3–5 splitting pods.

CONSOLIDA. Like *Delphinium*, with spurred flowers; fruits a single splitting pod.

ANEMONE. Flowers usually solitary, with up to 20 coloured segments (not true petals) and 3 leafy or sepal-like bracts below.

77

CLEMATIS. Woody climbers, opposite-leaved, climbing by the twisting of the leaf stalks; petals usually 4; fruits with long feathery styles.
ADONIS. Flowers usually red or yellow, usually solitary; petals 3–20; fruit a long conical head of many 1-seeded units; leaves deeply cut.
RANUNCULUS. Flowers usually yellow, but also red, pink, or white, carried singly or in spreading heads; distinguished from Anemone by the green sepals. Fruits of many 1-seeded units.
AQUILEGIA. Flowers with 5 petal-like outer segments and 5 long-spurred inner ones; stamens numerous; leaves once or thrice divided.

HELLEBORUS. ***H. cyclophyllus.*** GREEK HELLEBORE. A robust hairless perennial, with large dark green leaves deeply cut into 5–9 narrow, toothed segments. Flower stems up to 40 cm., carrying clusters of large green flowers. ⚘ Woods and bushy places in the mountains. Feb.–March. **36**
H. orientalis. EASTERN HELLEBORE. Resembles *H. cyclophyllus*, but the leaves persist throughout winter, and the flowers vary in colour from greenish-cream to purple. ⚘ Mountains of Thrace. Woods and thickets. March–May.
Hellebores are poisonous, very narcotic plants, used in medicine since ancient times. About 1400 B.C. *the soothsayer-physician Melampus used it as a purgative in cases of mania. It has been used in treating hysteria and other nervous disorders. Confused in the ancient literature with 'false hellebores', species of* Veratrum.

NIGELLA. ***N. damascena.*** LOVE-IN-A-MIST; DEVIL-IN-A-BUSH. This common annual, often grown in gardens, is 10–30 cm. tall, with blue flower segments, surrounded by leafy, finely cut bracts, and with finely dissected feathery leaves. Fruit inflated and globular. ⚘ Fields and waste places. May–June. **524**
N. arvensis. Like *N. damascena* but with smaller, paler flowers, usually not surrounded by an involucre of upper leaves. ⚘ Fields, rocky places; often seen as a cornfield weed. June–July. **525**

DELPHINIUM. ***D. halteratum.*** Annual, up to 40 cm., with branched hairy stems and bright blue flowers;

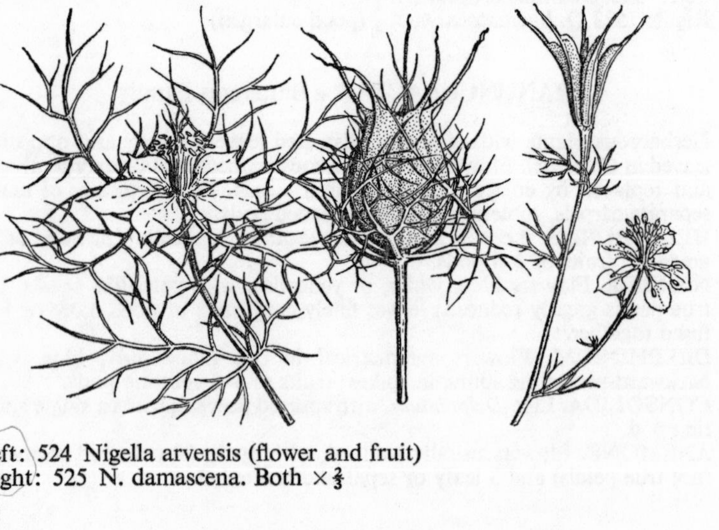

Left: 524 Nigella arvensis (flower and fruit)
Right: 525 N. damascena. Both ×⅔

spurs longer than sepals. ✤ Fields and stony places. May–Aug. **32**

D. peregrinum. VIOLET LARKSPUR. A taller annual, to 50 cm., finely hairy, with deeply cut lower leaves and spikes of bluish-violet flowers. Spurs slightly up-turned. ✤ Fields and stony places. May–June.

Drunk in wine, writes Dioscorides, the seeds help the scorpion-bitten. 'They say also that Scorpions grow faint, and become inactive and benumbed, the herb being put to them.'

D. staphisagria. Annual or biennial, with 5–9 lobed leaves and 1 m. flowering stems carrying dingy dark blue flowers with very short spurs. The whole plant very hairy. ✤ Field edges, stony places. May–August.

This very poisonous plant has been used as an insecticide and a cure for neuralgia and toothache.

CONSOLIDA. *C. ambigua.* LARKSPUR. A hairy annual to 60 cm., often grown in gardens, with branched stems, deeply divided lower leaves, and loose spikes of bright blue, pink, or white flowers. Seeds black. ✤ Fields, dry places. April–July.

C. orientalis. Like *C. ambigua,* but with shorter-spurred purplish-violet flowers and reddish-brown seeds. ✤ Cornfields and cultivated ground. June–July. **31**

ANEMONE. *A. blanda.* MOUNTAIN WINDFLOWER. With sky-blue flowers (occasionally pink, magenta, or white) of numerous very narrow 'petals', on 6–20 cm. stems above deeply cut leaves. ✤ Rocky places, often in the shelter of bushes, on hills and mountains. Jan.–April. **43**

A. coronaria. CROWN or POPPY ANEMONE. The 4–8 cm. flowers on 15–40 cm. stems have 5–8 elliptic or rounded overlapping 'petals' and vary from white to pale lavender through purple to shades of red, sometimes with a white or yellowish basal zone. Distinguished from *A. pavonina* by the stem-leaves below the flowers being cut into very narrow segments. The basal leaves are thrice-cut into narrow segments. ✤ Stony places, fields, olive groves, vineyards. Feb.–April.
38, 39, 40

Commonly cultivated in improved forms under the names de Caen, St Brigid, etc. This is one of several plants which lay claim to the title of the Biblical 'lily of the field' which 'surpassed Solomon in all his glory'. Valued according to Dioscorides for 'purging of the head' (for which the juice of the root was poured into the nostrils) and for curing skin ailments. The name anemone, literally wind-flower, comes from the ancient belief that the wind caused the flowers to open.

A. heldreichii. With small flowers of 12–19 narrow 'petals', white with bluish or pinkish backs, and entire stem-leaves. Sometimes almost flat on the ground, or on stems to 30 cm. ✤ Stony hillsides, grassy places, thickets. Ionian Islands, Crete, Karpathos. Feb.–April. **44**

See note after A. pavonina *below.*

A. pavonina. A brilliant spring flower very similar to *A. coronaria* and with a similar colour range, also often with a white basal zone. 'Petals' 7–12, usually a little less broad than in *A. coronaria.* Always distinguished by the stem-leaves which are entire or 3-lobed. ✤ Stony places, fields, olive groves, vineyards, climbing into the hills. Feb.–April. **41, 42**

The nomenclature of this species has suffered much confusion and argument. It was for long considered a sub-species of A. hortensis *(syn.* A. stellata*), which has typically 15 (12–19) 'petals', and is now considered a Central Mediterranean species not entering Greece – apart from* A. heldreichii *which is now technically* A. hortensis ssp. hortensis var. heldreichii. *Flora Europaea separates the two species. The name fulgens, once applied to the scarlet form of* A. pavonina, *is now referred to a supposed hybrid between the two species which does not breed true, and is presumably not found in Greece.*

CLEMATIS. *C. cirrhosa.* VIRGIN'S BOWER. A climbing or scrambling evergreen, with dark green leathery leaves of variable shape, and large solitary cream-coloured flowers. ✤ Woods and thickets. Dec.–March. **35**

According to Dioscorides, the seed of this beaten in water 'drives downwards

*phlegm and choler . . . the leaves being
laid remove leprosies. It is preserved in
salt with Lepidium, to be eaten'.*
C. flammula. A deciduous woody-
stemmed climber resembling Old
Man's Beard (*C. vitalba*), with twice-
or thrice-dissected leaves of oval to
narrow leaflets, and 1–3 cm. fragrant
white flowers in large loose heads.
⚘ Hedges, scrub, waste places. May–
Aug.   **37**

ADONIS. A. annua. PHEASANT'S EYE.
An annual reaching 40 cm., with
feathery leaves and small scarlet or,
less often, yellow flowers with black
central blotch, and dark purple
stamens and styles. ⚘ Cultivated
fields, waste places. May–Aug.   **45**
A. microcarpa. Very like *A. annua* but
usually with bright yellow, less often
reddish-violet flowers on branched
stems up to 40 cm. Technically distinguished from *A. annua* by a tooth on
the inside of the carpel. ⚘ Fields,
grassy and rocky places. March–April.
                                              46
A. cupaniana. This name is now
referred to *A. microcarpa* but the plant
in question is a very distinctive variant
with bicoloured red and yellow flowers.
⚘ Grassy and stony places. March–
April.   **47**

RANUNCULUS. R. asiaticus. TURBAN
BUTTERCUP. Tuberous-rooted, up to
30 cm. high, with variable, usually
lobed leaves, and large flowers of 6–12
petals. Several distinct colour forms
exist. The scarlet is usual in Rhodes,
while the white, pink, and yellow
forms predominate in Crete. ⚘ Not
on the mainland. Rocks, grassy and
stony places. Feb.–May.   **48, 49, 50**
R. creticus. A branched perennial to 60
cm., with shallowly lobed kidney-
shaped leaves and large yellow flowers.
⚘ Crete and Karpathos. Grassy and
rock places. April–June.
**R. ficaria ssp. ficariiformis (R. ficaria
var. grandiflora).** A large form of the
common LESSER CELANDINE with glossy
stalked heart-shaped leaves, and
flowers of a shining gold. ⚘ Damp
shady places. Feb.–April.   **51**
R. ficarioides. A compact CELANDINE to
7 cm. high, with slightly lobed heart-
shaped, dark-blotched leaves. Flowers

shining golden yellow. ⚘ Stony places
on mountains, often by melting snow.
Feb.–May.   **52**

AQUILEGIA. A. amaliae. A delicate
COLUMBINE with the deeply cut leaves
of the genus, and flowering stems of
30 cm. carrying long-spurred blue and
white flowers. ⚘ Shady rocks. Mountains of C. and N. Greece. July–Aug.
                                              33
A. ottonis. Closely allied to *A. amaliae,*
readily distinguished by having projecting stamens. ⚘ Shady rocky places.
Peloponnese. May–July.   **34**
    A. amaliae and *A. ottonis* have inter-
mediate forms sometimes called *A.
taygetea.*

PAEONIACEAE –
Peony Family

Large herbaceous plants with very
large solitary flowers with 5 sepals,
5–10 petals, and many stamens, followed by a fruit of 3 large carpels.

PAEONIA. P. clusii. A bushy, rather
spreading plant 40–50 cm. high, the
lower leaves with 30 or more narrow
segments; flowers white, occasionally
pink-flushed, 7–9 cm. across. ⚘ Open
stony hillsides; Crete and Karpathos.
April–May.   **53**
P. mascula. A strongly growing perennial up to 1 m. high with large dark
green leaves cut into 9–16 narrow oval
segments. The 8–14 cm. flowers are
deep red. ⚘ Woods and thickets in the
mountains. May–June.   **54**
P. rhodia. Up to 40 cm. high, with reddish stems and dark green leaves cut
into narrow leaflets. The pure white
flowers are up to 7 cm. across.
⚘ Woods, in the hills of Rhodes.
April–May.
*The two white-flowered peonies de-
scribed are possibly only variants of one
basic species. Other white peonies have
recently been found on other islands including Euboea.*

*Peonies were used medicinally in the
past, especially by monks. Dried roots
were used to treat convulsions and
epilepsy; it was also believed to cure
lunacy. One old herbal says, 'If a man*

layeth this wort over the lunatic as he lies, soon he upheaveth himself whole'. The peony was also a very magical plant, and some authors describe the need to dig it up in the same way as the Mandrake (page 128). Theophrastus and Pliny suggest the plant should be gathered at night 'for if any man shall pluck of the fruit in the daytime, being seen by the Woodpecker, he is in danger to lose his eyes; as, if he is cutting the root at the time, he gets prolapsos ani'.

BERBERIDACEAE –
Barberry Family

Usually shrubs, with yellow clustered flowers followed by berries; but including unexpected herbaceous plants with underground tubers and capsular fruits.
LEONTICE. Herbaceous perennial, with underground tuber and leafy stems. Flowers usually of 6 segments, sometimes 7–8.
BERBERIS. Woody shrubs, spiny and deciduous. Flowers of 6 large and 3 small segments.

LEONTICE. *L. leontopetalum.* With leafy stems up to 30–50 cm., carrying 3-lobed blue-grey leaves, subdivided into rounded leaflets. The branched flower heads carry long-stalked yellow flowers rising from the axils of leafy bracts. Fruit bladder-like, purplish. ⚜ Rocky places, ploughed fields. Feb.– April. **57, 58**
The tuber has been used as a cure for epilepsy, and soap is sometimes made from it. Dioscorides suggests that a paste of the root 'doth help ye bitings of ye shrew mouse'. The related Bongardia chrysogonum *is now believed to be extinct in Greece.*

BERBERIS. *B. vulgaris.* BARBERRY. A dense, very spiny shrub up to 3 m. high, with elliptic spiny-edged leaves, and drooping clusters of yellow flowers followed by coral-red oval berries. ⚜ Rocky hillsides. May–June. **55, 56**
B. cretica. A densely and intricately spiny shrub up to 1½ m. leaves 10–22

mm. long, oval and entire; flowers carried in drooping clusters of only 3–8 yellow flowers; fruit dark red oval berries. ⚜ Rocky places on mountains. April–May.

LAURACEAE – Laurel Family

Aromatic evergreen trees or shrubs with shining leaves and axillary clusters of small greenish or yellow flowers.

LAURUS. *L. nobilis.* SWEET BAY. A shrub or tree 2–15 m. high, with dark bark and dark green leathery aromatic leaves, broadly lanceolate. The small yellowish flowers are carried in loose clusters in the leaf axils. Fruit a black berry. ⚜ Damp rocky places, gullies, thickets. Often planted. March–April.
496, p. 61
This plant is the 'Daphne' of Greek legend – the nymph who was changed into a tree by other gods when amorously pursued by Apollo. After the transformation the repentant Apollo made himself a crown from the leaves and decreed that the tree should be held sacred to him. It was almost certainly bay laurel leaves that caused Apollo's priestess at Delphi to enter a state of inspiration before pronouncing oracles: she either chewed the leaves or inhaled smoke of burning laurel wood. Other oracles, including that at Dodona, used the same stimulant.

The laurel wreath was used by the Greeks to honour poets, military heroes, and the winners in the Olympic and Pythian Games. Greek military heralds carried a branch of laurel (or sometimes olive). Later laurel was equally important to the Romans. The word 'baccalaureate' and its English corruption bachelor (of arts, etc.) derives from a crown of laurel carrying berries (baccae) formerly bestowed on newly qualified doctors.

Laurel was a magically protective plant: the Greeks placed a bough over their doorways if anyone was ill, and Theophrastus records how superstitious people kept a bay leaf permanently in their mouths to avoid bad luck. Now-

adays bay is widely used as a flavouring herb. The fragrant oil of bay, made from the leaves, was recommended as a

general soothing remedy by Dioscorides. Bay wood was used for the drills of fire-sticks, and also for walking sticks.

PAPAVERACEAE – Poppy Family

Herbaceous plants, often with milky sap. Flowers often conspicuous with 4–6 delicate petals and 2–3 sepals falling as flowers open. Fruit a capsule with pores, or a long pod opening into long valves. The zygomorphic-flowered *Corydalis* and *Fumaria* were originally placed in the family *Fumariaceae*.

PAPAVER. Flowers often red, with 2 sepals; fruit with a cap of radiating stigmas, opening by pores below it.

ROEMERIA. Flowers poppy-like, often violet; fruit long and narrow, opening into 3–4 valves.

GLAUCIUM. Flowers poppy-like, yellow or red; sepals 2; fruit long and narrow, opening into 2 valves.

HYPECOUM. Flowers small, yellow, in spreading heads; petals 4, unequal in size. Fruit long and narrow, splitting into 1-seeded sections.

CORYDALIS. Flowers 2-lipped, clustered; petals 4, the upper hooded and spurred, the lower keeled and boat-shaped, the 2 lateral petals narrow; sepals 2. Fruit 2-valved with 2 to many seeds.

FUMARIA. Flowers similar to *Corydalis*. Fruit 1-seeded, not splitting open.

PAPAVER. *P. rhoeas.* CORN POPPY. A very variable plant with large (7–10 cm.) scarlet flowers usually blotched with black at the bases of the petals. Fruit almost round. Leaves segmented, and the whole plant hairy. ❧ Cultivated fields, waste places, roadsides, sand, and dunes. March–July.   **64**
A weed of cereal crops since the beginnings of agriculture: indeed, the satisfactory growth of corn was often believed to depend on the poppies. The Assyrians called it 'Daughter of the Field'; the Greeks considered it the flower of Aphrodite in her role as goddess of vegetation, the Romans as that of Ceres, goddess of the corn. This is the parent of our garden Shirley poppies.
P. dubium. LONG-HEADED POPPY. With 3–6 cm. flowers of a paler red than *P. rhoeas*, and fruits 2–3 times as long as broad. Leaves bluish. Sap white. ❧ Cornfields, waste places. March–July.
P. hybridum. BRISTLY POPPY. Flowers smallish (2–5 cm.), purplish or brick red, with black basal blotches. Stem and leaves hairy, fruits globular, ribbed, covered by stiff bristles.

❧ Cornfields, waste places. March–July.

ROEMERIA. *R. hybrida.* With large (4–5 cm.) poppy-like, violet flowers, with darker basal blotches, succeeded by long, narrow, hairy pods. Leaves deeply cut 2–3 times into narrow segments. Sap yellow. ❧ Fields and waste places. April–June.   **526**

GLAUCIUM. *G. corniculatum* (*G. grandiflorum*). RED HORNED POPPY. 25–50 cm. tall, densely hairy, with deeply cut leaves and smallish (3–5 cm.) flowers of red or orange-red, often black-blotched at the base. Pod hairy. ❧ Cultivated and waste places. April–June.   **62**
G. flavum. YELLOW HORNED POPPY. On erect or arching stems up to 1 m. high are carried deeply lobed and wavy-edged, blue-grey leaves and large (6–9 m.) flowers of pale gold. Fruit very long, curved. **Var. fulvum** has deep golden flowers with brown basal patches. ❧ Shingles and sea sands. April–July.   **63**
According to Theophrastus, the root

526 Roemeria hybrida × ½
(pod enlarged)

'has the property of purging the belly, and the leaf is used for removing ulcers on sheep's eyes'. Dioscorides recommends a root decoction 'to cure Sciaticas, and Liver griefs and to help such as piss thick, or cobweb-like matter'.

HYPECOUM. *H. imberbe* (*H. grandiflorum*). An erect 10–40 cm. annual with orange-yellow 1–1½ cm. flowers in loose heads. Petals 4, unequal in size, 3-lobed; the side lobes of the outer petals at least as large as the middle one. Leaves smooth, blue-grey, much cut. Fruit: a 4–6 cm. pod, barely jointed. ✲ Fields and stony places. March–April.   **61**
H. procumbens. A more delicate sprawling species with 10–40 cm. stems, and yellow flowers with side lobes of outer petals much smaller than middle one. Fruit curved, jointed. ✲ Fields, stony places. March–April.

CORYDALIS. *C. solida.* A soft herbaceous plant 10–20 cm. high, with tuberous roots and hairless blue-green leaves which are deeply cut into wedge-shaped segments (*var. densiflora* has narrow strap-shaped segments). There is a conspicuous scale below the lowest leaf. Flowers purplish, with long spurs, in spikes of 15–25. ✲ Hedgerows, woods, stony places, often in the mountains. March–May.   **59**

In some parts of Greece the plant is called chionistra, *or chilblain; the derivation is obscure.*
C. bulbosa (including **C. parnassica**). To 30 cm. tall, with dense spikes of 10–20 purplish flowers. Leaf segments pointed. No scale below lowest leaf. ✲ Stony places in the mountains. May–July.
C. uniflora. Above tufted blue-green dissected leaves rise 5–15 cm. flower stalks carrying 1–2, sometimes 3, spurred and hooded flowers of white veined with maroon. Sometimes referred to the similar but larger Asiatic *C. rutifolia.* ✲ Mountain shingles. Crete. May–June.   **508, p. 63**

FUMARIA. *F. capreolata.* RAMPING FUMITORY. A scrambling and climbing plant, with leaves cut into oblong segments and axillary clusters of creamy or pinkish flowers with dark red or purple petal-tips. ✲ Cultivated ground and waste places. April–June.   **60**

CAPPARIDACEAE – Caper Family

Shrubs (the family also includes trees) with alternate leaves and with stipules which are sometimes spiny. Fruit a berry.

CAPPARIS. *C. spinosa.* CAPER. A rather straggling spiny shrub, up to 1½ m. long, often sprawling over the ground, with oval spiny leaves and striking solitary flowers which are large, white or pinkish in colour, with many very long projecting stamens with purple stalks. Fruit a berry 5 cm. long which may split to reveal the red seeds. ✲ Stony, rocky places. June–September.   **65, 66**
The caper of cookery is the unopened flower bud, pickled. In Dioscorides' day 'the stalke and fruit of it are preserved in salt to be eaten'. He recommends various parts of the plant for the typical wide range of treatments, including killing 'ye wormes in the eares', and mentions several names given it by the Magi, including 'the heart of an Wolf', which suggests early magical uses.

CRUCIFERAE – Mustard Family

A large family of herbaceous plants with alternate leaves without stipules, and with small flowers, often carried in branched clusters, of characteristic cross shape, with 4 petals and 4 sepals. Fruit usually a pod, long and narrow, at least 3 times as long as wide (siliqua), or less than 3 times as long as wide (silicula). The pod usually splits longitudinally, but sometimes splits transversely into 1-seeded sections, or does not split at all.

Identification of this very large family can often only be made from the ripe fruit.

ERYSIMUM. Usually wallflower-like, though sometimes tufted plants. Flowers usually yellow or orange; stamens 6, surrounded by nectaries; Fruit a 4-angled siliqua.

MALCOLMIA. Flowers violet, purple, or white; stigma strongly 2-lobed; fruit a long narrow cylindrical pod. Leaves undivided.

MATTHIOLA. Flowers purple, red, or white; fruit a long narrow cylindrical pod ending in horn-like processes. Whole plant grey and hairy.

AUBRIETA. Flowers violet or pink; leaves undivided and hairy; fruit long and narrow, seeds in 2 rows.

RICOTIA. Flowers pink or violet; petals sometimes clawed. Leaves usually glabrous, entire or pinnatisect. Fruit siliqua or silicula, in some species much compressed.

LUNARIA. Flowers purple or white; fruit flat and disc-like; valves thin-walled and net-veined.

ALYSSOIDES. Flowers yellow; fruit globular, many-seeded; style long and slender. Leaves entire.

ALYSSUM. Flowers yellow; leaves usually entire; fruit globular, 1–2 seeds in each of the 2 cells; style often short.

DRABA. Often low-growing and tufted, with leaves entire, often in rosettes. Flowers yellow or white; fruit about twice as long as broad, with flattened valves becoming disc-like.

AETHIONEMA. Flowers white, pink, or violet; leaves undivided and hairless; fruit flattened and rounded with broad wing, notched at apex.

BISCUTELLA. Flowers yellow; fruit of 2 flattened disc-like lobes placed edge to edge; each disc is 1-seeded.

MORICANDIA. Flowers rather large, violet; leaves undivided, hairless, and fleshy; fruit long and narrow, 4-angled with short beak.

ERUCA. Hairy, with deeply lobed leaves; flowers yellow, violet-veined, sepals erect; fruit erect and narrow, with a beak half as long as the pod; seeds in 2 rows.

ERYSIMUM. *E. raulinii.* A much-branched biennial 15–50 cm. tall, with the lower part of the stem very strongly angled. Leaves narrow-oblong, toothed or wavy-edged. Flowers yellow, clustered, on short stalks; sepals with basal projection. ✲ Stony ground. Mountains of Crete. April. **67**

MALCOLMIA. *M. maritima.* VIRGINIAN STOCK. An annual, 10–35 cm. high, branched from the base, with elliptic or oblong leaves, entire or toothed, and pink to rosy purple flowers, often white-centred. Seed pods long and hairy, carried on narrow stalks. ✲ Coastal sands and cliffs; S. and W. Greece. Feb.–May. **70**

M. angulifolia is a mountain version of *M. maritima*, but has bracts in the lower part of the flower-heads. Leaves roundish. Flowers often very bright purple. ✲ Stony places. Mountains of C. and N. Greece. May–June.

M. flexuosa resembles *M. maritima*, but the stalks of the seed pods are as thick as the pods are wide; the flowers are often larger, and the leaves more fleshy. ❀ Coastal sands and cliffs, often replacing *M. maritima* in the eastern Aegean. Feb.–May.   **69**

M. chia differs from the species already described in its smaller flowers with shorter style. Feb.–April.   **68**

MATTHIOLA. *M. incana.* A biennial or perennial with woody-based stems, to 80 cm., with white-woolly mostly uncut leaves and heads of reddish-purple flowers. ❀ Sea cliffs. March–May.   **71**

In the English translation of Theophrastus this appears as the gilli flower which, with the 'wild wallflower', was the earliest flower to appear and 'of all the flowers that the garland-makers use, far outruns the others'.

M. sinuata. SEA STOCK. A biennial to 50 cm., grey-woolly, with wavy-edged and lobed leaves, and heads of sweet scented lilac flowers. ❀ Sand dunes and shingles. March–June.   **72**

M. tricuspidata. Resembles the Sea Stock, but with white-centred violet flowers and characteristic fruit with spreading conical horns at the apex. ❀ Coasts, often on sands and shingles. March–June.   **73**

AUBRIETA. *A. deltoidea.* A variable perennial, forming loose clumps up to 25 cm. high, or in rocky situations tight dwarf cushions. The hairy spoon-shaped leaves are often bluntly toothed, and the bright reddish-purple flowers are carried in clusters. ❀ Cliffs, rock crevices. March–May.   **74**

Parent of the familiar garden varieties.

RICOTIA. *R. isatoides.* A fleshy, hairless perennial, from 10–20 cm. high, with numerous delicate branching erect stems, entire or more usually segmented leaves, the 3–5 lobes being elliptic with rounded tips. The pale violet flowers are carried in terminal sprays. The fruit is compressed, about twice as long as broad, containing 1–2 seeds. ❀ Limestone screes. Mountains of Crete and Karpathos. April–May.

R. cretica. An annual, differing from *R. isatoides* in its height (up to 25 cm.), its more dissected leaves, its pink flowers and its fruit which is a siliqua 5–8 times as long as broad, containing up to 10 seeds. ❀ Rocky and stony places. Crete. March–April.

LUNARIA. *L. annua ssp. pachyrhiza.* A biennial with tuberous roots, reaching 1–1½ m., with opposite pairs of stalkless heart-shaped pointed leaves, toothed at the edges, and stalkless. The large, rich violet flowers, carried in terminal sprays, are very sweet-scented. ❀ In partial shade in woods and thickets, often in the hills. March–May. **78**

ALYSSOIDES. *A. cretica (Alyssum creticum).* A much branched woody perennial with rosettes of grey- or white-haired, blunt-edged leaves, golden flowers, and round to oval, grey-blue fruits. ❀ Rocks and cliffs. Crete. March–June.   **75**

A. graeca (A. utriculata) is a usually taller plant from the mainland, distinguished by the fruits having stalks.

ALYSSUM. *A. saxatile (Aurinia saxatile).* GOLDEN ALYSSUM. A branched perennial up to 40 cm., with silvery-hairy ovate leaves, and dense flat-topped clusters of golden-yellow flowers. Seed pods elliptic. ❀ Rocks, cliffs, and stony places. March–June. *The familiar alyssum of gardens.*

DRABA. *D. aizoides.* YELLOW WHIT-LOW-GRASS. A tufted perennial making dense rosettes of narrow, stiff, smooth leaves fringed with bristles. Flower stems up to 10 cm. carry rather dense clusters of bright yellow flowers. Seed pods ellipsoid and smooth. ❀ Rocks and cliffs. N. mountains. March–May. *D. cretica* is similar to *D. aizoides*, but with smaller flowers and hairy seed pods. ❀ Cretan mountains. March–May.

D. parnassica. Another dwarf, tightly-tufted plant, with dense clusters of rather large bright yellow flowers. Differs from *D. aizoides* in the hairy flower stems. ❀ Parnassus and other mountains. March–May.

D. scardica is smaller and more slender than *D. aizoides*, and not so tightly

tufted. The seed pods are inflated.
❀ Mount Olympos. May–July. **76**

AETHIONEMA. *A. saxatile* (*A. graeca*). BURNT CANDYTUFT. A cushion or mat-forming plant, 5–15 cm. high, with grey-blue, rather fleshy, pointed leaves. The pink and lilac flowers are carried in dense clusters. ❀ Rocky places, crevices, in the hills and mountains. March–May. **77**

BISCUTELLA. *B. didyma.* A slender annual, up to 40 cm. high, with oval more or less toothed leaves, and dense clusters of yellow flowers followed by twin-seeded flattened fruit with thick margins. ❀ Stony places, often in the hills. March–June. **527**

MORICANDIA. *M. arvensis.* A short-lived perennial with smooth, rather fleshy, grey-green rounded stem-clasping leaves, the branched stems up to 60 cm. high carrying sprays of purple flowers. ❀ Waste ground, stony hillsides. March–June. **529**

ERUCA. *E. vesicaria* (*E. sativa*). ROGNETTE. A mustard-like plant, hairy and branched, 20–100 cm. tall. Leaves deeply lobed. Flowers of a dingy yellowish-white, veined with purple. Pods

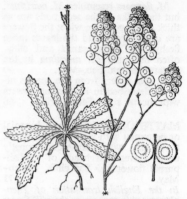

527 Biscutella didyma × ½
(siliquae enlarged)

short, erect, and beaked. ❀ Waste places, fields. Feb.–June. **528**
Cultivated for salad, and for oil produced from the seeds and often naturalised. Dioscorides remarks 'This being eaten raw in any great quantitie doth provoke Venery, and the seed of it also doth work ye like effect, being ureticall and digestive, and good for ye belly. They doe also use the seed of it in making of Sawces.'

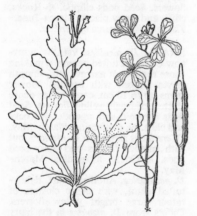

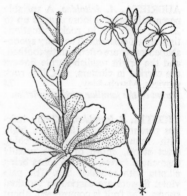

Left: 528 Eruca vesicaria.
Right: 529 Moricandia arvensis (siliquae enlarged). Both × ½

RESEDACEAE – Mignonette Family

Herbaceous plants with dense spikes of numerous small irregular flowers. Sepals and petals 4–8. Fruit a capsule.

RESEDA. *R. alba.* WHITE MIGNONETTE. Up to 80 cm. high, with deeply cut wavy-edged leaves and spikes of white flowers 9 mm. across, usually with 5 sepals and petals. ❈ Waste land, stony places, walls, and cliffs, often on the coast. March–June.
R. lutea. WILD MIGNONETTE. Like *R. alba*, but with spikes of yellow flowers. 6 mm. across, usually with 6 sepals and petals. Leaves cut into 5–8 pairs of lobes. ❈ Stony places and roadsides, on limestone. April–July.

CRASSULACEAE – Stonecrop Family

Herbs with fleshy undivided leaves. Flowers in clusters or spikes; petals and other flower parts in whorls, variable in number but often 5.
UMBILICUS. Basal leaves rounded with centrally placed stalk; flowers numerous, in elongated spikes.
SEMPERVIVUM. Leaves in rosettes. Flowers pink, purple, or yellowish. Petals and sepals 8–16.
JOVIBARBA. Leaves in rosettes; flowers pale yellow, sepals and petals 5–7 – usually 6.
SEDUM. Leaves fleshy, flat, or cylindrical, usually alternate, on elongated stems; flower parts usually 5.

UMBILICUS. *U. horizontalis* (Cotyledon horizontalis). A Mediterranean PENNYWORT with basal fleshy rounded leaves, erect stems 10–40 cm. tall carrying narrow crowded leaves, and the flowering spikes which are not more than half the length of the stem. Flowers reddish, horizontally carried and almost stalkless. ❈ Rocky and shady places. April–May.   **79**

SEMPERVIVUM. *S. marmoreum* (*S. schlehanii*). A HOUSELEEK with rosettes 6 cm. across, olive green, sometimes reddish, with smooth oblong leaves edged with fine hairs. Flowering stem up to 20 cm. carrying clusters of pink or reddish flowers with parts in 12s. ❈ Rocky places in the mountains. July–Aug.
  S. reginae-amaliae is like *S. marmoreum*, but smaller, and with finely hairy leaves. ❈ Mount Olympos, N. Pindos. July–Aug.
  S. ballsii is a very local species with open, 3 cm. shining green, thick-leaved rosettes and flowers with 12 pink, red-striped petals. ❈ Smolikas, Grammos mountains. July–Aug.

JOVIBARBA. *J. heuffelii* (*Sempervivum heuffelii*). Rosettes 5–7 cm. across, leaves dark green with white and bristly edged margins. Stolons absent; unique in increasing by the splitting of the rosette. Flowers pale yellow, on stems to 20 cm. high. ❈ Limestone mountains. N. Greece. June–Aug.   **80**

SEDUM. *S. dasyphyllum.* A creeping perennial producing many upright shoots in loose tufts. The usually opposite leaves are 3–5 cm. long and almost globular. Flowers pinkish white in small clusters on 5–8 cm. stems. ❈ Rocks in the mountains. June–Aug.   **530**
S. sediforme (*S. altissimum, S. nicaeense*). A smooth blue-grey perennial with rather large overlapping oval, pointed leaves. Flat-topped flower heads of pale yellow flowers are carried on clustered stems up to 60 cm. ❈ Rocky and stony places. June–Aug.   **531**
S. stellatum. STARRY STONECROP. An annual 3–15 cm. high, with smooth rounded leaves and flat-topped clusters

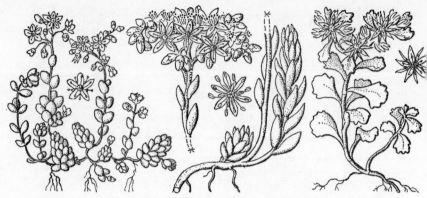

Left to Right: 530 Sedum dasyphyllum. 531 S. nicaeense. 532 S. stellatum. All × ⅔ (single florets enlarged)

of pink flowers. ❧ Rocky and stony places. May–June. **532**

SAXIFRAGACEAE

Herbs with simple or lobed leaves, often rosette-forming. Flowers usually in branched clusters; sepals and petals 4 or 5.

Lax, frail plants

SAXIFRAGA. *S. rotundifolia*. ROUND-LEAVED SAXIFRAGE. From basal tufts of rounded or kidney-shaped hairy leaves arise flowering stems up to 40 cm. high, carrying rather narrow branched clusters of white flowers, often yellow spotted. ❧ Damp and shady places in the mountains. May–July. **81**
***S. graeca*.** Similar to the British Meadow Saxifrage, *S. granulata*, with kidney-shaped, glandular-hairy leaves, and compact terminal sprays of large white flowers. ❧ Grassy places in the mountains. April–June.

Rosette-forming mountain plants

***S. marginata*.** A tightly cushioned dwarf plant. The overlapping leaves are variable, but often of narrow-oblong shape edged with white; stems reddish, up to 9 cm., carrying loose heads of 2–8 white or pinkish flowers. ❧ Rocks. High limestone mountains. June–Aug. **83**

S. spruneri resembles *S. marginata*, but has very numerous leafy shoots with smaller leaves and rather smaller white flowers. ❧ High mountains of N. and C. Greece, including Olympos and Parnassos. June–August.
***S. scardica*.** Forming tight cushions of rosettes of silvery-grey broad-pointed leaves, with 10 cm. stems carrying clusters of white trumpet-shaped flowers. ❧ Limestone rocks. Mountains of C. Greece and Peloponnese. March-May. **82**
***S. sempervivum* (*S. porophylla var. sibthorpiana*).** Forming cushions of lime-encrusted rosettes, of narrow blue-grey pointed leaves. Stems up to 14 cm. high carry heads of 7–20 pinkish-purple flowers. ❧ Limestone rocks. High mountains. June–Aug. **84**
***S. taygetea*.** Tightly tufted, with stalked, rounded, soft leaves, and 10 cm. high heads of pink and white flowers. ❧ Rocks and cliffs. High mountains, C. Greece and Peloponnese. March–May.

PLATANACEAE – Plane Family

Trees, with flaking bark and deeply lobed leaves. Flowers in clusters; fruits forming round bristly heads.

PLATANUS. *P. orientalis*. ORIENTAL PLANE. A tall spreading tree, up to 30

m. high with grey mottled bark and large deeply-cut and toothed leaves of 5–7 lobes. Flowers unisexual in drooping catkins. ⚘ Widely planted as a shade tree, but a true native in Crete and some E. Aegean islands, where it grows in rocky valleys and along streams. March–April.

491, p. 60

A tree prized since earliest times for its beauty and shade-providing. Xerxes so admired the Lydian planes that he hung them with golden ornaments. The wood, to quote Theophrastus, 'is fairly tough . . . moist in character . . . A proof of this is that, if it is set upright after being cut, it discharges much water.' It takes a high polish and is hence valued by cabinet-makers. Dioscorides gives a number of remedies, including relief of eye discharges, inflammations, toothache, and snake bite.

ROSACEAE – Rose Family

Trees, shrubs, or herbaceous plants with alternate leaves. Radially symmetrical flowers usually of 5 sepals and petals.

ROSA. Shrubs, often with prickles; leaves compound (pinnate); sepals and petals 5; fruit fleshy, often flask-shaped.

SARCOPOTERIUM. Spiny shrubs with compound leaves; flowers unisexual.

CRATAEGUS. Trees or shrubs, usually with thorns. Flowers in flat-topped clusters. Leaves lobed. Fruit fleshy.

PYRUS. Deciduous shrubs or trees, often somewhat spiny; leaves undivided; flowers white or pinkish in clusters; fruit fleshy and gritty.

PRUNUS. Trees or shrubs, often deciduous, sometimes spiny; flowers white or pink in clusters or solitary; fruit fleshy.

ROSA. *R. pendulina* **(R. alpina).** ALPINE ROSE. Stems up to 2 m., yellowish-green, without prickles. Leaflets oblong-oval and toothed. The solitary flowers are bright carmine, and the fruit is longish, drooping, and bright red. ⚘ Rocky semi-shaded places. N. mountains. June–July. **85**

R. sempervirens. An evergreen rose, with shining pointed leaves of 5 leaflets. Clusters of 3–7 white flowers, followed by rounded smooth red fruit. ⚘ Hedges, especially in damp places. Feb.–July. **86**

Theophrastus refers to wild roses as having 'many differences, in the number of petals, in roughness, in beauty of colour, and in sweetness of scent . . . there are some, they say, which are even called "hundred-petalled" '. These multi-petalled roses were dug up and planted in gardens. Theophrastus also discusses growing roses from seeds and cuttings, and pruning by either cutting or burning to improve flower production.

The Romans used roses by the million for festoons and garlands. At banquets their petals were dropped from the ceiling to carpet the floors. The emperor Heliogabalus is reputed to have suffocated some of his guests by over-generous use of rose petals in this way. Sybarites filled their couches with rose petals and complained if any were on edge rather than flat! Virgil mentions that the dried petals are used to make a medicine for sick bees.

SARCOPOTERIUM. *S. spinosum* **(Poterium spinosum).** THORNY BURNET. A dense, very spiny shrub up to 60 cm. high, bearing oval heads of very small reddish flowers. Leaves with 4–7 pairs of small leaflets. Fruit fleshy, becoming bright red. ⚘ Dry limestone hills. March–May. **87**

An important constituent of phrygana, often the only shrub to survive fires. At one time it was widely cut for fuel, especially for lime-kilns and bread-ovens where its tight bushy growth could be rammed in where required. Branches would also be pushed into the tops of water jars to act as a crude filter. Dioscorides remarks that the leaves and seed have binding properties, and a de-

coction cures dysentery, purulent ears, 'bloody flux', and blood-shot eyes.

PYRUS. *P. amygdaliformis.* A deciduous shrub or small tree to 6 m., often spiny, with grey twigs, often woolly in their young growth, and with narrow lance-shaped leaves. Flowers white, in clusters. Fruits small, globular, reddish-brown. ❧ Dry rocky places. March–April.

P. pyraster. WILD PEAR. A deciduous tree to 15 m., with somewhat spiny branches, thin oval leaves, and clusters of long-stalked white flowers followed by small hard fruit, rounded or pear-shaped. ❧ Stony hillsides. March–April.

Theophrastus, remarking how hard woods help to sharpen tools, mentions that 'cobblers make their strops of wild pear'.

CRATAEGUS. *C. azarolus.* MEDITERRANEAN MEDLAR. A shrub or small tree up to 10 m., white-downy on twigs and both surfaces of leaves. Leaves deeply 3–5 lobed. Flowers in tight clusters, white with purple anthers. The rounded 2 cm. fruits are orange-red or yellow, with 1–3 nuts. ❧ Dry hillsides, thickets. Crete. April–May.   **533**

Sometimes cultivated for its edible fruits. Of oxuacantha – probably referring to hawthorns in general – Dioscorides states that the bruised root helps to draw out splinters and thorns, and 'it is sayd also that the roote, hath the power to cause abortments, the belly being thrice smitten therewith gently'.

PRUNUS. *P. dulcis (P. amygdalus, P. communis).* ALMOND. A tree to 10 m. with elliptic leaves and flowers varying from near white to deep pink. ❧ Widely cultivated and equally widely naturalised. Feb.–March.   **88**

Introduced from W. Asia in very ancient times. Wild almonds have bitter fruits containing prussic acid, and the oil from them is narcotic. From the cultivated almond a sweet edible oil is produced. The reddish wood is used in veneering.

P. prostrata. A dwarf shrub, growing to 1 m. but often closely pressed against rocks. The oval leaves are small and toothed and the almost stalkless flowers are rose-pink. ❧ Rocks, cliffs, stony places. Hills and mountains of N. Greece. April–May.   **89**

533 Crataegus azarolus × ½

LEGUMINOSAE – Pea Family

A large family of trees, shrubs, and herbaceous plants, usually with compound leaves; the many climbing species have tendrils. Stipules (scaly or leaf-like organs at the base of leaf-stalks) are usually present. Flowers symmetrical in one plane only, with 5 petals and sepals: one broad upper petal (standard), two spreading lateral petals, and two lower petals (keel). Fruit a many-seeded pod (legume) splitting longitudinally.

CERCIS. A tree; leaves rounded, undivided; flowers reddish-purple.

CERATONIA. A tree; leaves leathery with 4–8 leaflets; pods large.

ANAGYRIS. A bush; leaves trifoliate; calyx toothed.

CALICOTOME: A shrub; leaves trifoliate; branches terminating in spines; calyx with short teeth.

CYTISUS. Non-spiny shrubs; leaves usually trifoliate; calyx 2-lipped.

GENISTA. Shrubs, usually spiny; leaves simple or reduced to spines; calyx 2-lipped, upper lip deeply divided.

SPARTIUM. Non-spiny shrubs; leaves simple or absent; smooth rush-like branches. Flowers yellow with single calyx lip.

LUPINUS. Herbaceous plants or sub-shrubs. Leaves with 4–11 leaflets; flowers in long spikes; calyx 2-lipped.

COLUTEA. Non-spiny shrubs: leaves with 7–15 leaflets; pod bladder-like and membranous when ripe.

ASTRAGALUS. Herbaceous or shrubby. Flowers white, pink, or bluish in axillary spikes or clusters; calyx tubular and 5-toothed.

PSORALEA. Herbaceous; flowers bluish in dense rounded clusters; leaves trifoliate; pod ovoid.

VICIA. Climbing or scrambling plants; leaves of many pairs of leaflets and usually a terminal tendril; pod flattened.

LATHYRUS. Climbing plants similar to *Vicia* but usually with fewer leaflets; stems winged or angled; flower heads usually long-stemmed.

PISUM. Climbing plants. Stems rounded; stipules leafy and larger than the leaflets; tendrils branched.

ONONIS. Herbaceous or shrubby. Flowers rose-pink or yellow; leaves simple or trifoliate; stipules conspicuous; calyx bell-shaped and 5-toothed.

TRIGONELLA. Herbaceous. Leaves trifoliate; flowers in short clusters; pod straight or curved, often flattened.

MEDICAGO. Herbaceous or shrubby. Leaves trifoliate; flowers orange or yellow; pod spirally coiled or sometimes sickle-shaped.

TRIFOLIUM. Herbaceous. Flowers in dense rounded heads, pink, white, or purple; leaves trifoliate; pods very small.

DORYCNIUM. Herbaceous. Flowers white with blackish keel, in stalked rounded axillary heads.

TETRAGONOLOBUS. Herbaceous. Flowers yellow or reddish-purple, and axillary; pod 4-angled and winged; leaves trefoil.

ANTHYLLIS. Herbaceous or shrubby. Flowers in dense heads or clusters; calyx long-tubed and inflated at base.

CORONILLA. Herbaceous or shrubby; flowers yellow, purple, or white; pods long and narrow.

HIPPOCREPIS. Herbaceous. Flowers yellow, calyx 5-toothed; pod flattened, narrow, and deeply indented into horse-shoe-shaped segments.

HEDYSARUM. Herbaceous. Flowers pink, purple, or whitish, in dense, stalked axillary clusters; pod broad, flattened, and segmented.

EBENUS. Shrubs with divided leaves and axillary flower heads of pink or purple; calyx bell-shaped, tubular, 5-toothed.

CERCIS. *C. siliquastrum.* JUDAS TREE. A deciduous tree to 10 m. The flowers, of a rich pink to purple, are carried in thick clusters on the bare branches in early spring, before the kidney-shaped leaves appear. ✤ Stony hills and mountain sides. March–April. **90**
This is traditionally the tree on which Judas Iscariot hanged himself after denouncing Christ. Legend has it that the originally pale flowers blushed pink with shame; or, more luridly, that the flowers – emerging from the wood direct – represent Judas's entrails. The ancient Greeks, of course, had no such legends, and Theophrastus's only comment is that the wood is used for walking sticks. It is in fact very hard and beautifully veined, taking a high polish. The flower buds, which are slightly acid, are sometimes added to salads.

CERATONIA. *C. siliqua.* CAROB or LOCUST TREE. A thick-trunked tree to

10 m. The shining leathery, dark green leaves are divided into 2 rows of oval leaflets, and are carried on widely spreading branches, giving deep shade. Flowers minute, greenish; the long pods appear to spring direct from the branches. ✣ Rocky places on the coast. Naturalised or cultivated elsewhere. Sept.–Nov. **500, p. 61**

The pods are the 'husks' in the parable of the prodigal son, and almost certainly the 'locusts' which fed John the Baptist in the desert. Early Greek writers mention the pods as a regular source of food especially to the poor. The ripe pods have a sweet syrupy pulp and were, earlier this century, occasionally sold as delicacies on the Riviera. They were also used for making syrups, sherbets, and fermented drinks. However, the main use of the pods is to feed horses and cattle. The seeds were used as the original carat of jewellers – a weight of 4 grains (Arabian kirat from the Greek keration, the word for the tree). The hard, shiny wood is used in marquetry and for walking sticks.

ANAGYRIS. *A. foetida.* An evil-smelling deciduous shrub 1–3 m. high, with trifoliate leaves, the leaflets being narrow-elliptic, green above and sil-

very beneath. The rather large flowers, yellow with a black blotch, are carried in clusters. Feb.–March. **534**

A poisonous plant, once used as a purge and an emetic.

CALICOTOME (often spelt *Calycotome*). *C. villosa* (*C. infesta*). SPINY BROOM. Shrub of 1–2 m., much branched, very spiny; the under-surface of leaflets and pods covered with silky hairs. The brilliant golden flowers are carried in clusters of 6–8 all along the branches. ✣ Rocky barren hillsides. March–June. **91**

The leaves and pods were once used for their astringent qualities, although the whole plant, especially the seeds, is poisonous to ruminant animals at least. The spiny branches were bound into brooms.

CYTISUS. *C. villosus* (*C. triflorus*). A branching broom relation to 2 m. high, with trifoliate leaves of 3 elliptic leaflets, and yellow flowers streaked with

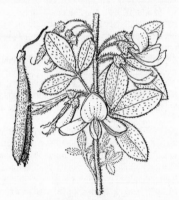

535 Cytisus villosus ×½
(pod enlarged)

red carried in the axils of the leaves, singly or in pairs. Pods: densely hairy. ✣ Open woodland and thickets, avoiding limestone. April–May. **535**

GENISTA. *G. acanthoclada.* A low growing shrub to 1 m., often prostrate, dense and spiny, with trefoil leaves of 3 very narrow leaflets, and yellow

534 Anagyris foetida ×½

flowers carried at the ends of the branches in the axils of bracts. Pods egg-shaped, silky-haired. ✿ Stony ground, rock crevices. June–July. **92**

SPARTIUM. *S. junceum.* SPANISH BROOM. A tall graceful shrub, of many erect grey-green, almost leafless, branches growing to 2½ m., carrying spikes of large golden, sweet-scented flowers at the ends. ✿ Stony open hillsides, sea cliffs. May–June. **93**

The seeds and flowering shoots contain an alkaloid and are diuretic in small doses, purging and emetic in larger ones. A yellow dye was made from the flowers, while the stems are used in basket-making and yield a fibre used for weaving.

LUPINUS. *L. angustifolius.* NARROW-LEAVED LUPIN. An annual to 60 cm. The leaves have 5–9 narrow leaflets, and the clear blue flowers are carried in long terminal spikes. ✿ Sandy and rocky places. March–May. **95**

L. micranthus (*L. hirsutus*). An annual up to 40 cm. Leaves with leaflets 1–5 cm. wide; flowers dark blue. Whole plant hairy. ✿ Fields, vineyards, olive groves, and roadsides. Feb.–April. **96**

L. varius (*L. pilosus*). A white-hairy annual growing to 50 cm. The blue and white flowers are carried in flowering spikes 5–10 cm. long. The Greek plant is *ssp. orientalis.* ✿ Stony places and cultivated ground. April–June.

L. albus. Annual, up to 120 cm., with leaves smooth above, slightly hairy below, and dark blue flowers. The Greek plant is *ssp. graecus.* ✿ Cultivated ground. April–June.

Sometimes cultivated for its edible seeds, and for fodder. Theophrastus says the seed must be planted immediately after threshing, and prefers sandy or poor soil to cultivated.

The yellow *L. luteus,* growing up to 80 cm. high, is a W. Mediterranean species, but is sometimes grown as a fodder crop in Greece, and is occasionally naturalised. May–June.

COLUTEA. *C. arborescens.* BLADDER SENNA. A deciduous shrub to 3 m., with pale green compound leaves of 7–15 oval leaflets, and erect axillary clusters of 2–8 large yellow flowers followed by the characteristic inflated papery seed pods. ✿ Woods and thickets on limestone hills. April–July. **94**

The leaves have been used as a mild substitute for true senna (a species of Cassia). An infusion of the seeds was used as an emetic; they are in fact poisonous, containing an alkaloid which can kill cattle.

ASTRAGALUS. *A. angustifolius.* A densely tufted spiny plant growing to 20 cm., with 6–10 pairs of narrow leaflets, and clusters of 3–12 white flowers. ✿ Rocky places in the mountains. May–July.

A. hamosus. A greyish green, hairy, sprawling annual to 40 cm., with small white flowers in stalked globular clusters, immediately recognisable by the cylindrical, sickle-shaped pods. ✿ Waste places, field edges. March–July. **102**

A. lusitanicus. IBERIAN MILK VETCH. A strong-growing plant up to 70 cm. high, with leaves of 8–11 pairs of oval leaflets, hairy below, and dense oblong clusters of many white flowers. The Greek plant is *ssp. orientalis.* ✿ Waste places and field edges; Peloponnese. March–May. **101**

A. parnassi. Forms dense low-growing cushions, with compound leaves of 5–8 pairs of narrow leaflets, smooth above, somewhat hairy beneath; flowers purplish-pink in stemless heads. ✿ Rocky places in the mountains. April–June. **103**

PSORALEA. *P. bituminosa.* BITUMEN PEA. A straggling perennial 50–100 cm. high, smelling of tar when crushed. Leaves trifoliate, dark green and long-stalked, with narrow to oval leaflets. The 10–15 dark blue-violet flowers are carried in heads on very long stalks. ✿ Dry banks, waste places, fields. April–July. **97**

The Bitumen Pea used to figure widely in herbal medicine. Dioscorides mentions many uses, including treatment of ague, epilepsy, dropsy, and the 'serpent-bitten'. He adds, 'if another having an ulcer be fomented in ye water [containing the plant juice] wherein another was healed, he feels ye same pains as ye bitten did'.

VICIA. ***V. dasycarpa*** **(*V. villosa ssp. varia*).** An annual or biennial vetch, climbing and scrambling, with leaves of 5–8 pairs of narrow leaflets, and terminal tendrils. The clusters of numerous violet and white coloured flowers are borne in profusion. ⚘ In bushes and among herbage at roadsides, and in stony, rocky places. March–May. **104**

V. hybrida. Climbing and scrambling to 50 cm. Its leaves have 4–8 pairs of oval leaflets and terminal tendrils, and the rather large pale yellow flowers are carried singly in leaf axils. ⚘ Fields, waste and cultivated ground. March–May. **107**

V. lutea. YELLOW VETCH. Resembles *V. hybrida*, but the 3–10 pairs of leaflets are narrower, and end in a fine point. Flowers sulphur-yellow. ⚘ Fields, waste and cultivated ground. March–May.

LATHYRUS. ***L. aphaca.*** YELLOW VETCHLING. A slender hairless annual, 25–100 cm. tall, with true leaves replaced by broad leaf-like stipules and long tendrils. The solitary yellow flowers are carried singly on long stalks. ⚘ Fields and waste places. April–June. **98**

L. cicera. A prostrate or scrambling vetch-like plant. The leaves have paired leaflets, long and narrow, with tendrils. Flowers large, single, of an unusual brick-red colour. ⚘ Rough, grassy, and bushy places, sometimes on cultivated ground. March–May. **100**

L. grandiflorus. EVERLASTING PEA. A finely hairy perennial scrambling or sprawling to 1½ m., stem unwinged. Leaves with 1–3 pairs of ovate leaves. Axillary clusters of 1–4 large (3 cm.) purple and bright pink flowers. ⚘ Shady places in the mountains. May–July. **99**

L. ochrus. A hairless blue-grey annual up to 80 cm. high, with broadly winged stems and solitary pale yellow flowers carried on short stalks. Lower leaves egg-shaped, upper leaves with 1–2 pairs of egg-shaped leaflets, and with branched tendrils. ⚘ Cornfields and waste places. March–June.

PISUM. ***P. elatius*** **(*P. sativum ssp. elatius*).** WILD PEA. A hairless blue-green annual, climbing to 1 m. or more. The 1–3 oval leaflets are smaller than the leaf-like stipules, and the large flowers are rosy-purple with darker wings. ⚘ Thickets. April–June. **108**

ONONIS. ***O. pubescens.*** A hairy and sticky annual to 35 cm. Leaves of 1 or 3 elliptical leaflets. The yellow flowers are carried in dense terminal spikes. Calyx teeth 5-veined. ⚘ Waste land and stony places. April–June.

O. spinosa. RESTHARROW. A dwarf shrub 30–80 cm. high, spiny, and with trifoliate leaves of variable shape. The short-stalked pink flowers are carried in loose leafy clusters. Seed smooth. The Greek plant is ***ssp. leiosperma.*** ⚘ Waste and stony places. April–June.

O. viscosa. A variable, erect annual up to 80 cm., softly hairy, and sticky. Leaves simple or with 1–3 leaflets. Flowers yellow streaked with red. Similar to *O. pubescens* but calyx teeth 3-veined. ⚘ Stony and waste places. May–July. **118**

TRIGONELLA. ***T. balansae.*** An annual, growing to 50 cm., with pale green trifoliate leaves, the leaflets being oval, toothed, and stalked. The yellow flowers are carried in rounded heads, and the seed pods are sickle-shaped. ⚘ Cultivated ground and sandy places. March–May. **105**

T. caerulea. An unbranched almost hairless annual, growing up to 50 cm. with trefoil leaves and globular heads of bluish flowers. ⚘ Grown as a fodder crop but widely naturalised. March–April.

T. coerulescens. A low-growing hairy annual up to 40 cm., with trifoliate leaves, the oval leaflets being toothed. Flowers blue, in tight round heads. Pods straight. Looks like a small blue clover. ⚘ Dry stony hills, coasts. March–April. **106**

MEDICAGO. ***M. arborea.*** TREE MEDICK. A densely growing shrub, up to 3 m. high, with bright green leaves divided into 3 oval leaflets. The pale orange flowers are carried in clusters. Pods in a single flat spiral. ⚘ Rocks and cliffs. March–July. **109**

Often planted as a decorative shrub.

M. marina. SEA MEDICK. A spreading prostrate plant densely covered by soft white woolly hairs. The bright lemon yellow flowers are carried in clusters of 5–10. ⚘ Sea shores, often in pure sand. March–May.   **110**

TRIFOLIUM. *T. purpureum.* PURPLE CLOVER. A branched annual up to 60 cm. high, with narrow leaflets and long-stalked, large and handsome conical rosy-purple flowers. ⚘ Fields and dry sandy places. March–July.
T. stellatum. STAR CLOVER. A silky-haired annual 5–20 cm. high, with trefoil leaves and rounded pinkish-white flower heads followed by the outspread calyx teeth forming a star shape, often crimson in the centre. ⚘ Sandy and stony places. March–June.   **111**
T. tomentosum. WOOLLY TREFOIL. A low-growing annual with smooth trefoil leaves. The small rounded white or pinkish flower heads are white-woolly, and enlarge to 1–1½ cm. in fruit. ⚘ Grassy and stony places. April–May.
T. uniflorum. A low growing plant forming usually flat tufts or mats, the trefoil leaves formed of egg-shaped leaflets, and the rather large solitary pinkish-white flowers carried tightly packed just above the leaves. ⚘ Stony and rocky places. March–May.   **112**

DORYCNIUM. *D. hirsutum (Bonjeanea hirsuta).* A grey-hairy perennial up to 50 cm. high, with trifoliate leaves of oval leaflets, and tight rounded heads of white or pinkish flowers with darker keels. Calyces very hairy. ⚘ Stony and sandy places. April–July.
536

TETRAGONOLOBUS. *T. purpureus (Lotus tetragonolobus).* WINGED or ASPARAGUS PEA. A softly hairy annual up to 40 cm. high, with trefoil leaves and dark crimson flowers carried singly or in pairs, succeeded by characteristic pods with 4 broad crinkled wings. ⚘ Cultivated ground and by pathsides. March–May.   **114**
The small pods can be cooked and eaten, and seeds are available in Britain.

ANTHYLLIS. *A. hermanniae.* A densely branched spiny shrub up to

50 cm., with simple or trefoil leaves composed of narrowly oval leaflets, hairy beneath. The small yellow flowers are carried in axillary clusters of 1–3. ⚘ Stony ground and rocky places. May–August.   **117**
A. tetraphylla (Physanthyllis tetraphylla). BLADDER VETCH. A prostrate annual, softly hairy, with 1–2 pairs of pale green rounded leaflets, and axillary clusters of pale yellow flowers touched with red. The large very hairy calyces become strikingly swollen in fruit, and turn reddish. ⚘ Fields and cultivated ground. March–July.   **115**
A. vulneraria ssp. praepropera (ssp. spruneri). This form of the well known and widely distributed KIDNEY VETCH is most likely to be found in Greece. The leaves have 1–6 pairs of leaflets, and the large flowers are rose-coloured with white-silky, purple-tipped calyces. ⚘ Dry fields, hillsides. March–June.
116

536 Dorycnium hirsutum × ½
(floret and pod enlarged)

CORONILLA. *C. emerus (C. emeroides).* SCORPION SENNA. A much-branched leafy shrub growing up to 2 m., with dark green hairless leaves of 2–4 oval leaflets, and large bright yellow flowers in clusters of 2–7. The Greek plant is *ssp. emeroides.* ⚘ Shady woods on limestone. March–May.
497, p. 61
The bitter leaves have been used to

adulterate true senna (Cassia acutifolia) *and it has been grown for this purpose in Britain since the sixteenth century.*

C. varia. A perennial growing up to 1 m., with hairless pinnate leaves of 7–12 pairs of elliptic leaflets. The variably coloured flowers – white, pink, or purple – are carried in axillary clusters of 10–20. ✣ Thickets, often on the hills. April–June.   **113**
Often cultivated for fodder.

HIPPOCREPIS. *H. unisiliquosa.* HORSE-SHOE VETCH. A slender annual up to 30 cm. high, with pinnate leaves of 3–7 pairs of oblong leaflets, and small almost stalkless yellow flowers carried in the upper leaf axils. The characteristic hairless pods are curved, with 7–10 deep horse-shoe shaped constrictions. ✣ Sandy and stony places. March–May.

The similar *H. multisiliquosa* has long flower stalks and more strongly curved pods. ✣ Sandy and stony places. March–May.

HEDYSARUM. *H. coronarium.* ITALIAN SAINFOIN. A branched perennial growing up to 1 m., with pinnate leaves of 3–5 pairs of leaflets, smooth above and hairy beneath. The bright carmine flowers, with hairy calyces, are carried in long-stalked oval clusters in the leaf axils. Pods: rough and spiny. ✣ Grown as a fodder crop, and often naturalised. April–June.
H. glomeratum (H. capitatum). Resembles *H. coronarium*, but has larger

flowers of pinkish-purple. ✣ Dry scrub. April–May.

EBENUS. *E. cretica.* CRETAN EBONY. A woody-based shrub with drooping branches carrying greyish-white downy leaves of 3–5 elliptic leaflets, and rose-pink flowers in dense erect terminal spikes. ✣ Stony hillsides, rock crevices. Crete. May–June.   **119**

OXALIDACEAE – Wood Sorrel Family

Low growing herbs, many with fleshy rootstock, and with clover-like leaves of 3 leaflets. Flowers with 5 sepals and petals, in umbels or solitary.

OXALIS. *O. pes-caprae (O. cernua).* BERMUDA BUTTERCUP. With bright green, purple-spotted trefoil leaves, and heads of 6–12 lemon-yellow flowers on 20 cm. high stems. A double flowered form (*fl. pl.*) is often seen and sometimes predominates locally. ✣ On agricultural land, in vineyards, and olive groves. Jan.–April.   **120, 121**
A native of South Africa, introduced from Bermuda (hence its name) to Malta for ornament, whence it has spread throughout the Mediterranean by means of its numerous bulbils. The form which has become such a universal weed is, ironically, sterile and never sets seed. Neither cultural practices nor weed-killers can destroy it.

GERANIACEAE – Geranium Family

Herbs with lobed or compound leaves. Flowers with 5 petals and sepals. Ovary ends in a long beak formed by the fused styles, splitting on maturity into 1-seeded sections.
GERANIUM. Leaf lobes as broad as long; seeds released by splitting of styles.
ERODIUM. Leaves usually pinnate with leaflets longer than broad; style twists in corkscrew shape before splitting.

GERANIUM. *G. cinereum.* A grey-hairy low-growing perennial up to 15 cm., with deeply 5–7 segmented leaves and deep reddish-purple flowers, the sepals bearing long white hairs. The

Greek form is *ssp. subcaulescens.* ✣ Limestone rocks and screes in the mountains. June–August.   **122**
G. macrorrhizum. A hairy perennial with stout creeping rhizome growing

to 10–30 cm., with lobed leaves divided into 5–7 oval-toothed segments. The dense clusters of flowers are usually pale flesh-pink, sometimes carmine, with projecting stamens and style. ✤ Rocky places in the mountains, on limestone, usually in semi-shade. June–Aug. **123**

G. molle. DOVE'S-FOOT CRANESBILL. A hairy annual with rounded, deeply cut leaves, growing up to 50 cm., with small pink flowers, the petals deeply 2-lobed, and beaked fruit. A larger flowered form (*forma grandiflorum*) is commonly seen in Greece. ✤ Roadsides, grassy places. March–June.

G. sanguineum. BLOODY CRANESBILL. A spreading hairy and bushy perennial with a creeping rhizome, growing to 40 cm. Leaves rounded, deeply cut into 5–7 narrow lobes which are still further divided. The large bright crimson-purple flowers are borne singly. ✤ On hills, in rocky and stony places. June–Sept. **124**

G. tuberosum. TUBEROUS CRANESBILL. With slender, finely hairy stems 20–40 cm. high arising from a small nut-like tuber. Leaves cut into 5–7 narrow segments. The pinkish-purple flowers, carried in terminal clusters, have notched petals. ✤ Cultivated ground, vineyards, olive groves. March–June. **125**

Pliny mentions that the root is a useful tonic for convalescents.

ERODIUM. *E. chrysanthum.* YELLOW STORKSBILL. A small plant, white-hairy, only 5 cm. high, with dissected leaves and umbels of 3–7 yellow flowers. ✤ Stony places in the mountains. May–June. **131**

E. gruinum. LONG-BEAKED STORKSBILL. Annual or biennial, up to 40 cm. The lower leaves are heart-shaped, the upper divided into three leaflets. The lilac or bluish flowers are carried in clusters of 2–6 on long stalks; but the outstanding feature of the plant is the fruit, which has very long beaks, up to 11 cm. long. ✤ Field margins, sandy downs, stony places. Feb.–May. **134**

LINACEAE – Flax Family

Herbs with simple alternate leaves. Flowers with 4 or 5 sepals and petals. Fruit a capsule containing the shining seeds.

The flax of commerce is Linum usitatissimum, *the fibres of which have been used since Egyptian times for making linen. The Greeks used this material especially for shrouds. Linseed oil is made from the seeds.*

LINUM. *L. arboreum.* TREE FLAX. A shrub up to 1 m. high. Leaves spoon-shaped, thick. Flowers 3–4 cm. across, bright yellow, in small clusters. ✤ Limestone rocks. S. Greece, Crete, Rhodes. March–May. **132**

L. leucanthum. A branched woody-based plant up to 15 cm. The thick spoon-shaped leaves are in basal rosettes, and alternate on the stems; usually densely covered with short hairs, though smooth-leaved varieties also occur. Flowers white, in loose clusters of up to 10. ✤ Rocky places, often on mountains in S.E. Greece. April–May. **133**

L. pubescens. A hairy annual with lance-shaped leaves and stems 7–20 cm. high, carrying a few large pink flowers. ✤ Fields and stony places. March–April. **135**

EUPHORBIACEAE – Spurge Family

Herbs or shrubs with milky juice. (Many of the Greek names include the word *gala*, meaning milk, e.g. *galastoiri*.) Leaves often narrow and spirally arranged. Flowers small and green, sexes on separate flowers, with or without petals and sepals, and often with accompanying glands. Flowers often in umbels (umbrella-shaped heads) composed of several stems (rays), sometimes with bracts at various points.

EUPHORBIA. *E. acanthothamnos.* A low-growing domed shrub, up to 30 cm., composed of densely intertwined spiny branches. In spring the bush is covered with bright yellowish-green little leaves, and heads of golden-yellow flowers. Fruit warty. ⚹ Rocky places, cliffs. March–April.   **136**

E. apios. Low-growing, sometimes sprawling, the stems 5–20 cm. long. Leaves narrow-lanceolate to oval, radiating from centre. Flowers in an umbel of 3–5 rays. Unique among the Euphorbias in having a rounded underground tuber. ⚹ Dry, rocky places, thickets. April–June.

E. characias. Shrub-like plants with stout erect stems. The lance-shaped leaves are leathery, while the lower part of the woody stems are scarred by the bases of fallen leaves. There are two easily distinguished sub-species:

Ssp. characias. To 80–100 cm., with large, rather cylindrical flower heads of green flowers, usually with brownish-purple glands having short 'horns'.   **129**

Ssp. wulfenii (E. wulfenii, E. veneta). To 100–180 cm., with large rounded flower heads of golden-yellow, the glands long-haired. ⚹ Dry ground in open places, often in the hills. March–May.   **126**

The word tithymallos *which basically means spurge appears frequently in* Theophrastus *but seems usually to refer to other plants. Dioscorides however gives numerous uses of the 'dwarf mountain pine' and other species of which he recognises seven. It was used as a purge, an emetic, a depilatory, to cure toothache, and destroy 'hanging warts'. He says of the seeds 'some also do pickle them, mixing with ye milky juice Lepidium and bruised Cheese'. He explains how important it is to avoid getting the acrid juice on to one's skin or in the eyes when preparing 'tithymal'.*

E. dendroides. TREE SPURGE. A woody-stemmed shrub, making rounded bushes up to 2½ m. The much-branched stems are reddish, showing the scars of shed leaves. The leaves are narrow and the yellow flowers are carried in terminal clusters. Glands half-moon-shaped. ⚹ Coastal hills and cliffs, often on rock. March–June.   **128**

E. myrsinites. With spreading 20–40 cm. stems and broad fleshy overlapping blue-green leaves. Flowering heads of 5–12 rays, flowers yellow, distinctive from their reddish-brown involucral glands. ⚹ Rocky and stony places, especially in N. Greece. March–June.   **130**

Another 'tithymal' specified by Dioscorides, with similar faculties to E. characias.

E. rigida (E. biglandulosa). Many stout 30–50 stems carry blue-green leaves, narrow and pointed. The golden yellow flower heads are spreading of 6–12 rays. ⚹ Stony places, especially in the Peloponnese. March–May.   **127**

RUTACEAE – Rue Family

In Greece, sub-shrubs or herbaceous plants, with simple or pinnate glandular leaves. Flowers with 4–5 sepals and petals. Fruit fleshy.

This family includes all the Citrus *grown in Greece – oranges, lemons, citrons, etc., small trees which are not native.*

RUTA. Shrubs. Flowers yellow; petals with toothed or fringed margins.

DICTAMNUS. Herbaceous. Flowers irregular, white or pink.

RUTA. *R. chalepensis.* FRINGED RUE. A small highly aromatic shrub, growing to a height of up to 80 cm., with leaves deeply cut into wedge-like segments; the yellow green-tinged flowers with fringed petals are carried in branched clusters. ⚹ Rocky hillsides, cliffs, and low thickets. March–June.   **137**

R. graveolens. COMMON RUE. A low shrub, with woody base, growing up to 80 cm. The very bluish leaves are twice subdivided deeply into oval segments, and the yellow flowers with toothed petals are carried in branched clusters. The whole plant is pungently aromatic. ⚹ Stony places on limestone. May–July.

According to Dioscorides both these rues are 'caustical, warming, exulcerating, ureticall, bringing out ye menstrua, and being eaten or drank do bind ye belly; . . . ye seed being drank in wine, is an Antidot of deadly medicines'. He goes on with numerous other attributes, explaining that the wild rue is stronger in action than the cultivated or common species. The latter, the 'Herb of Grace', was long used as a bitter pot-herb, and widely in herbal medicine; it was also considered efficacious against infectious diseases and to ward off fleas and other insects.

DICTAMNUS. *D. albus* (*D. fraxinella*). BURNING BUSH. A glandular aromatic perennial up to 1 m. high, with pinnate leaves of 5–9 oval, leathery, finely toothed leaflets. The pink or white, purple-marked flowers are carried in long spikes, and the 5 petals are unequal, the upper 4 being erect, the lowest deflexed. ✲ Stony and rocky hillsides, in woods and bushy places. May–June. **138**
Called Burning Bush because of the aromatic oil given off which, on a really calm, hot day, can be briefly ignited without harm to the plant.

SIMAROUBACEAE –
Quassia Family

Trees or shrubs with alternate pinnate leaves, bitter bark, and small flowers with 5–6 petals. Fruit winged.

AILANTHUS. *A. altissima* (*A. angulosa*). TREE OF HEAVEN. A fast growing tree to 20 m., with smooth bark, large compound leaves, and clusters of small green-yellow flowers followed by reddish-brown fruits. ✲ Native of China, often planted for ornament and occasionally naturalised. July–Aug.

MELIACEAE – Mahogany
Family

Trees or shrubs, with pinnate leaves. The wood is often hard and scented. Flowers in small clusters, sepals and petals 4 or 5. Fruit a berry.

MELIA. *M. azederach.* INDIAN BEAD TREE, PERSIAN LILAC. A tree reaching 15 m. Leaves large and pinnate; flowers sweet-scented, bluish, flowers carried in loose clusters, followed by globular yellow fruit. ✲ A native of China, this ornamental tree is widely grown, and occasionally naturalised in Crete. May–June. **139, 140**
The name Bead Tree (also Arbor Sancta) derives from the use of the fruits as rosary beads. Parts of the plant were used in herbal medicine, although the fruit is poisonous. The leaves were believed to keep off mosquitoes, a use which has been proven in modern times when close relations with similar properties are being used in the tropics as 'poor farmers' insecticides'.

POLYGALACEAE –
Milkwort Family

Usually herbaceous plants, with simple leaves without stipules. Flowers asymmetrical, with 5 sepals, 2 of which are petal-like, and 3–5 petals.

POLYGALA. *P. monspeliaca.* A slender annual, up to 15 cm., with loose spikes of narrow-oval whitish flowers, and very narrow leaves. ✲ Stony and bushy places. May–July. **537**
P. nicaeensis. A perennial with slender

Left: 537 Polygala monspeliaca
Right: 538 P. nicaeensis. Both ×½
(florets enlarged)

stems up to 35 cm. high, with small narrow leaves and loose spikes of oval pink, blue, or white flowers, larger than in *P. monspeliaca*. The Greek plant is usually *ssp. tomentella*. ⚜ Dry grassy and stony places. May–June.　**538**

P. venulosa is similar to *P. nicaeensis*, but differs in having its blue petals longer than the sepals, which are white. Flower spikes with few flowers. ⚜ Rocky and stony places. S. Greece and the islands. May–July.

ANACARDIACEAE – Cashew Family

Trees or shrubs with resinous or acrid milky juice and resinous bark. Leaves simple or compound; flowers small, in clusters. Fruit usually fleshy. *This mainly tropical family includes cashew nuts, hog plums, mangoes, and lacquer trees.*
RHUS. Shrubs or small trees with pinnate leaves; flowers bisexual.
COTINUS. Leaves simple, toothed; flowers bisexual, style at side of fruit.
PISTACIA. Leaves pinnate of 3–25 leaflets; flowers unisexual; petals absent; style on summit of fruit.

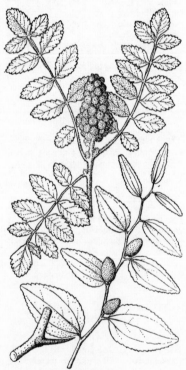

RHUS. *R. coriaria.* SUMACH. A softly hairy almost evergreen shrub of 1–3 m. The thick velvety leaves are divided into 7–15 oval leaflets. Flowers small and whitish in long, erect, compact spikes. Fruit hairy and purple-brown. ⚜ Thickets in dry stony places. May–June.　**539**
Bark and leaves are prized for tanning fine grades of white leather as used for gloves and fancy shoes, and also produce a yellow dye. The sap is poisonous, but the fruits are sometimes eaten like capers, both as a spice and a tonic. Dioscorides describes a number of varied medicinal uses.

COTINUS. *C. coggygria (Rhus cotinus).* SMOKE BUSH, WIG TREE, VENETIAN SUMACH. A dense shrub up to 3 m., with smooth long-stalked simple leaves, rounded or egg-shaped, turning brilliant red in autumn. The small yellowish flowers are carried in loose pyramidal clusters, and the large fruiting clusters have a yellowish or reddish colour given by the long hairs on the stalks. ⚜ Dry stony and rocky places, and open woodland on limestone. May–July.　**141**
Another plant whose leaves are used in tanning, while an extract of the wood produces 'young fustic', a yellow-orange dye used on leather and also for yarn.

PISTACIA. *P. lentiscus.* MASTIC TREE, LENTISC. A dense aromatic shrub of 1–3 m., with dark green leaves of 2–6

Left: 539 Rhus coriaria
Right: 540 Zizyphus jujuba.
Both × ½

100

pairs of elliptic leaflets without a terminal one. The small tightly clustered, dull red flowers, are in the axils of the leaves. Fruit red, finally black, pea-sized. ⚘ Bushy and rocky places. March–May. **142**

Mastic, a gummy resin obtained from the punctured stems, has been valued since classical times as a kind of chewing gum which also preserves the gums and sweetens the breath. It is also used to make a sweetmeat called masticha, *a liqueur,* mastiche, *and for incense tablets. The resin is further used for varnish-making and as a cure for toothache, rheumatism, and gout. Dioscorides also mentions the removal of spots, healing of broken bones, and the use of the twigs to clean teeth. The hard, beautifully veined wood is used in cabinet-making and joinery; it burns especially well and makes excellent charcoal.*

P. terebinthus. TEREBINTH, TURPENTINE TREE. A deciduous shrub of 2–5 m., with resinous-scented compound leaves of 2–5 pairs of leaflets with a terminal one, resembling those of ash, and branched clusters of reddish flowers followed by red and finally brown pea-sized fruit. ⚘ Stony hillsides. April–July. **143**

A tree of great importance since classical times, notably for its resin, which Theophrastus regarded as the best, fragrant and setting firm. The wood is hard and polishes well, and is valued in cabinet making and marquetry. Theophrastus says it was used for dagger-handles in Syria, 'and by means of the lathe-chisel they also make of it "Theriklean" cups, so that no one could distinguish these from cups made of pottery'. Oil is extracted from the seeds which are edible, like the true Pistachio. The plant often bears large irregular horn-shaped galls, which are used in tanning, and medicinally as an astringent and against asthma. Of the galls Theophrastus observed 'it bears also some hollow bag-like growths, in which are found little creatures like gnats; and resinous sticky matter is found also in the bags'.

The PISTACHIO, ***P. vera*** from Asia, is sometimes cultivated in Greece; it is similar to its wild relations, on which it is often grafted, but there are only 1–5 large leaflets. Its large nuts are eaten fresh and prized in confectionery and pastry-making.

ACERACEAE – Maple Family

Usually deciduous trees or shrubs with lobed or pinnate leaves. Small greenish-yellow flowers in clusters; sepals and petals 4 or 5. Fruit winged.

ACER. *A. monspessulanum.* MONTPELLIER MAPLE. A shrub or small tree to 6 m., with grey fissured bark, and long-stalked 3-lobed leaves, leathery and shining green above and blue-grey below. Flowers small and yellowish-green in erect clusters. ⚘ Open woods and rocky places, usually on limestone. April–May. **541**

Theophrastus notes that the wood is used for making beds and yokes for oxen.

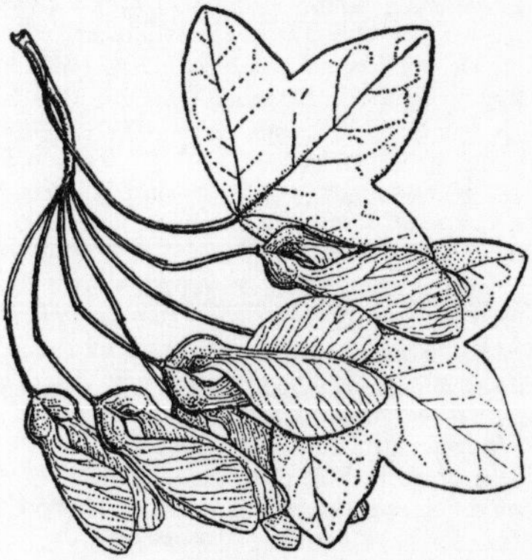

541 Acer monspessulanum (fruit) $\times \frac{1}{2}$

BUXACEAE – Box Family

Evergreen trees or shrubs with simple leaves and small 1-sexed clustered flowers.

BUXUS. *B. sempervirens.* BOX. An evergreen shrub or small tree, 2–5 m. high, with shiny and leathery dark green elliptic leaves, and axillary clus-

ters of small whitish-green stalkless flowers, each cluster containing both male and female flowers. ⁕ Dry hillsides, mainly on lime-free soils, up to 1,500 m. altitude. March–April.
A tree of 'cold, rough places', producing a close, heavy wood used like ebony.

Theophrastus notes it is 'used for some purposes; however that which grows on Mount Olympus is useless, because only short pieces can be obtained and the wood is full of knots'. Virgil describes its uses as a frame for ivory, for spinning tops and musical pipes.

RHAMNACEAE – Buckthorn Family

Shrubs or small trees, often spiny, with simple leaves and small greenish flowers in axillary clusters. Sepals and petals 5. Fruit: a berry or capsule.
PALIURUS. Fruit dry, surrounded by broad flattened disc; stipules spiny.
ZIZYPHUS. Fruit fleshy containing 2–3 nuts; stipules spiny; leaves 3-nerved from base.
RHAMNUS. Stipules not spiny but branches may end in spine; fruit fleshy with 2–3 nuts; leaves pinnately veined.

PALIURUS. *P. spina-christi.* CHRIST'S THORN. A straggling and very spiny shrub, up to 2 m., the flexible zig-zag branches carry short-stemmed oval leaves, in the axils of which are the small yellow flower clusters which are followed by disc-shaped fruits. ⁕ Makes thickets on dry stony ground. June–Sept. **144, 145**
It seems quite possible that Christ's Crown of Thorns was made from this very spiny, pliant shrub, which also grows in Palestine. According to Dioscorides 'it is said that the branches, being layd in gates or windowes, doe drive away the enchantments of witches . . . and against devils and their assalts'. He describes its value against erysipelas and herpes; in recent times it was used as a remedy for diarrhoea, and its seeds for lung ailments. Columella recommends it, not surprisingly, as a good hedge plant.

ZIZYPHUS. *Z. jujuba.* COMMON JUJUBE. A spiny shrub up to 8 m. high, with zig-zag green branches, oval, shining finely toothed leaves, and axillary clusters of small yellowish flowers followed by oval purplish fruits. ⁕ An Asiatic native, but cultivated for the edible fruits and sometimes naturalised in Greece and Crete. April–May.
540, p. 100

RHAMNUS. *R. alaternus.* An ever-green shrub 2–5 m. high, with variable but usually oval, leathery leaves, sometimes toothed at the margins. Branched clusters of small yellowish flowers, in which petals are absent, are carried in leaf axils, and are followed by globular fruit, red turning to black. ⁕ Thickets on stony and rocky hillsides. March–April. **159**
The rank-smelling wood 'is the easiest for turning, and its whiteness is like that of the holly' (Theophrastus); although elsewhere he says it 'is only useful for feeding sheep; for it is always leafy'. The fine-grained wood is still used in cabinet making and marquetry; the leaves were used to relieve angina and the berries as a mild purgative.

VITACEAE – Vine Family

Climbing plants, with leaves simple, palmate, or pinnate. Clusters of small greenish flowers arising at the leaf nodes. Branched tendrils arise opposite the leaves. Sepals and petals 4–5. Fruit a berry.

VITIS. *V. vinifera ssp. sylvestris.* COMMON VINE. A woody climbing plant, the wild form of the cultivated vine (*ssp. vinifera*) with the same deeply lobed alternate leaves, branched tendrils, and clusters of small greenish flowers. Male and female plants are differentiated by slightly different depth of the leaf lobation. The fruit is small and bluish-black. ⚘ Damp woods, stream-sides, climbing up trees and bushes. May–June.

The vine has been cultivated since ancient times; it was grown by the ancient Egyptians, and is the first cultivated plant recorded in the Bible. It was extensively grown in Palestine and further east, and probably arose, as a mutation from the wild species, in ancient Armenia. Noah is credited in the Bible as the first wine-maker – and drunkard. Its products – wine, grapes, currants, raisins, and sultanas – are all of antique origin. Currants – small seedless grapes which are dried – derive their name from Corinth, the Greek city from which they were first imported into Europe. The Romans introduced the grape into S.E. Europe.

MALVACEAE – Mallow Family

Shrubs or herbaceous plants with alternate leaves, simple or lobed, and with star-shaped hairs. Flowers large, solitary or clustered. Sepals and petals usually 5; flowers often with an 'epicalyx' of 3 or more sepal-like bracts below. Fruit a capsule.

MALOPE. Differs from other genera in its strawberry-like fruit of many carpels around a central axis; epicalyx of 3 heart-shaped lobed.

MALVA. Epicalyx of 3 separate segments.

LAVATERA. Epicalyx of 3 lobes fused at base to form a cup.

ALTHAEA. Epicalyx of 6–9 lobes fused at base to form a cup.

ALCEA. Flowers large in long spikes; epicalyx usually 6-lobed.

ABUTILON. Epicalyx absent.

HIBISCUS. Epicalyx of 6–13 narrow segments, not fused; fruit oval.

MALOPE. *M. malacoides.* A hairy perennial up to 40 cm. high, with oval leaves, sometimes lobed or toothed, and with large long-stalked rose-coloured flowers in the upper axils of the leaves. ⚘ Fields and waste places. June–July.   **148**

MALVA. *M. cretica.* A hairy annual to 40 cm. with rounded lower leaves and upper leaves deeply divided into 3–5 narrow toothed lobes. The small pink flowers are carried on long stalks in the leaf axils. ⚘ Cultivated and stony ground. April–June.

M. sylvestris. COMMON MALLOW. Biennial or perennial, reaching 50–120 cm. The leaves are broad and deeply lobed, and the flowers, carried in clusters in the upper leaf axils, are large and of a rose colour, striped with purple. ⚘ Stony and waste places. March–May.   **146**

Dioscorides recommends Mallow, and likewise Hollyhock, for various disorders. Not only did they relieve bee and wasp stings but, 'if a man beforehand be anointed therewith . . . he remains unstrikable'. Further, 'being applied with urine, it cures the running sores of the head', while, with seeds of 'wild Lote' in wine, it 'doth assuage the griefs about ye bladder'.

LAVATERA. *L. arborea.* TREE MALLOW. A tall-growing thick-stemmed branched biennial or perennial, growing to 3 m. Leaves large, rounded and shallowly lobed, softly downy. The large rose-purple flowers are carried in simple or branched clusters. ⚘ Rocky and sandy places on the coast. April–Sept.   **149**

L. cretica. An annual or biennial up to 1½ m., with rounded or heart-shaped lower leaves, shallowly 5–7-lobed; and deeply 5-lobed and toothed upper leaves densely hairy on the lower surface. Clusters of 2–8 lilac-coloured flowers carried in leaf axils. ⚘ Waste places and roadsides. April–June.

ALTHAEA. *A. cannabina.* HEMP-LEAVED MALLOW. A perennial with 5-lobed green, hairy leaves, and tall flowering stems which are often

branched and reach up to 2 m.; the large flowers are rosy-purple, the petals being very deeply notched. ✲ Dry open places, in waste or cultivated ground. May–July.　**150**
A. hirsuta. HAIRY MALLOW. A branched and stiffly hairy annual or biennial up to 60 cm., with large solitary long-stalked pink flowers, becoming bluish. Lower leaves rounded and shallowly lobed, upper leaves deeply 5-lobed. ✲ Fields and grassy places. May–July.　**147**

ALCEA. A. pallida (Althaea pallida). Perennial with 2 m. spikes carrying rounded leaves, with shallow lobes, and large stalkless flowers up to 9 cm. across, varying from a very pale to a quite dark pink. The plant usually seen in Greece and Crete is *ssp. cretica*, which is grey-woolly with bright pink to purple flowers; *ssp. pallida* is less woolly and the flowers are pale pink with yellow centres. ✲ Steep hillsides; often at the edges of terraced olive groves. May–July.　**151**

Alcea (Althaea) rosea is the cultivated HOLLYHOCK, grown widely and often locally naturalised. It resembles *A. pallida ssp. cretica*, but is distinguished by the fewer petals, which touch each other. Its origins are obscure. ✲ Waste places. May–July.　**152**

ABUTILON. A. theophrasti. A tall softly hairy annual to 2 m. Leaves long-stalked, heart-shaped, and pointed. Rather small solitary yellow flowers in the leaf axils. ✲ Cultivated ground and waste places. July–Oct.　**542**

HIBISCUS. H. trionum. BLADDER KETMIA. A branched annual to 60 cm. The hairless leaves are usually deeply divided into 3–5 lobes which themselves are further subdivided. The large solitary flowers are yellow with dark purple centres. The fruit is enclosed by the calyx which becomes inflated and bladder-like. ✲ Cultivated ground and waste places. June–Sept.　**543**

Left:　542 Abutilon theophrasti.　Right:　543 Hibiscus trionum (fruit enlarged). Both × ½.

THYMELAEACEAE – Daphne Family

Shrubs with simple stalkless leaves without stipules. Calyx tubular with 4–5 spreading petal-like lobes. True petals absent or scale-like.
DAPHNE. Calyx tube cylindrical, often swollen at base, with 4 spreading petal-like lobes; flowers sweet scented; fruit fleshy.
THYMELAEA. Evergreen. Flowers small, greenish or yellow; fruit dry.

DAPHNE. *D. gnidium.* A much-branched evergreen shrub, up to 1½ m. The small white fragrant flowers are borne in terminal clusters. The red fruits often start ripening with flowers still present. ❧ Rocky or stony places, woods, often on hillsides. June–Oct.

157

Theophrastus comments that the tough root 'is used for binding and to put round things, like the withy'. Virgil commends the plant to bee-keepers. The entire plant is poisonous, containing a bitter alkaloid. Despite this it was used medicinally, sometimes as a purge, though in recent times only externally for skin ailments.

D. jasminea. A small evergreen shrub up to 30 cm. high, with much branched semi-prostrate branches, small oblong pointed leaves, and terminal clusters of small pinkish-purple flowers. ❧ Rocky places and cliffs in the mountains. April–May.

158

D. laureola. SPURGE LAUREL. An evergreen shrub to 1 m. high, with thick glossy-green oblong leaves. The small, greenish-yellow, fragrant flowers are carried in drooping clusters, and are followed by black fruit. ❧ Open woods on mountain slopes in the North. Feb.–April.

D. mezereum. MEZEREON. A deciduous shrub to 1 m. high carrying bright green lance-shaped leaves in clusters at the ends of the branches. The small, very sweet-scented pink to purple flowers are carried in dense clusters on the bare stems before the leaves appear, and are followed by scarlet fruit. ❧ Open woodland on mountain slopes in the North. Feb.–May.

D. oleoides. A low-growing evergreen shrub to 50 cm., with oval leathery leaves and clusters of 5–10 mm. white or creamy (rarely purplish) flowers. ❧ Scrub and open rocky slopes in the mountains, most commonly in the North. April–May.

154

D. sericea (D. collina). A dense evergreen shrub to 70 cm., with oval-lanceolate leaves, smooth above and more or less hairy beneath. The very fragrant buff to pink flowers are carried in terminal clusters. A rather variable plant of which two or three forms have been described. ❧ Rocky places

in the hills and mountains. Crete. May–June.

155

THYMELAEA. *T. hirsuta.* A small much-branched shrub up to 1 m., with white-woolly branches and small thick overlapping leaves pressed closely to the stems. Very small yellowish flowers are borne in clusters. ❧ Stony hillsides. Oct.–May.

158

The very strong stem fibres were once used for making ropes.

T. tartonraira. More resembling a Daphne than *T. hirsuta:* a 60 cm. shrub with flat, spreading oval leaves, densely silky and of a leathery texture. The small yellowish flowers are carried in clusters in the upper leaf axils. ❧ Stony and sandy places. March–May.

156

GUTTIFERAE (HYPERICACEAE) – St John's Wort Family

Shrubs or herbaceous plants, with simple opposite or whorled leaves, often glandular. Yellow flowers, solitary or in clusters. Sepals and petals 5; stamens numerous. Fruit a capsule.

HYPERICUM. *H. apollinis.* With creeping woody much-branched 5–40 cm. stems, small narrow leaves, and flowers of a deep coppery-gold. (Possibly only a form of *H. rumeliacum.*) ❧ Rock crevices in full sun. April–June.

160

H. empetrifolium. A shrub with erect stems to 50 cm. The narrow heath-like leaves, with recurved margins, grow in groups of 3, and the many smallish yellow flowers are carried in branched heads. ❧ Dry rocky places. May–June.

161

H. kelleri. A small perennial with prostrate slender stems of 5–25 cm., small narrowly ovate leaves, and yellow, black-dotted petals. ❧ At high altitudes in the Cretan mountains. May–July.

544

H. olympicum. From a woody base spring wiry stems up to 20 cm. high carrying blue-grey narrow-oblong leaves, and terminal clusters of 4–5

544 Hypericum kelleri × 1

large golden flowers. ❀ Rocky and stony places in the mountains. June–Aug. **162**

VIOLACEAE – Violet Family

Herbaceous plants or rarely small shrubs. Flowers solitary, spurred, symmetrical in one plane only. Sepals and petals 5.

VIOLA. *V. delphinantha*. A dwarf shrubby violet with twiggy shoots carrying very narrow leaves. Flowers reddish-lilac, long-stalked, with long slender and curved spur. ❀ Rock crevices in the high mountains of the North. June–July. **163**

V. gracilis. Makes leafy tufts up to 15 cm. or more, the leaves being bluntly elliptic and the flowers large, blue, violet, or yellow, varying somewhat in shape. ❀ Rocky places in the C. and N. mountains. April–June. **164**

V. hymettia. Tufted, very dwarf, with variable but often oval and slightly lobed leaves, and short-stemmed flowers of a bright yellow and white. ❀ Stony ground, pastures, often at the edges of woods and in light shade, in the mountains. March–May. **165**

V. magellensis (*V. albanica*). A tufted plant up to 10 cm. high, with rounded leaves and flowers of violet, pink, or reddish-violet. ❀ Mountain pastures and screes on limestone. N. Greece. May–June.

V. poetica. A small tufted violet, with small fleshy rounded leaves and stems up to 10 cm. carrying 1–4 flowers of violet or blue. ❀ Rock crevices in the high mountains. S.C. Greece. May–June.

V. fragrans is a similar plant, but more or less hairy, with pale violet or yellow flowers. ❀ Mountain rocks. Greece, Crete. May–June.

V. scorpiuroides. A woody-based plant with erect 10–20 cm. stems carrying grey-green ovate leaves and small yellow flowers marked with brown blotches. ❀ Scrambles among small shrubs. Crete and S. Aegean. Feb.–March.

CISTACEAE – Rockrose Family

Herbs or shrubs with simple, usually opposite leaves. Flowers solitary or in loose clusters, the 5 petals falling during the day of opening. Fruit a capsule.

CISTUS. Shrubs with large flowers, white, pink, or purple; fruit on erect stalks, splitting by 5–10 valves.

TUBERARIA. Like *Helianthemum*; yellow-flowered, style very short.

HELIANTHEMUM. Herbs or dwarf shrubs with yellow, white, or rarely pink flowers; style elongated.

FUMANA. Like *Helianthemum*, yellow-flowered; leaves very narrow; a ring of sterile stamens outside the inner fertile stamens.

CISTUS. *C. incanus* (*C. villosus*) (including *C. creticus*). A much branched shrub, up to 1 m. high, with oval wavy leaves, hairy on both surfaces. The 4–6 cm. pink flowers are borne in loose clusters of 1–6. The Greek and Aegean plant is *ssp. creticus* (*C. creticus*). ⚘ Stony bushy places. March–June. **169**

From this cistus especially is obtained the gum ladanum, still occasionally used in medicinal plasters and in perfumery. An old Greek name for the plant is ladanes. *The gum exudes from the plant, and was collected by pulling a kind of leather-thonged flail through the plants in the hottest part of the day. Also, as Herodotus and Dioscorides recorded, it sticks to the beards and legs of goats feeding among the bushes, and was collected from these by the shepherds. An aromatic 'tea' is made from the leaves.*

C. monspeliensis. A very sticky and aromatic cistus reaching 1½ m., with narrow rolled dark green leaves. The 2–3 cm. white flowers are carried in heads of 2–10. ⚘ Garigue and other dry areas. March–May. **170**

C. parviflorus. Similar to *C. incanus ssp. creticus*, but with smaller 3-nerved leaves and 2–3 cm. pink flowers, 1–6 together. ⚘ Macchie. March–May. **171**

C. salvifolius. A spreading or even procumbent shrub to 1 m. high, with soft oval leaves, wrinkled green above and whitish below. The 3–5 cm. white, golden centred flowers are usually carried singly or up to 4 together. ⚘ Open stony hillsides. March–May. **172**

A decoction of the flowers was used against dysentery in ancient Greece, and is still so used in Morocco.

TUBERARIA. ***T. guttata.*** ANNUAL ROCKROSE. A slender-stemmed hairy annual growing to 25 cm. from a basal rosette; leaves narrow. The small yellow flowers, carried in loose heads, carry maroon spots at the base of each petal. ⚘ Sandy, bushy places. March–May. **166**

HELIANTHEMUM. ***H. oelandicum*** (including ***H. alpestre***). A shrublet with branches to 20 cm. long, varying from sprawling to compact, with more or less elliptical, slightly downy leaves, and bright yellow 1–2 cm. flowers in clusters of 2–10. ⚘ Stony places in the mountains. June–July. **167**

H. salicifolium. SUN ROSE. A branched annual up to 30 cm. high, with small oblong or lance-shaped grey-green hairy leaves, and terminal clusters of yellow flowers. ⚘ Dry sandy places. March–June.

FUMANA. ***F. procumbens.*** A spreading wiry-stemmed shrub up to 20 cm., hairy and sticky, with alternate narrow leaves. The usually solitary flowers on short stalks arise in leaf axils, and are yellow, spotted with darker yellow at base. ⚘ Stony and sandy places. May–June. **168**

F. thymifolia. A miniature shrub reaching up to 25 cm. The wiry stems carry numerous small and very narrow leaves, inrolled at the edges, and the yellow flowers are carried in terminal clusters. ⚘ Dry stony places in full sun. March–June. **545**

545 Fumana thymifolia ×⅔ (calyx enlarged)

TAMARICACEAE – Tamarisk Family

Small trees or shrubs with slender branches and little scale-like or needle-like leaves. Flowers small, in dense elongated clusters. Sepals and petals 4–5. Seeds with long silky hairs.

TAMARIX. ***T. tetrandra.*** TAMARISK. A shrub or small tree up to 5 m. high with slender, very dark branches, the twigs clothed in overlapping scale-like pointed leaves. The small flowers, usually rose-pink, are carried in cylindrical spikes on the previous year's shoots. Sepals entire. ⚘ Coastal sands and marshes. Usually spring-flowering.

T. parviflora is similar but with smaller flowers of a pale pink in slender spikes. Sepals toothed. Leaves hard-pointed. ⚘ Usually spring-flowering. **173**

T. smyrnensis has reddish-brown bark. ⚘ Coastal marshes. Spring-flowering.

T. hampeana is another similar species, but with smooth reddish-brown bark and pinkish-white flowers in racemes which often form loose sprays. ⚘ Coastal sands, marshes. Usually spring-flowering.

T. dalmatica forms a small tree with smooth blackish bark and white flowers, usually 4 petalled. ⚘ Coastal marshes and river banks. Usually spring-flowering.

A decoction of tamarisk leaves is recommended by Dioscorides to 'meet ye spleen' and for 'such as breed lice, and nitts'. He also says that 'there be somme that make cups of ye stock of it . . . for such as are troubled with ye spleen'.

CUCURBITACEAE – Cucumber Family

Herbaceous plants, usually climbing or scrambling, often with tendrils. Leaves lobed. Flowers 1-sexed with 5 sepals and petals. Fruit fleshy and swollen.

ECBALLIUM. *E. elaterium.* SQUIRTING CUCUMBER. A hairy, non-climbing plant, with sprawling stems up to 60 cm., and large thick triangular leaves, grey on the under-surface, and small yellow flowers in the axils of the leaves. The fruit, shaped like miniature hairy cucumbers, when ripe discharge their seeds with violence from the basal end. ⚘ Waste ground, rubbish heaps, and stony places, usually by the sea. March–August. **174**

A poisonous plant; the juice with which the seeds is ejected is acrid. An ancient medicine, the root was used, according to Theophrastus, for 'white leprosy' and

mange in sheep, and the juice from the fruit to make a drug called 'the driver' – 'the older it is, the better it is . . . also of all drugs . . . it effects a thorough purge upwards'. Dioscorides goes into great detail as to the making of this drug, which he calls elaterium. The root has also been used for treating rheumatism, shingles, dropsy, and paralysis.

CACTACEAE – Cactus Family

Spiny succulent plants, with leaves replaced by scales or spines. Stems often flattened and jointed. Large flowers, solitary or clustered, sepals and petals fused to form a basal cup or tube. Fruit dry or fleshy.

OPUNTIA. *O. ficus-indica.* PRICKLY PEAR. A much branched spiny cactus, reaching 3–4 m., and composed of many fleshy compressed joints, rounded or oval in outline. The yellow stalkless flowers are carried at the margins of the upper joints, and succeeded by pulpy fruit, purplish-red or yellow. ⚘ Much used for boundary hedges and widely naturalised in rocky places. April–July.

175, 176

Apparently introduced from the New World by Christopher Columbus, this plant is to be seen all round the Mediterranean. Since any part roots quickly, stem segments are commonly set around gardens and fields and soon form dense, impenetrable hedges not even eaten by goats. The fruits are edible and often sold in markets.

MYRTACEAE – Myrtle Family

Trees or shrubs, with opposite and entire evergreen leaves, glandular and aromatic. Flowers with 4–5 sepals and petals. Besides *Myrtus* the family includes the widely planted *Eucalyptus*.

MYRTUS. *M. communis.* MYRTLE. A dense shrub up to 2½ m. high, with opposite oval leaves which are dark green, leathery, and shiny. The long-stalked flowers, white with prominent stamens, are carried singly in the leaf axils, and are very sweet-scented. The whole shrub is most aromatic. The flowers are followed by black berries. ❧ Thickets and woods. May–July. **177**

Myrtle was a classical symbol of love, peace, and honour: wreaths of it were worn by Greek magistrates, and victors in the Olympic Games. The bark, leaves, and flowers are all aromatic and from them is made an essential oil called Eau d'Anges, *used in perfumery. The berries are sometimes fermented into an alcoholic drink, or put into brandy. Remedies based on myrtle were recommended by Dioscorides for many ailments. The reddish-grey wood is hard and heavy with very fine grain, and is used for turnery and marquetry; it burns well and makes good charcoal.*

PUNICACEAE – Pomegranate Family

Typically spiny trees with narrow shining deciduous leaves, and large solitary flowers of 5–7 petals. Calyx bell-shaped. Fruit a large fleshy berry.

PUNICA. *P. granatum.* POMEGRANATE. A bush or low tree, much branched, with shiny lance-shaped leaves, and large scarlet flowers carried singly or in clusters of 2 or 3. The flowers are followed by the familiar large pomegranate fruits. ❧ Much cultivated, and naturalised in rocky places, hedges, and thickets, usually near habitations. May–July. **178**

A fruit esteemed since earliest times, and a symbol of fertility; reputed to be the fruit given to Aphrodite by Paris. It occurs often as a decoration in Eastern art, and is frequently mentioned in the Bible, while Theophrastus refers to it extensively, especially with regard to its cultivation. Breaking a pomegranate on the threshold is an ancient Greek New Year custom. In some localities, e.g. Arachova, a stone and a pomegranate

are left outside on New Year's Eve, and the person who draws water in the morning throws them into the house, saying 'Strong as stone, full as pomegranates.' The pulp has been used for making cool drinks, sherbets, and syrups; Marret extols a dessert of the seeds in sweet red wine, although Dioscorides reminds us that the fruit is flatulent, 'wherfore unfitting for such as are aguish'. It is useful, too, a red dye used in tanning morocco leather being obtained from the rind of unripe fruits; another red dye is made from the flowers. Medicinally these materials are strongly astringent, and the bark of the root has been used effectively against tapeworms.

CORNACEAE – Dogwood Family

Trees or shrubs with simple leaves. Small flowers clustered in umbels. Sepals 4, petals 4 or absent. Fruit a berry.

CORNUS. *C. mas.* CORNELIAN CHERRY. A shrub or small tree up to 5 m. high with greyish trunk and branches, and long oval deciduous leaves. The small clusters of bright yellow flowers open early in the year before the leaves appear. Fruit scarlet. ❧ Open woodland, mountain thickets. March–April. **179, 180**

The fruit is edible, and was formerly esteemed in Europe and even England; it has also been used to flavour sherbets. Pliny remarks disparagingly that it was dried in the sun, like prunes. Medicinally it was recommended for bowel disorders and against cholera, while the flowers were used against diarrhoea. The tree provides a red dye used in Turkey for the fez.

In early Roman times the trunks of the tree were made into lance shafts, and Virgil uses the name cornus *to mean a lance at one point in the Aeneid. The trunk was too thin for many other uses, but its hardness made the wood valued for wedges and wheel-spokes.*

UMBELLIFERAE – Cow Parsley Family

Herbaceous plants with hollow stems and usually much-divided leaves. Flowers small and numerous, usually arranged in flat-topped umbels which are formed from numerous branches arising from the top of the main stem. The paired fruits separate when ripe into 2 one-seeded parts.

ERYNGIUM. Flowers in dense rounded heads surrounded by rigid spiny bracts; leaves thistle-like and spiny.

SMYRNIUM. Hairless yellowish-green plants; basal leaves thrice divided into broad rounded segments; umbels yellowish with few or no bracts.

CRITHMUM. Leaves compound and fleshy; umbels compound; fruit ovoid with prominent ribs.

FERULA. Tall-growing, with large leaves usually subdivided into very narrow segments; petals pointed and oval, not notched.

TORDYLIUM. White or pinkish flowered; outer petals of outer flowers larger than the others, with deeply divided lobes; fruits hairy or warty with thickened edges.

ORLAYA. Flowers white or pink with outer petals of outer flowers large and notched. Fruit oval and ribbed with spines along the rib lines.

ERYNGIUM. *E. amethystinum.* Perennial to 50 cm., with basal leaves deeply cut and spiny. Upper leaves lanceolate with a few teeth at base. Flower heads rounded, 1–2 cm. across, with amethyst-blue flowers. ❧ Dry places. June–Aug.

E. creticum. Usually perennial, to 1 m., much branched above, the whole being violet-blue. Basal leaves not divided. The amethyst-blue flowers are carried in ½–1 cm. rounded heads. ❧ Dry stony places. May–Aug. **181**
The roots were used against snake bite. When dry the flowering stems break off in the wind and are carried along as 'tumble-weeds', shedding seeds as they go.

E. maritimum. SEA HOLLY. A very bluish, branched, prickly plant, up to 80 cm., with bluish-white flowers in oval heads surrounded by wide bracts. ❧ Coastal sands. May–Aug.
The name Eryngium derives from the Greek eruggarein, to eructate, and this was a supposed remedy for flatulence. The root, 'eryngo', was at one time widely sold candied in Europe and was reputed to be an excellent aphrodisiac.

SMYRNIUM. *S. rotundifolium.* A striking biennial plant 50–150 cm. tall with rounded stalkless upper leaves, of a greenish-gold colour, clasping the stem. The golden-yellow flowers are arranged in tight compound umbels. ❧ Open places, olive groves, edges of cultivated ground. April–June.

S. perfoliatum resembles *S. rotundifolium*, but differs in the leaves which are bright green and often toothed at the margins, and the prominently winged stem. ❧ Open places, olive groves, edges of cultivated ground. April–June. **187**
Theophrastus called smyrniums 'horsecelery' which he says is 'serviceable in cases of strangury and for those suffering from stone, being administered in sweet white wine'.

CRITHMUM. *C. maritimum.* ROCK SAMPHIRE. A fleshy plant, 15–30 cm. tall, much branched, with narrow segmented leaves of bluish-green, and umbels of pale yellow flowers. The whole plant has a curious aromatic smell. ❧ Coastal rocks, cliffs, and sand dunes. July–Oct. **182**
The use of samphire as a pot-herb is ancient: Dioscorides says it is eaten 'either sod [boiled] or raw, and it is also preserved in brine'. At one time it was very extensively gathered for pickling in Britain, with the result that the samphire-gatherer's was, to quote Lear, a 'dreadful trade' as the only plants to survive were on cliffs. It was eaten both for its distinctive flavour and its good effect on the digestion. The English name

110

Samphire is derived from 'herbe de Saint Pierre' – it was the plant of St Peter, patron saint of fishermen.

FERULA. *F. communis.* GIANT FENNEL. A perennial 2 m. or more tall, with thick, branched, hollow stems, feathery bright-green leaves much divided into narrow green segments up to 1 mm. wide, mainly at the base, and yellow flowers in large umbels. ⚘ Waste ground, dry hills. March–June.   **183**
The dried pith was used as tinder, and because it smoulders very slowly within the stem it could be carried from one place to another. This explains why Prometheus, bringing to earth the fire stolen from heaven, did so 'in a ferula' (Hesiod). Bacchus, god of wine, recommended that his votaries should carry the light stems rather than wooden sticks, so that if they brawled under the influence they would not injure one another.
F. chiliantha (*F. communis ssp. glauca*). Very like *F. communis* but leaf segments more fleshy, green above and bluish below, to 3 mm. wide; the upper leaves forming large inflated stem-clasping sheaths. The flowers are orange and in rounded heads. ⚘ Rocky places, coastal limestone cliffs, especially in the Aegean. March–May.   **184**

TORDYLIUM. *T. apulum.* An annual of 20–50 cm. The leaves, softly hairy, are deeply divided into narrow segments, and the white flower heads are bordered by flowers with a single greatly enlarged and deeply lobed petal. The flat, rounded fruits with thickened edges are very characteristic. ⚘ Roadsides, field edges, and waste land. March–May.   **185, 186**

T. officinale is very similar to *T. apulum*, but the outer flowers of the umbel have 2 large petals divided into very unequal lobes.

ORLAYA. *O. grandiflora.* An annual, up to 50 cm. high, with deeply dissected smooth leaves and terminal umbels of white flowers, the outermost flowers having long and striking 2-lobed outer petals, and 5–8 bracts under the umbel. Fruit egg-shaped, long-hairy. ⚘ Fields and waste places. April–June.   **546**

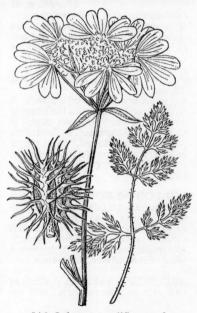

546 Orlaya grandiflora × ⅔
(fruit enlarged)

ERICACEAE – Heather Family

Usually shrubs, with simple evergreen leaves without stipules. Flowers solitary or in clusters, with 4–5 sepals and petals, the petals being usually fused in a bell-like tube. Fruit a capsule or a berry.
ERICA. Evergreen shrubs with small narrow leaves in whorls; flowers small; calyx 4–10-lobed, corolla usually bell or flask-shaped with 4 small lobes.
RHODODENDRON. Shrubs or trees, usually evergreen, though in our

111

species deciduous; large bell or funnel-shaped flowers in terminal clusters; corolla lobes 5.

ARBUTUS. Evergreen shrubs or small trees; flowers flask-shaped in terminal clusters; fruit a round berry.

ERICA. *E. arborea.* TREE HEATHER. An erect shrub up to 4 m. high, with dense woody branches carrying little narrow leaves in whorls, with large terminal pyramidal clusters of very small sweet-scented white or pinkish flowers. ⚘ Hillsides, streamsides, evergreen scrub, on siliceous soils. March–May.
499, p. 61

Like other heathers, an important source of nectar for honey bees. The dried branches are used as brooms, and also for screening against wind and sun. A species of silkworm was until recently grown on the plant. Briar pipes are made from the rootstock, mainly in North Africa.

E. verticillata (E. manipuliflora). A bushy shrub to 1 m., with the leaves in whorls of 3, and the flowers carried in tight terminal clusters. The flowers are pink and bell-shaped, with purple anthers slightly projecting. ⚘ Sandy, rocky places, evergreen scrub. Sept.–Dec.

RHODODENDRON. *R. luteum (Azalea pontica).* YELLOW AZALEA. A deciduous shrub up to 4 m. with lanceolate leaves and clusters of 10–12 soft yellow, sweetly scented flowers. ⚘ Streambeds. Lesbos. (Otherwise a plant of Asia Minor.) May–June.

ARBUTUS. *A. andrachne.* A shrub or tree with smooth red bark, oval un-toothed leathery grey-green leaves, and erect clusters of whitish flowers. Fruits yellow with rough surfaces. ⚘ Rocky hillsides, evergreen scrub. Feb.–April.
188

According to Theophrastus parts of looms were made from this wood.

A. unedo. STRAWBERRY TREE. A shrub or small tree, rough-barked, much branched, bearing leathery elliptic toothed leaves of a shining dark green above, paler below. The urn-shaped waxy white or pinkish flowers are carried in drooping clusters, and the globular rough-surfaced fruits, at first yellow, then rosy-red, are often carried simultaneously. ⚘ Evergreen scrub, rocky hillsides, edges of woods, usually on siliceous soil. Oct.–April.
189

The fruit looks attractive but is very uninteresting, full of seeds and almost tasteless; indeed the word 'unedo' means 'eat one', implying that that is enough. In some Mediterranean countries it is used to make a brandy-like liqueur, and also a conserve. The wood is good for turnery and also produces good charcoal. In Greece flutes are made of it.

A. × andrachnoides, a hybrid between these two species, is often to be found if both parents are present. It has the reddish bark of *A. andrachne* and a few hairs on the young growth.

This hybrid was recognised as such by Theophrastus, who states that it was used for stakes and for burning.

PRIMULACEAE – Primrose Family

Herbaceous plants with simple or broad leaves. Flowers solitary or in an umbel. Sepals and petals usually 5. Petals fused at the base to form a tube.

PRIMULA. Flowers in terminal clusters, or less commonly solitary; corolla tube long, often with spreading lobes; calyx tubular, 5-lobed.

SOLDANELLA. Flowers in terminal clusters, or solitary; bell or funnel-shaped with lobes deeply cut into fringe of narrow segments.

CYCLAMEN. Leaves triangular or kidney-shaped rising from large underground tubers. Flowers solitary, long-stalked, corolla lobes strongly reflexed.

LYSIMACHIA. Flowers yellow or purple, 5–7-lobed. Corolla bell-shaped with spreading lobes. Leaves usually opposite or whorled.
ANAGALLIS. Flowers red, pink, or blue, arising in axils of leaves; corolla tube short.

PRIMULA. *P. veris ssp. columnae.* A form of the widely distributed COWSLIP, distinguished by the leaves which are white-hairy beneath, and by the heads of rather large yellow flowers, with corolla up to 2 cm. across. ⚜ Mountain meadows in the North. April–May.
P. vulgaris. PRIMROSE. This well-known plant is found widely in Greece where the conditions favour it, and there are several colour and other variations.
Var. alba differs from the type in the leaves, which are less corrugated and of a lighter green, and in the flowers which are white with an orange centre. *The botanical status of this quite common white primrose is confused: it has been referred to as* P. komarovii, *but for our purposes it seems simpler to treat it, as did older botanists, as a variety of* P. vulgaris. **192**
Ssp. sibthorpii has red or purple flowers. ⚜ Rocky gullies, damp places, mainly in the mountains. March–April.

SOLDANELLA. *S. pindicola.* Forms clumps of rounded leathery dark green leaves scalloped at the edges, and with the under-surface a pale grey. On stems of up to 30 cm. are carried 2–6 funnel-shaped fringed flowers of a deep purple. ⚜ Damp meadows, stony places, in the mountains, N.W. Greece. Very local. May–July. **507, p. 63**

CYCLAMEN. *C. creticum.* Leaves variable, but often ivy-shaped, toothed, dark green. The small white, scented flowers have rather narrow upright petals. ⚜ Woods, damp rocks in shade. Crete. March–May. **193**
C. graecum. Tuber large and globe-shaped. Leaves large, very variable, often heart-shaped, velvety in texture, with a hard border, and beautifully marked with silver. Flowers varying from palest pink to deep carmine. ⚜ Stony ground, rocky hillsides, in full sun or partial shade. ⚜ Mainland, Crete, and Aegean. Sept.–Dec. **194**

C. hederifolium (*C. neapolitanum*). SOWBREAD. With flowers closely resembling those of its near relative *C. graecum*, and varying in colour from white to shades of pink. The leaves, which appear later than the flowers, are very variable, but often heart-shaped, shallowly lobed, and marked with silvery-grey in an infinite variety of patterns. The tuber is flattish with the roots springing from the upper surface. ⚜ Woods and thickets, often in partial shade, usually on limestone. Sept.–Nov. **195**
As its English name implies this was once used for feeding pigs, and its absence in parts of Provence, for instance, is due to wild boars. In ancient times cyclamens had many uses: according to Theophrastus 'the root is used for suppurating boils; also as a pessary for women and, mixed with honey, for dressing wounds; the juice for purgings of the head . . .; it also conduces to drunkenness, if one is given a draught of wine in which it has been steeped. They say also that the root is a good charm for inducing rapid delivery and as a love potion.' To these attributes Dioscorides adds plenty more, adding that 'if a woman great with childe doe goe over ye roote, she doth make abortion, and being tyed about her it doth haste the birth'. Further, 'it is dranck with wine against deadly poysons, and especially against the Sea-Hare'.
C. persicum. With heart-shaped leaves with a variety of lighter green markings and toothed edges. The large (25–45 mm.), usually perfumed flowers are carried on stems up to 15 cm. high and have long extremely reflexed twisted petals; the colour varies from pure white to a light pink and, less often, carmine. ⚜ Woodlands, rocky hillsides, sometimes in rock crevices. Rhodes, Crete, Karpathos, and a few places in the Peloponnese. March–May. **196**
Our cultivated winter-flowering cyclamens were derived from this species by selection. Recent breeding has returned

113

scent to some strains and produced very silvery or highly patterned leaves in others, while there is now a trend towards miniature varieties more like the elegant original.

C. repandum. The fragrant flowers are crimson, less often pink or white. Leaves variable, but often angular, bright green, shallowly lobed, and marked with silver. ✤ S. Greece. Scrub, shady and rocky places. March–May. **197**

Var. rhodense has very large leaves; flowers almost always white or pink-flushed, with a carmine ring at the base. ✤ Woods, rocky places. Rhodes. March–May. **198**

LYSIMACHIA. L. atropurpurea. With stems up to 65 cm., sparingly branched, arising from rhizomes. The alternate leaves vary from narrow to spoon-shaped, and are wavy-edged. The small dark purple flowers are carried in spikes, typically leaning sideways at the top. ✤ Sandy, damp places in the North. June–August. **190**

L. serpyllifolia. A woody-based creeping shrub, with spreading stems carrying small opposite egg-shaped leaves and axillary yellow flowers on rather long stalks. ✤ Boulders and rocks; mountains of C. and S. Greece and Crete. May–June.

ANAGALLIS. A. arvensis. PIMPERNEL. A low-growing spreading annual, with small oval leaves and stalked flowers arising from leaf axils. Flowers red, pink, or blue (the latter form has been called *A. foemina*). ✤ Dry soil, cultivated ground. March–Sept. **191**

Useful, according to Dioscorides, for relieving inflammations and toothache and extracting splinters or thorns. He considered the red forms to be male and the blue female. The herbalist Gerard records the uses of these: "Pimpernell with the blew flower helpeth up the fundament that is fallen downe; . . . red Pimpernel applied, contrariwise bringeth it down."

PLUMBAGINACEAE –
Sea Lavender Family

Herbs or shrubs with simple, usually spirally arranged leaves, often in a basal rosette. Sepals and petals 5. Calyx tubular, often coloured, and 'everlasting'.

LIMONIUM. L. sinuatum (Statice sinuata). WINGED SEA LAVENDER. From rosettes of lobed, wavy-margined leaves rise three-winged stems which carry flat-topped sprays of flowers in which the blue papery calyces form the prominent feature, while the central corolla is very small, pale yellow, or white. ✤ Coasts, on sand and shingle. April–Sept. **199**

A popular 'everlasting' which keeps its colour for well over a year if dried.

STYRACACEAE –
Storax Family

Trees or shrubs with alternate leaves, entire or toothed, without stipules. Flowers in axillary or terminal clusters. Sepals and petals 4–5.

STYRAX. S. officinalis. STORAX. A shrub or small tree up to 7 m. in height, with alternate, egg-shaped, deciduous leaves, bright green above and grey-woolly beneath. Clusters of 2–4 cm. white, pendant flowers are followed by the cherry-sized fruit which is ovoid and white-felted. ✤ Woods and thickets, often by streams. April–May. **200**

The gum storax has been used since ancient times, and is today in the Roman Catholic Church, for incense; also in perfumery. It is obtained by making cuts in the branches, resulting in what Dioscorides calls 'lachrymae' or drops of gum. Medicinally he explains 'it hath a warming, mollifying and concocting facultie'.

OLEACEAE – Olive Family

Trees or shrubs with entire or pinnate leaves without stipules. Flowers in axillary or terminal clusters. Calyx 4-lobed. Calyx and corolla bell-shaped or tubular. Fruit dry or fleshy.

JASMINUM. Shrubs or climbers with compound leaves; flowers yellow or white; corolla funnel-shaped; fruit a berry.

FRAXINUS. Trees with compound leaves; petals 4 or absent; fruit 1-seeded, with a long 'wing'.

SYRINGA. Shrubs or small trees with simple leaves; flowers lilac; calyx bell-shaped with 4–9 lobes; corolla funnel-shaped with 4–5 spreading lobes. Fruit a dry capsule.

OLEA. Evergreen trees with simple leaves, silvery beneath; corolla tube short with stamens projecting; fruit fleshy with hard stone.

PHILLYREA. Evergreen shrubs or small trees with simple leaves, not silvery beneath; corolla tube short with stamens projecting; fruit fleshy without a hard stone.

JASMINUM. *J. fruticans.* SHRUBBY JASMINE. A shrub reaching 1 m. The much branched angular stems carry shining dark green leaves of 3 leaflets, and terminal clusters of tubular golden-yellow flowers. ❊ Stony hills, on limestone. April–June. **201**

FRAXINUS. *F. ornus.* MANNA ASH. A tree to 10 m., with smooth grey bark, large compound leaves of 5–9 oval-toothed leaflets, and dense clusters of white flowers appearing with the leaves, followed by winged seeds. ❊ Thickets, woods, on limestone. April–May. **202**
The name Manna Ash refers to a sweetish exudation for which the tree is actually cultivated in Sicily and Italy. The moist wood, according to Theophrastus, was valuable for making 'elastic bedsteads'. Dioscorides considered it efficacious for skin infections and against snake bite.

SYRINGA. *S. vulgaris.* LILAC. A deciduous shrub up to 6 m. high with heart-shaped leaves and pyramidal clusters of sweet-scented lilac flowers. ❊ Mountain thickets. N. Greece. May–July.

OLEA. *O. europaea.* OLIVE. This, the most typical tree of the Mediterranean, reaches up to 10 m. with grey bark; old trees may have very thick, sometimes perforated trunks. The leaves are dark grey-green above, whitish underneath, narrow-oblong, 2–8 cm. long. The whitish flowers are carried in small upright clusters, to be followed by green oval fruit ripening to black. ❊ Grown on a variety of soils from sea level to the lower slopes of the mountains. Sometimes naturalised. May–June.
503, p. 62
Olea europaea ssp. sylvestris. WILD OLIVE. The wild form of the Olive, from which the cultivated tree was derived in antiquity, is usually seen as a branched and somewhat spiny shrub, with smaller shorter leaves and smaller, harder fruit than the cultivated plant. ❊ Rocky hillsides, stony hillsides, maquis, garigue. May–June. **504, p. 62**
The oil pressed from olive fruits has been used since the dawn of civilisation for cooking, lighting, and anointing the body. All Mediterranean peoples since the Minoans have cultivated olives and based their economy on them at least in part. Olives are habitually preserved and still form a vital part of the diet of Mediterranean peasants. The oil is still used for cooking, making soap, and treating wool, although cheaper vegetable oils are ousting it from its pre-eminence.

Olives are frequently referred to in the Bible and an olive branch is, of course, the symbol of peace. The oily wood is strongly patterned and widely used for making bowls, beads, and souvenirs. Theophrastus remarks on its capacity to produce shoots long after being cut. He also states that hammers and gimlets were made of wild olive. Of the latter Dioscorides considered the leaves to be valuable for many purposes, notably treating boils and ulcers.

The olive branch is an age-old symbol of peace, and equally the envoy's white flag, as mentioned several times in the Aeneid. When Athene and Poseidon were disputing over the possession of Athens, Poseidon made a salt water spring gush from the rock of the Acropolis. Athene, however, caused the olive tree to appear, and the other gods considered this the more valuable gift. Thus Athens received its name, Athene became its particular goddess, and the olive tree – a twig of which is portrayed on early Attic coins – became her tree. Indeed Virgil refers to Athene as oleae inventrix. Olive was used for victors' crowns at the Olympic Games, and was as important as the bay laurel in this respect.

PHILLYREA. *P. latifolia.* A grey-stemmed evergreen shrub growing to a height of up to 4 m., with paired stalked oval toothed leaves, indented at the apex, of leathery texture, 6–30 mm. broad. The axillary clusters of small sweet-scented yellowish flowers are followed by globular, fleshy, pea-sized, bluish-black fruit. ❀ Dry thickets, hillsides, rocky places, mainly on limestone. April–May.   **502,** p. 62

Very similar are *P. media*, with 8–20 mm. broad, finely-toothed, blunt-tipped leaves, and *P. angustifolia* (**501,** p. 62) with pointed leaves never more than 10

mm. broad. They grow in similar places.

The leaves, according to Dioscorides, were valued to treat mouth ulcers.

GENTIANACEAE – Gentian Family

Herbaceous plants with opposite and entire leaves. Calyx 4–5 lobed. Corolla tube with 4–5 lobes.

GENTIANA. *G. lutea.* GREAT YELLOW GENTIAN. A stout erect perennial up to 2 m. in height, with broadly oval strongly veined bluish leaves, and tall flowering stems carrying tight terminal and axillary clusters of starry yellow flowers. The Greek plant is *ssp. symphyandra.* ❀ Mountain meadows. June–Aug.

G. verna. SPRING GENTIAN. Two variants of this familiar alpine are found in Greece. Both have 'wings' on the calyx 2–4 mm. wide compared with the 1–2 mm. of the species.

Ssp. pontica. With broad, blunt rosette leaves, about twice as long as wide. ❀ Grassy places on limestone mountains. N.E. Greece and the Peloponnese. June–Aug.

Ssp. tergestina. KARST GENTIAN. Forming looser mats of rosettes, leaves pointed, 4 times longer than wide. ❀ Grassy places on limestone mountains. Mainly in N.W. Greece. June–Aug.

APOCYNACEAE – Periwinkle Family

Trees, shrubs, or herbs, with milky juice. Leaves entire, opposite or in whorls. Calyx and corolla 5-lobed; corolla tubular at base.
NERIUM. Bushes or small trees; flowers large in terminal clusters, pink or white; throat of corolla fringed with long petal-like projections.
VINCA. Trailing herbs; flowers usually blue, large and solitary.

NERIUM. *N. oleander.* OLEANDER. A large spreading shrub growing to 2–4 m., with lance-shaped leathery grey-green leaves, and terminal clusters of large scented flowers, usually rose pink but rarely white. ❀ Stream beds, stony water courses, where dense thickets may be formed. May–July.   **205**

The name *N. kotschyi* has been applied to a smaller-flowered, Cretan form of *N. oleander*, with narrower leaves.

Widely cultivated in various colour forms, sometimes double-flowered. A poisonous plant; as Dioscorides writes, having 'a power destructive of dogs and of asses and of mules and of most four-footed creatures'. Despite this Theophrastus describes the root as giving off a fragrance like wine when dried and, added to wine, making 'the temper gentler and more cheerful'.

VINCA. *V. major.* GREATER PERIWINKLE. Trailing, partly erect stems 30–50 cm. long carry paired evergreen egg-shaped leaves with hairy margins; the blue flowers are 4–5 cm. across. ✣ Woods, hedges, and shady streamsides. Corfu, Crete; rarely native elsewhere in Greece. March–June.

V. minor. LESSER PERIWINKLE. The trailing stems root at the nodes and carry hairless, elliptic, leathery, evergreen leaves; the solitary blue-violet flowers, 2½–3 cm. across, are borne on stalks longer than the leaves. ✣ Woods, hedges, and rocky places. Feb.–May.

V. herbacea is similar but the non-rooting stems die back in winter. The narrow leaves are hairy, with rough margins. ✣ Thickets, shady places. Feb.–April.   **203**

ASCLEPIADACEAE – Milkweed Family

Shrubby or herbaceous plants, often with milky juice. Flowers radially symmetrical, 5-parted. Stamens often fused into a ring round the stigma. Fruit a pod-like follicle containing white-tufted seeds.

CIONURA. *C. erecta* **(***Cynanchum erectum, Marsdenia erecta***).** Herbaceous, with sprawling stems to 1 m., often twining at the tips. Leaves heart-shaped, stalked, shiny. Flowers white, 1 cm. across, in rounded clusters. ✣ Rocky places, river sides, coastal sands. June–July.   **204**

RUBIACEAE – Madder Family

Herbaceous plants or small shrubs with whorled or opposite leaves, entire, and with stipules. Flowers small and clustered. Sepals 4–5. Corolla tubular and 4–5 lobed. Fruit a berry or capsule.
PUTORIA. Leaves opposite, stipules very small. Corolla with long tube.
ASPERULA. Leaves whorled, with leaf-like stipules. Corolla funnel-shaped, usually 4-lobed; stamens arising from the tube or corolla throat.

PUTORIA. *P. calabrica.* A rank-smelling dwarf shrub, prostrate and spreading, with opposite narrow leaves, the edges inrolled. The pink flowers with long tubes are carried in dense terminal clusters. ✣ Rocky and stony places on limestone, usually in the mountains. May–July.   **206**

ASPERULA. *A. arcadiensis.* Forms mats of tufted grey-woolly narrow leaves, and stems up to 10 cm. high carrying heads of 6–8 small rose-pink, waxy trumpets. ✣ Rocks and screes. Peloponnese mountains. March–May.   **207**

A. incana resembles *A. arcadiensis,* like it becoming woody at the base, but is more densely white-woolly, and its flowers are a little longer. ✣ Rocks and screes. Crete, from coast to mountains. June–July.

CONVOLVULACEAE – Bindweed Family

Herbs, shrubs, or climbing plants, with alternate simple leaves without stipules. Flowers large; sepals 5. Corolla deeply funnel-shaped, with or without 5 spreading lobes.

117

CUSCUTA. Parasitic plants without green leaves, attached to the host plant by suckers; flowers small, pink, white, or yellow, in rounded clusters. **CONVOLVULUS.** Flowers funnel-shaped; sepals 5; fruit a capsule.

CUSCUTA. *C. europaea.* LARGE DODDER. Forming a mesh over the host plant of delicate branched red or yellow-red stems on which scales take the place of leaves. The pinkish-white flowers, very small and stalkless, are carried in globular clusters. Parasitises a variety of plants, on which it scrambles and climbs up to 1 m. high. June–Aug. **213**
An example of the 11 species of Dodder found in Greece, some specialising in parasitising herbaceous plants, a few on shrubs; they were known as 'vetch-stranglers' to the ancient Greeks. Dioscorides tells us they were eaten as pot-herbs, either raw or cooked, and 'purgeth downward Phlegm, and black choler . . . properly good for ye melancholicall, and ye puffed up with wind'.

CONVOLVULUS. *C. althaeoides.* A scrambling bindweed with hairy stems to 1 m. long. Flowers 1–3 together, 25–40 mm. across, pink.
Ssp. althaeoides. A robust plant. The leaves with fairly wide, shallow lobes, dark green, and sparsely hairy. Flowers often deep pink or purplish. **208**
Ssp. tenuissimus (C. elegantissimus). A much more slender plant. The leaves deeply lobed and silvery with dense hairs. Flowers clear soft pink. **209**
⚜ Both ssp. grow in dry, stony, and sandy places, often among and over dwarf shrubs, at lower altitudes. April–June.
The Greeks sometimes aptly call these plants foustanaki, *or petticoats; in Crete usually* chonaki, *meaning funnels. Used in the past as a purgative.*
C. cantabrica. A non-climbing, bushy plant with woody stock and 10–50 cm. erect stems. Leaves narrow and silvery haired: flowers 15–25 mm. across, pink,

carried on long stalks in clusters of 1–4 in axils of the leaves. ⚜ Rocky and sandy places, dry hillsides. April–June. **210**
C. dorycnium. A small upright shrub, branched and somewhat hairy, growing to 50–100 cm. The leaves are narrow or spoon-shaped and the flowering stems carry 1 or more pink flowers. ⚜ Dry stony places. S. Greece and the islands. May–July.
C. oleifolius. A shrub growing up to 1 m. Stem and narrow pointed leaves are intensely silvery with long silky hairs, and flowers are carried in terminal heads; they are pink or white flushed pink, 15–25 mm. across, with softly hairy calyces. ⚜ Dry sunny places on rocky ground and cliffs. May–July. **211**
Very similar to the white-flowered C. cneorum which is often grown in gardens.
C. scammonia. SCAMMONY. A scrambling or low-climbing convolvulus, with dark green leaves of elongated arrow-shape. The flowers are large (25–45 mm.), of a clear pale yellow, carried on delicate stalks in the leaf axils. ⚜ Among low scrub in full sun. May–July.
Still employed as a drastic purgative, one of several uses known to the ancient Greeks.
C. tricolor. A spreading hairy annual up to 60 cm. with almost stalkless oval-lance-shaped leaves. The stalked 20–40 mm. solitary flowers are tricoloured, with yellow, white, and blue bands. ⚜ Dry open places, cultivated ground. April–June. **212**
A plant much grown as a hardy decorative annual, and developed into improved forms; sometimes naturalised as a result.

BORAGINACEAE – Borage Family

Herbaceous plants, usually rough and hairy, with alternate entire leaves. Flowers on upper sides of outwardly coiled branches (cymes). Calyx tubular and 5-lobed. Corolla bell or funnel-shaped, 5-lobed.

118

HELIOTROPIUM. Flowers white or lilac; corolla lobes separated by longitudinal folds; leaves soft and hairy.

BUGLOSSOIDES. Flowers white, blue, or purple, corolla funnel-shaped or tubular with spreading petals, and with 5 longitudinal hairy bands within.

LITHODORA. Dwarf shrubs; flowers blue, purple, or white; corolla funnel-shaped or tubular without scales or folds in throat.

ONOSMA. Plants covered with stiff spiny hairs; corolla cylindrical with 5 short lobes and without hairs in throat. Some of the species differ only in minute detail.

CERINTHE. Leaves usually smooth, the upper clasping the stem; corolla cylindrical without scales in throat.

ALKANNA. Corolla funnel-shaped without scales in throat, but with 5 small transverse swellings alternating with the stamens.

ECHIUM. Plants with stiff hairs; corolla funnel-shaped with mouth obliquely cut, the upper lip entire or 2-lobed, the lower lip 3-lobed, without scales in throat.

ANCHUSA. Plants rough-hairy; corolla long and funnel-shaped, throat closed by scales or hairs; nutlets wrinkled.

BORAGO. Corolla with short tube and widely spreading lobes. Stamens projecting forward in a cone.

CYNOGLOSSUM. Corolla funnel-shaped, throat closed by scales or lobes; fruit of 4 nutlets covered by bristles or hooks.

HELIOTROPIUM. *H. europaeum.* A low-growing grey, softly hairy annual, with oval leaves and numerous arched 1-sided spikes of closely packed little white or pale lilac flowers, rather sweetly scented. ✢ Cultivated and waste land. June–Oct. **214**
The curling flower-head, 'winding about like ye tail of a Scorpion', was naturally considered to be remedial for scorpion stings. Furthermore, Dioscorides says 'it is hanged about one to cause barrenness', although pounded leaves will 'expel ye Embrya'.

BUGLOSSOIDES. *B. purpurocaerulea (Lithospermum purpurocaeruleum).* BLUE GROMWELL. A perennial with creeping stems from which rise erect flowering stems up to 50 cm. high, bearing narrow hairy dark green leaves and terminal clusters of funnel-shaped dark blue flowers. ✢ In the shade of woods and under hedges. April–June. **215**

LITHODORA. *L. hispidula (Lithospermum hispidulum).* A small bush, dense, much branched, and spiny, growing up to 70 cm. Leaves small, leathery, and narrow, of a dark green.

The numerous small flowers are of a rather dull blue. ✢ In open woods and thickets. Crete, Karpathos, and Eastern Islands. March–May. **216**

ONOSMA. *O. frutescens.* GOLDEN DROP. A very bristly perennial with woody base, narrow grey-green leaves, and many clusters of pendulous, golden-yellow tubular flowers. ✢ Rocks and cliffs. C. and S. Greece, Aegean. March–May. **219**
O. graeca. An erect, much branched biennial to 30 cm. Leaves narrow and hairy. Flowers pale yellow tinged with purple. ✢ Rocky and stony places. April–June. **220**
O. montana. A tufted, very bristly perennial with spoon-shaped basal leaves and erect stems up to 30 cm., carrying pale yellow, almost stalkless flowers. ✢ Dry mountain slopes. April–May. **217**
O. erecta is similar, but usually shorter, with basal leaves narrowly lance-shaped, flowers yellow, often hairless on 1–5 mm. stalks. ✢ Dry mountainsides. S. Greece and Crete. April–May. **218**
O. taurica. Very similar to *O. erecta*, with oblong basal leaves, and almost

stalkless yellow flowers. ⚘ Dry rocky places in the mountains. June–July.

CERINTHE. *C. major.* HONEYWORT. A hairless blue-grey annual, growing to 20–40 cm., with rounded overlapping leaves clasping the stem, and drooping heads of large cylindrical flowers, usually a pale yellow, sometimes marked with brown at the base. A variable plant; the bracts around the flowerhead may be dark purple. ⚘ Roadsides, field edges, and stony places. Feb.–April. **221**
C. minor. LESSER HONEYWORT. Like *C. major* but with smaller yellowish-white flowers, pinched in at the opening. ⚘ Cultivated ground and waste places. April–July.
C. retorta. 20–40 cm. tall, with rounded blue-green, hairless leaves clasping the stems; the yellow and violet-tipped flowers are surrounded by broad violet bracts. ⚘ Stony soil, in olive groves and vineyards, often in partial shade. March–May. **222**

ALKANNA. *A. graeca.* A spreading, narrow-leaved plant 15–50 cm. tall, with leafy sprays of golden trumpet-shaped flowers.
Ssp. graeca is rather sticky with calyx and corolla both about 6 mm. long.
Ssp. baeotica is densely covered in soft white hairs, and the corolla is twice as long as the calyx at 10–12 mm. ⚘ Rocky places in the hills, often on walls and cliffs. *Ssp. graeca* mainly below 1,500 m., March–May. *Ssp. baeotica* mainly above 1,500 mm. April–June. **223**
A. orientalis. Very like *A. graeca*, but with wavy edges to the leaves. ⚘ Rocky places in the mountains. April–June.
A. tinctoria. DYER'S ALKANET. A low-growing perennial, densely white-haired, whose much-branched stems form dense leafy mats. The leaves are narrow and white-bristly, and the brilliant blue flowers are carried in short leafy spikes. ⚘ In gravelly or sandy places on chalky soil, often near the sea. March–May.
The plant gets its name from the red dye obtained from the roots, which ladies in ancient Greece used as a cosmetic, and was once an important article of trade.

The Greeks still call it vaphoriza, *or 'dye-root'.*

ECHIUM. *E. angustifolium (E. diffusum).* A densely grey-hairy perennial, with several flowering stems up to 40 cm. high carrying tubular red-purple flowers with 4 projecting stamens. Leaves narrow. ⚘ Dry stony and sandy places. April–Aug. **225**
E. italicum. A stiff, grey, very bristly biennial with usually single erect flowering stems up to 1 m., carrying short lateral branches with many small pinkish or bluish flowers, sometimes yellowish, with 4–5 long-projecting stamens. Basal leaves lance-shaped, stem leaves narrow, with dense stiff white hairs. ⚘ Dry stony and sandy places. April–Aug. **224**
E. plantagineum (E. lycopsis). PURPLE VIPER'S BUGLOSS. Biennial, very hairy, with stalked oval leaves, and stems reaching 60 cm. The flowers start blue, changing to purple and finally pink; they are tubular with 2 projecting stamens, densely arranged in narrow spikes. ⚘ Dry sandy or stony places. April–July. **226, 227**

ANCHUSA. *A. azurea (A. italica).* A perennial with hairy lance-shaped leaves, and tall branched stems up to 1 m. high, carrying sprays of bright blue open flowers, white-hairy in the throat. ⚘ Fields, waste places. May–Aug. **228**
A well-known garden plant.
A. arvensis (Lycopsis arvensis). SMALL BUGLOSS. A 10–40 cm. annual, bristly-haired, with narrowly lanceolate wavy-edged leaves. The small blue flowers with white base are carried on stems up to 40 cm. high, the flower cymes with bracts throughout. ⚘ Cultivated and waste ground. May–Aug.
A. caespitosa. From the prostrate tufts of rather long bristly leaves spring a cluster of almost stalkless flowers of intense dark blue. ⚘ Stony places. High Cretan mountains. May–June.
509, p. 63
A. undulata ssp. hybrida (A. hybrida). A bristly biennial with narrow wavy-edged leaves, and heads of dark purple flowers. Grows to 60 cm. high, with the leafy stems branched and the flowers arranged along one side of the flower-

ing stems. ❋ Waste land, edges of cultivated fields. March–June. **229**
A. variegata (Lycopsis variegata L.). A small hairy annual with procumbent stems to 30 cm. long with oblong bristly leaves, slightly toothed, and clusters of upright funnel-shaped, strongly scented flowers, purple becoming variegated with reddish markings on blue; flowers with a corolla-tube curved to one side. Flower cymes with bracts only near base (in which this differs from *A. arvensis*). ❋ Roadsides, cultivated ground. Feb.– May. **548**

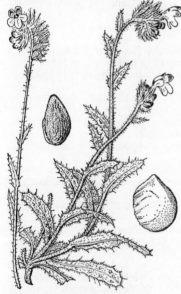

Left: 547 Anchusa cretica
Right: 548 A. variegata. Both × ½
(nutlets enlarged)

A. cretica (Lycopsis variegata auct.) is very similar but is more or less erect, the flowers ending up blue with white lines. ❋ Track sides, cultivated ground. Feb.–May. **547**

BORAGO. *B. officinalis.* BORAGE. A branched annual up to 70 cm., very bristly, with oval wavy-edged rough-surfaced leaves, the lower stalked, the upper clasping the stem. The bright blue open flowers with stamens projecting in a cone are carried in loose branched heads. ❋ Waste places, cultivated ground. April–Sept. **230**
Widely cultivated as a culinary herb.

CYNOGLOSSUM. *C. columnae.* A grey-hairy annual or biennial Hounds-tongue up to 70 cm. high, with stalked elliptic leaves and long clusters of dull purple flowers. Fruits flat, roundish, with raised border, and covered with hooked spines and warty swellings. ❋ Stony ground. March–July. **233**
C. creticum. A softly hairy biennial up to 60 cm., with lance-shaped leaves, shortly stalked, and heads of pale blue flowers. Fruits rounded, without border, covered with short spikes and conical swellings. ❋ Open dry places, thickets. May–June. **231, 232**

VERBENACEAE – Verbena Family

Herbs, trees, shrubs, or climbers, with usually opposite leaves without stipules. Calyx tubular with 4–5 lobes; corolla tubular with 4–5 lobes, sometimes 2-lipped. Fruit often fleshy.

VITEX. *V. agnus-castus.* CHASTE TREE. A shrub up to 3 m. high, with dark green leaves, white-felted below, cut deeply into 5–7 narrow leaflets. The small sweet-scented flowers are carried in long terminal spikes like a miniature buddleia; they vary from lilac to pale or deep blue. Fruit 2 mm. across, fleshy, purplish. ❋ Streams, gullies, and damp places near the sea. June–Sept. **234**
From early times this shrub, sacred to Hera, was associated with chastity. The seeds were originally believed to subdue the 'inclination natural' between the sexes – hence the names Chaste Tree and Monk's Pepper. Despite this the aromatic seeds were later considered to be aphrodisiac. Dioscorides writes, somewhat obscurely, 'It is called Agnus, because in the sacrifices of Ceres the chast matrons did use it for a strawing

121

LABIATAE – Mint Family

Herbs or shrubs with quadrangular stems and opposite paired leaves, without stipules, the plants being usually glandular and hairy. Flowers in whorls in the axils of the upper leaves or bracts. Calyx tubular, 5-lobed, and often 2-lipped. Corolla tubular, 5-lobed and 2-lipped, the upper lip being large, the lower lip divided into 3 or occasionally 5 lobes.

This is the family above all others of aromatic and culinary herbs, and we have not mentioned such uses in every familiar case. The Greeks use even more of them than we do as herbs and some, like Sideritis *species, to make* 'tea'.

AJUGA. Corolla with very short upper lip and conspicuous 3-lobed lower lip; corolla tube with a ring of hairs within.

TEUCRIUM. Corolla without an upper lip, the lower lip 5-lobed with middle lobe much the longest; corolla tube without a ring of hairs.

PRASIUM. Upper lip of corolla convex and arched; stamens 4, projecting; calyx 2-lipped.

SIDERITIS. Corolla with flat upper lip, often entire or 2-lobed; lower lip 3-lobed. Calyx bell-shaped, with 5 spiny teeth.

MELITTIS. Corolla with upper lip entire; lower lip with 2 rounded lobes. Calyx upper lip 3–4 lobed; lower lip 2-lobed.

PHLOMIS. Flowers rather large; corolla with upper lip large and hooded; calyx with 5 equal teeth.

LAMIUM. Flowers rather large; corolla 2-lipped, upper lip hooded, lower lip 3-lobed with 2 lateral tooth-like projections; calyx funnel-shaped, 10-veined, usually 5-lobed.

BALLOTA. Corolla 2-lipped with upper lip concave; calyx funnel-shaped, 10-veined, usually 5-lobed.

STACHYS. Calyx tubular or bell-shaped, 5- or 10-veined, 5-lobed; corolla 2-lipped, upper lip flat or arched, lower lip 3-lobed, with middle lobe the longest.

MELISSA. Corolla 2-lipped, upper lip erect and notched, lower lip 3-lobed; calyx 13-veined, 2-lipped; upper lip 3-lobed, lower lip 2-lobed.

SATUREIA. Corolla 2-lipped with upper lip flat or convex, lower lip 3-lobed; calyx 2-lipped.

MICROMERIA. Calyx bell-shaped with 13–15 veins and 5 equal pointed lobes.

ORIGANUM. Flowers clustered on spreading terminal heads; calyx bell-shaped, hairy within, 13-veined and 5-lobed.

THYMUS. Calyx 2-lipped, upper lip 3-toothed and hairy, lower lip with very narrow lobes.

ROSMARINUS. Corolla 2-lipped, the upper deeply divided, the lower spreading and 3-lobed; stamens 2, projecting; calyx 2-lipped, lower lip 2-lobed.

LAVANDULA. Flowers blue in tight leafless spikes; corolla tube longer than calyx, stamens not projecting.

SALVIA. Calyx tubular or bell-shaped, upper lip entire or 3-lobed, lower lip 2-lobed; corolla tubular, 2-lipped, upper lip usually hooded, lower lip 3-lobed with middle lobe longer and often notched; stamens 2.

AJUGA. *A. chamaepitys.* GROUND PINE. A hairy annual up to 20 cm. with resinous smell when crushed; with branched stems and sticky leaves deeply divided into 3 very narrow segments. The bright yellow 7–25 mm. flowers, sometimes streaked with red or purple (occasionally entirely purple) are carried in pairs in the leaf axils. The Greek plant is *ssp. chia.* ✳ Fields and dry hillsides, usually on limestone. March–April. **235**
A general-purpose remedy according to Dioscorides. The Arabs know it as a cure for paralysis in animals, and hysteria in horses.
A. orientalis. EASTERN BUGLE. This is the Eastern form of the widely distributed Pyramidal Bugle. It shares with it the same dense pyramidal head of broad overlapping blue-violet bracts and pale bluish flowers. The oblong leaves are variably lobed and densely hairy. ✳ Grassy places in the hills. April–Aug.

TEUCRIUM. *T. fruticans.* SHRUBBY GERMANDER. A shrub growing to 1½ m., much branched, with narrow leaves, dark green above, white-felted below, and large pale blue flowers with long lip and very prominent stamens and style. ✳ Rocky hills by the coast. Feb.–June. **236**
Sometimes grown as a hedge; it can be clipped.
T. polium. A small shrub up to 40 cm. high, much branched, with oval leaves with inrolled margins, and dense heads of stalkless white or pinkish flowers. The whole plant is white-felted. Rather variable. ✳ Dry stony places. June–Aug. **549**
Dioscorides recommends a decoction against bites from venomous beasts and to drive away such creatures; also for stomach ache, fevers, and colds, being given in a steam bath for the latter.

PRASIUM. *P. majus.* A small shrub up to 1 m. high, with branched stems, hairless oval, toothed leaves, and leafy flower clusters in which white or pinkish 2-lipped flowers are carried in the

leaf axils. ✳ Bushy places, often among rocks. Feb.–June. **237**

SIDERITIS. *S. syriaca.* A densely white-woolly perennial shrub up to 50 cm., with ovate-lanceolate leaves, sometimes wavy-edged, and 6–10-flowered whorls of smallish yellow flowers. ✳ Stony places in the mountains. S. Greece and Crete. June–Aug. **550, p. 124**

MELITTIS. *M. melissophyllum.* BASTARD BALM. A robust strongly aromatic perennial, up to 70 cm., with stalked oval leaves, coarsely toothed and softly hairy. The 25–40 mm. pink, white, or variegated flowers are carried in whorls. ✳ Shady places, woods. May–July. **242**

PHLOMIS. *P. fruticosa.* JERUSALEM SAGE. A shrub to 1–1½ m., with large oval leaves covered with dense white-woolly hairs. The golden-yellow, hooded 2–4 cm. flowers are carried in whorls. ✳ Dry places, often on the hills, where it is often the dominant plant. March–June. **238**
The flowers of this often cultivated shrub form a rich source of nectar for honey bees.
P. herba-venti. A hairy branched peren-

549 Teucrium polium ×½

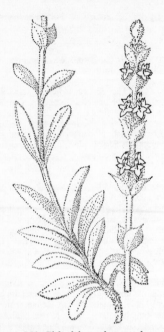

550 Sideritis syriaca × ½

nial up to 60 cm., with toothed lance-shaped leaves, shining green above and white-woolly beneath; 2–5 dense whorls of 2 cm. purple flowers are carried in leaf axils. ❋ Dry and stony places, usually on chalk or clay. May–July. **239**
P. samia. A herbaceous perennial up to 1 m., with lanceolate-ovate leaves, rather leathery and toothed, hairy above and white-woolly below. 3–4 cm. purple flowers in whorls. ❋ Dry stony places. May–July.

LAMIUM. *L. garganicum.* A handsome deadnettle growing up to 50 cm. Leaves hairy, heart-shaped, and toothed. The 25–40 mm. rosy-red flowers are carried in whorls. ❋ Stony places; often in the mountains. April–June. **240**
Ssp. pictum does not grow over 10 cm.; leaves barely hairy. ❋ Mountains of C. and S. Greece. May–June.

BALLOTA. *B. acetabulosa.* FALSE DIT-TANY. A stout erect Horehound growing to 50 cm., with densely packed paired leaves, heart-shaped, coarsely toothed, and densely woolly, white when young, becoming grey. Its striking characteristic is the calyx which, after the purple flowers fade, becomes grossly enlarged and umbrella-shaped. ❋ Stony places. April–May. **241**
The name False Dittany was given for its slight resemblance to Cretan Dittany (Origanum dictamnus), *whose qualities it could not emulate. The seed vessels are used by peasants as floating wicks in lamps of olive oil, and the plant is therefore sometimes called* louminia.

STACHYS. *S. candida.* A woody-based, branched Woundwort, perennial, up to 10–20 cm. high, white-woolly, with oval leaves and whorls of white flowers with purple sepals. ❋ Stony rocky places. M. Taygetus, Peloponnese. April–July. **243**
S. cretica. A densely grey-hairy perennial up to 80 cm., the leaves being oval-oblong and white-woolly on the lower surface. The whorls of numerous flowers are purplish. ❋ Stony places. May–July. **551**
S. tournefortii. A densely white-woolly perennial shrub growing up to 100 cm., with ovate-oblong leaves and many-flowered whorls of small pink flowers. ❋ Dry and rocky places. Crete. May–July.

MELISSA. *M. officinalis.* BALM. A branched and usually hairy perennial up to 1 m. The oval lemon-scented leaves are stalked and toothed, and the white flowers are carried in axillary whorls. Bracts leaf-like. ❋ Bushy and shady places. June–Sept.
Virgil describes how a mixture of leaves of balm and honeywort (cerinthe) *was used to persuade bees to swarm. A decoction of balm was until recently valued as a tonic.*

SATUREIA. *S. thymbra.* SUMMER SAVORY A very aromatic shrublet up to 40 cm. The oblong leaves are hairy, and the small rose-coloured flowers are arranged in whorls along the wiry upright stems. The calyces become black in summer. ❋ Dry stony hillsides. April–June. **553**

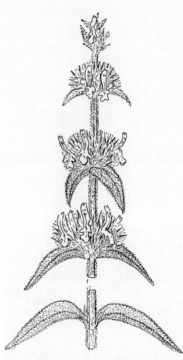

551 Stachys cretica × ½

MICROMERIA. *M. nervosa.* A perennial woody-based shrublet up to 40 cm. The stems and the paired stalked-egg-shaped leaves are rough-hairy, and the many-flowered whorls of pinkish flowers are carried in cylindrical spikes. The calyces are bristly-toothed, with long thin spreading hairs. ❊ Stony and rocky places. April–July.

M. graeca is similar, but the narrower leaves are not stalked. The flowers are carried in loose clusters, and the hairs on the calyces are pressed to the surface. **552**

M. juliana has very small stalkless purple flowers in densely packed whorls, the leaves are short and narrow, and the calyx throat is hairless.

ORIGANUM. *O. dictamnus.* CRETAN DITTANY. A white-woolly shrublet up to 25 cm., with egg-shaped or rounded leaves; loose terminal or lateral hop-like heads of pink flowers; bracts larger than calyx, and purple in colour. ❊ Rocky places. Cretan mountains. June–Aug. **554**, p. 126

Much prized as a herb by the natives. Of it Theophrastus writes 'this plant is marvellous in virtue and is useful for many purposes, but especially for women in childbirth . . . If goats eat it when they have been shot, it rids them of the arrow.' He adds that the bunches of dittany are put into the hollow stems of giant fennel or reed 'so that it may not exhale its virtue'.

O. scabrum. A rhizomatous perennial with thin wiry stems up to 45 cm., erect or drooping, branched above, and carrying small paired stalkless leaves, smooth and ovate or rounded. Flowers pink, small, and hop-like in lax narrow sprays with numerous overlapping purplish bracts. ❊ Dry stony place. Mountains of S. Greece. **555**, p. 126

O. vulgare. MARJORAM. A very aromatic perennial, growing up to 80 cm. high. The leaves are oval, stalked, and shallowly toothed. The rosy-purple flowers are carried in terminal and

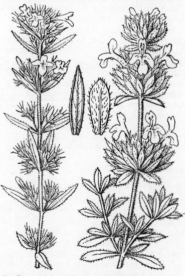

Left: 552 Micromeria graeca
Right: 553 Satureia thymbra
Both × 1 (leaf undersides enlarged)

125

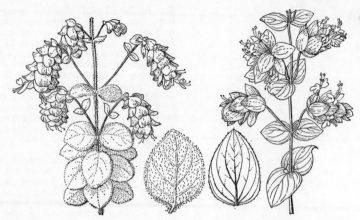

Left: 554 Origanum dictamnus. Right: 555 O. scabrum. Both ×⅔
(leaf undersides enlarged)

axillary clusters, dense, spreading, and rather rounded. ❧ Dry meadows and stony places. July–Sept.

THYMUS. *T. capitatus* (*Coridothymus capitatus, Thymbra capitata*). A low-growing, very compact shrublet, seldom exceeding 25 cm. The small narrow, stiff leaves are arranged in clusters along the woody, almost spiny stems, and the purplish-pink flowers are borne in rounded clusters at the ends; the individual flowers show very prominent stamens. ❧ Limestone outcrops, stony places. May–August. **244** *Much worked by honey bees, and a source of ethereal oil used in medicine and perfumery. Even in Theophrastus' day it was exported from Athens as a herb. It also had much medicinal value, according to herbalists.*

ROSMARINUS. *R. officinalis.* ROSE-MARY. A dense aromatic shrub to 1½ m., with narrow leaves, green above and white below, and clusters of pale mauve flowers, from which the 2 stamens and curved style project. ❧ Dry hills, macchie, near the sea. Flowers throughout the year. **245** *To the Greeks, as later the Romans, rosemary played an important part in religious ceremonies and festivities, both public and private. The Greeks*

burned it like incense. Later it became a symbol of fidelity, because it was supposed to enhance memory; and it was used at both weddings and funerals. A good honey plant, it is often cultivated, sometimes as an easily clipped hedge. Its essential oil is used in perfumery and making conserves; it has many medicinal properties and has been employed as an antiseptic and an insecticide.

LAVANDULA. *L. angustifolia* (*L. spica*). COMMON LAVENDER. The well-known Lavender of cultivation, growing up to 1 m., with narrow downy grey-green leaves, inrolled at the margins. The very fragrant grey-blue flowers are carried in crowded spikes. ❧ Dry stony hillsides. June–Sept.
L. stoechas. FRENCH LAVENDER. A sub-shrub up to 60 cm. with narrow grey-green hairy leaves, and compact quadrangular flowerheads of dark purple, topped with large purple bracts. The whole plant is very aromatic. ❧ Dry hills, macchie, phrygana, on siliceous soils. Feb.–June. **246** *This very aromatic plant was anciently known as a soothing medicine, and like other lavenders is used to scent clothes and linen and keep away moths.*

SALVIA. *S. glutinosa.* A perennial 50–100 cm. tall, distinguished by its strongly smelling, sticky leaves, which are pointed and oval, coarsely toothed and with basal lobes; and by its spikes of a few large pale yellow flowers. ✲ Woods, mainly in mountainous areas. June–Sept.   **247**

S. horminum. RED-TOPPED SAGE. An annual up to 40 cm., with pairs of stalked oval leaves, hairy, wrinkled, and toothed. The small violet or pinkish flowers are carried in numerous whorls. Broad purple or pink bracts crown the flowering stem. ✲ Dry stony places. April–June.

S. pomifera. A sub-shrub up to 1 m. high, with stalked leaves, which are egg-shaped, rounded, or heart-shaped, and with whorls of violet-blue flowers. Calyx reddish-purple. ✲ Stony hillsides. May–July.   **248**
The name pomifera – *apple-bearing – is derived from the round, smooth galls which this plant often carries, which are eaten by the Arabs, and are said to quench thirst. In Greece peasants collect them on May 1 and candy them in sugar as a sweetmeat.*

S. sclarea. CLARY. A sticky aromatic biennial growing to 1 m., with grey-green leaves, wrinkled and hairy, and branched flowerheads of whorled whitish-violet flowers with long papery bracts. ✲ Dry stony places, roadsides. May–Sept.   **249**

S. triloba. THREE-LOBED SAGE. A large woody-based shrub, very aromatic, and reaching 1½ m. The stalked leaves are of a greyish-green, wrinkled above and downy white below, frequently with 2 small lobes at the base. The hooded flowers carried in whorls, are a light bluish-purple, while the calyx is often tinged with pinkish-purple. ✲ Bushy, rocky places, often on sea cliffs. March–June.   **251**
Like S. pomifera *this plant may carry insect-produced apple-like galls. 'Tea' is made from the dried leaves and is sold in cafés in Greece under the name* faskomelo. *The fresh leaves are also infused with sugar or honey. The plant is sometimes burned in a house to cleanse it. The flowers give much nectar.*

S. verbenaca. WILD CLARY. A perennial up to 50 cm. with wrinkled hairy leaves, ovate and irregularly lobed, and spikes of small blue flowers arranged in whorls. *Ssp. clandestina* is lower growing, with deeply divided leaves almost confined to a basal tuft. Flower heads denser and of a pale blue. ✲ Dry stony hillsides, roadsides. March–June.   **250**

SOLANACEAE – Nightshade Family

Herbs, shrubs, small trees, or climbing plants with alternate and often entire leaves without stipules. Calyx and corolla both fused at the base and 5-lobed. Fruit a berry or capsule.
Most members of this family are poisonous in some part, although they include important food plants like potatoes, tomatoes, capsicums, and cayenne pepper, as well as tobacco.

ATROPA. Flowers axillary, single or paired; corolla and calyx bell-shaped; fruit a berry.

HYOSCYAMUS. Flowers axillary or coiled in leafy branches; corolla funnel- or bell-shaped, asymmetrical; calyx tubular; fruit a capsule.

MANDRAGORA. Flowers short-stalked, arising from rootstock in centre of leaf rosettes; corolla bell-shaped; fruit a berry.

DATURA. Corolla long, funnel-shaped, with short lobes; calyx long and tubular; fruit a spiny capsule.

NICOTIANA. Flowers in clusters; corolla tube long and narrow, petals often spreading; fruit a capsule.

ATROPA. *A. belladonna.* DEADLY NIGHTSHADE. A branched, leafy perennial to 1½ m., carrying large, stalked oval leaves and large solitary bell-shaped flowers of a brownish-purple in the leaf axils. The fruit is rounded and

127

black. ✤ Woods, thickets, clearings, mainly in the mountains. May–Aug.

A very poisonous plant. The name 'belladonna' comes from its use by Roman ladies for dilating the pupils of their eyes to make them more attractive; and it remains an invaluable aid in medical treatment of the eye. In ancient times it was very much a magician's plant, reputed to belong to the devil.

HYOSCYAMUS. *H. albus.* WHITE HENBANE. A sticky and hairy, coarse-growing 20–50 cm. perennial with large oval leaves, stalked and with blunt lobes. The pale yellow tubular flowers, often purple in the throat, grow in the leaf axils. ✤ Waste places, among rocks, often near habitations. March–June. **252**

The poisonous, narcotic henbanes were associated with witchcraft since earliest times. The Assyrians recommended hanging them on one's door to ward off sorcery. Witches found them valuable especially due to their trance-inducing capabilities. They have been used to lessen pain, neuralgia, diminish convulsions, and so on. Dioscorides recommended them largely for external pain-killing use. The leaves are made into a kind of cigarette to relieve asthma and other respiratory ailments.

H. aureus. GOLDEN HENBANE. Like *H. albus,* but with more striking flowers of a golden-yellow with violet throat. ✤ On rocks and in walls. Crete, Rhodes. Possibly naturalised. March–July. **253**

MANDRAGORA. *M. officinarum.* MANDRAKE. From a flat rosette of large, wrinkled, and broadly oval leaves, ranging from mid to dark bluish-green, and either woolly or smooth, rise a cluster of short-stalked flowers, sometimes bell-shaped, sometimes of long narrow lobes, varying in colour from dull to light blue. Roots thick, fleshy, and often forked. ✤ Fields and stony places. Flowers in spring and autumn. Fruit usually oval, green becoming yellow.

A variable species. Modern botanical authorities have split it into '*M. autumnalis*' and '*M. vernalis*' but expert opinion suggests such variability in inter-connected populations that the diagnoses of these new 'species' are in effect meaningless. **254, 255, 256**

A moderately narcotic plant favoured in myth and magic largely because its shape often resembled a human figure when the tap-root forked; 'male' and 'female' mandrakes were recognised and the plant was typically depicted as having a human head. In Theophrastus' day 'it is said that one should draw three circles round mandrake with a sword, and cut it with one's face towards the west; and at the cutting of the second piece say as many things as possible about the mysteries of love'. Later, it became believed that when dug up mandrakes uttered a shriek to hear which spelt death. Hence it was considered necessary to loosen the root and tie a dog to it to carry out the final extraction; presumably 'the dog it was that died'. Apart from employment in sorcery mandrake was, during the Middle Ages, a prized painkiller during operations. The leaf was valued for healing wounds and the root for gout, sleeplessness, and love potions. The fruit is edible and has an interesting flavour.

DATURA. *D. stramonium.* THORN APPLE, JIMSON WEED. A densely branched plant usually 50–80 cm. tall, sometimes more with large oval leaves toothed at the margins. The 5–10 cm. white trumpet-shaped flowers are borne singly and are followed by oblong spiny green fruits, like horse chestnuts, containing a mass of black seeds. The plant is rank-smelling if touched. ✤ A world-wide weed of unknown origin. Waste ground. April–Oct.

This plant was known to Theophrastus who wrote how, if three-twentieths of an ounce is given, the patient 'becomes merely sportive and thinks himself a fine fellow'; with twice this dose, he goes mad outright and has delusions; thrice the dose, he becomes permanently insane; four times the dose, the man is killed. Thorn apple is very poisonous and narcotic, and has many uses in modern medicine, resembling those of henbane.

D. metel resembles *D. stramonium,* but has much larger (10–20 cm.)

flowers, rarely pinkish. It is a greyish, hairy plant with only shallowly-lobed leaves, and the roundish, slender-spined fruit is drooping, not erect. ❋ An introduction from Central America, naturalised on roadsides and stony waste places; sometimes cultivated in a double form. Flowers spring and summer. **257**

NICOTIANA. *N. glauca.* TREE TO-BACCO. A straggling branched shrub up to 3 m. high, with oval hairless blue-green leaves, and terminal clusters of long narrow tubular yellow flowers. ❋ A native of S. America, but long naturalised in waste places, on cliffs and rocky slopes on the coast. Flowers all the year round. **258**

SCROPHULARIACEAE – Figwort Family

Herbs or shrubs with entire or toothed leaves. Flowers symmetrical in 1 plane only. Calyx 4–5 lobed. Corolla very variable, fused at base, often bell-shaped or tubular with spreading lobes, or 2-lipped. Fruit a capsule.
VERBASCUM. Flowers in a long terminal spike; corolla a spreading 5-lobed cup; stamens 4 or 5; calyx deeply 5-lobed.
ANTIRRHINUM. Corolla 2-lipped, the lower lip 3-toothed with a swelling in throat closing the corolla mouth.
LINARIA. Like *Antirrhinum* but corolla with a downward projecting spur.
DIGITALIS. Corolla long and tubular, 2-lipped, the upper lip shorter than the lower; calyx deeply 5-lobed.
PARENTUCELLIA. Corolla 2-lipped, the upper lip forming a hood, the lower lip 3-lobed; calyx cylindrical with sharp teeth.
BELLARDIA. Corolla 2-lipped, the upper lip forming a hood, the lower lip 3-lobed; calyx bell-shaped and swollen, deeply divided into 2 toothed lobes.

VERBASCUM. MULLEIN.

Flowers carried singly in the axil of each stem bract, usually on distinct stalks

V. arcturus (Celsia arcturus). A woody-based perennial with numerous stems to 70 cm. Leaves divided into a large oval terminal lobe and 2–4 smaller lateral lobes, green above and white-woolly beneath. The hairy flowering spikes carry short-stalked (15–25 mm.) yellow flowers with 4 stamens on violet filaments. ❋ Limestone rock crevices, walls. Crete. April–June. **259**
V. phoeniceum. PURPLE MULLEIN. A perennial, smooth above and hairy beneath, with rosettes of oval leaves, the violet, rarely yellow flowers are carried on flowering spikes up to 1 m. high, on 10–25 mm. stalks. Stamens 4 or 5 on violet filaments. ❋ Stony hillsides. May–Sept.
V. blattaria, the MOTH MULLEIN, is similar to *V. phoeniceum*, with yellow

or whitish flowers, biennial. Flower stalks 5–25 mm. Stamens 5, with white and purple filaments. Leaves smooth and coarsely toothed. ❋ Damp places on uncultivated ground and roadsides. May–Sept.
V. spinosum. SPINY MULLEIN. A branched spiny shrub up to 50 cm., with narrowly oblong white-woolly leaves, toothed or lobed. Flowers yellow, 10–18 mm., almost stalkless; stamens 5 on lilac filaments. ❋ Stony hillsides. Crete. May–July. **556**, p. 130

Flowers several in each axil, usually virtually stalkless

V. graecum. A white-woolly perennial up to 1½ m., with ovate-lanceolate untoothed leaves up to 10 by 30 cm., and branched flowering spikes of yellow flowers with 5 stamens. Filaments white. ❋ Stony and rocky places. May–July. **260**
V. sinuatum. Biennial. From large rosettes of short-stalked wavy-edged greyish leaves rise the stately 1 m.

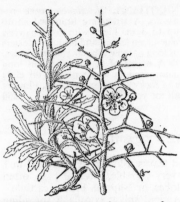

556 Verbascum spinosum ×½

stems bearing stalkless spoon-shaped leaves and clusters of 15–30 mm. yellow flowers on slender spreading branches. Stamens 5 on violet filaments. ✳ Uncultivated ground. May–July. **261**

V. speciosum. A massive plant 50–200 cm. tall, densely covered in white or yellow wool, and with flower head of numerous erect branches. Flowers 18–30 mm. Stamens 5 on white filaments. ✳ Stony places in mountains. C. and S. Greece (*ssp. megaphlomos*). June–Aug. **262**

V. undulatum. A biennial, forming large handsome rosettes of wavy-edged leaves densely covered with white, grey, or pale yellow hairs. The flower stems, about 1½ m. high, carry stemless clusters of bright yellow flowers. Stamens 5 on white filaments. ✳ Stony places, cliffs, and hillsides. March–May.

263, 264

In the medieval herbal of Apuleius Platonicus there is an apocryphal version of Ulysses' skirmish with the sorceress Circe, in which Mercury gives him a mullein which protects him against her spells. In this period mulleins acquired many such protective attributes. Most mulleins are covered in woolly 'felt' which is very unpalatable to animals; hence they often appear in quantities on heavily grazed ground. They are still occasionally used as fish poisons, and the very woolly leaves of some species were formerly used as

130

lamp wicks. As well as various medical remedies cited by Dioscorides, he states that they attract woodworms and, if placed with figs, stop the latter from rotting.

ANTIRRHINUM. *A. majus.* SNAPDRAGON. A perennial, growing to 30–60 cm., with spikes of reddish-purple flowers, yellow in the throat. Leaves dark green, smooth and narrow. The form commonly seen in Greece, often growing at some distance from human habitation, is usually *ssp. tortuosum.* ✳ A plant naturalised from the W. Mediterranean. Dry stony places, walls, banks. April–Oct.
The familiar garden flower in its original form.

LINARIA. *L. triphylla.* A hairless annual up to 40 cm., with whorls of 3 oval leaves and compact terminal heads of tricoloured flowers of yellow, orange, and purple. ✳ Cultivated ground near the coast. April–June.

Among other common TOADFLAX species in Greece are *L. chalepensis* (265) with very narrow pointed leaves and small white flowers distinguished by their long thin curved spurs; *L. pelisseriana* with narrow alternate leaves and violet flowers; and *L. micrantha*, with tiny lilac-blue flowers.

DIGITALIS. *D. ferruginea.* RUSTY FOXGLOVE. Up to 1 m., with narrow hairless leaves and spikes of 1½ cm. reddish-yellow flowers marked with brown. ✳ Woods, thickets. July–Sept. *D. lanata.* Up to 1 m. with oval leaves and greyish downy spikes of whitish, purple-veined flowers. ✳ Thickets, rough ground. July–Sept. **266**

PARENTUCELLIA. *P. latifolia.* SOUTHERN RED BARTSIA. A hairy sticky annual growing up to 20 cm., reddish in colour, with small oval toothed leaves, and small reddish-purple flowers with a white tube, carried in short leafy spikes. ✳ Grassy and sandy places especially near the coast. March–June.

BELLARDIA. *B. trixago.* A stout glandular hairy annual, up to 30 cm. high, with narrow toothed hairy leaves, and short dense leafy flowering spikes of creamy yellow and pink. ⚘ Sandy places and damp roadsides. April–June. **267**

GLOBULARIACEAE –
Globularia Family

Shrubs or herbs with alternate simple leaves. Flowers in rounded heads surrounded by numerous bracts. Calyx tubular and 5-lobed; corolla tubed and 2-lipped.

GLOBULARIA. *G. alypum*. A small, much branched shrub reaching 60 cm. It bears small, narrow, leathery leaves, spiny-tipped, and small rounded heads of pale blue fragrant flowers, on long stems. ⚘ Dry rocky places. Nov.–April. **268**
A poisonous plant once used as a drastic purgative.
***G. meridionalis*.** An evergreen shrublet to 10 cm., with small dark green spoon-shaped leaves, the flowers in small rounded heads of powder-blue. ⚘ Rocks in full sun. High limestone mountains in N. June–August.

ACANTHACEAE – Acanthus
Family

Herbs or shrubs with opposite leaves. Resemble *Scrophulariaceae*

but the bracts on the flowering spikes are often conspicuous and coloured.

ACANTHUS. *A. balcanicus*. A spreading perennial, with 20–60 cm. dark green leaves cut into segments to the midrib, and toothed at the edges. The stout unbranched flowering stems grow up to 1 m. in height, and carry numerous $3\frac{1}{2}$–5 cm. white flowers, veined with purple. The bracts are broad and spiny. ⚘ Shady and rocky places, roadsides. N. Greece. May–July.
This plant is very similar to A. mollis, *often grown in gardens, in which the leaves are only cut half-way to the midrib;* A. mollis *does not appear to enter Greece.*
***A. spinosus* (*A. spinosissimus*, *A. caroli-alexandrae*).** Like *A. balcanicus* but the leaves with stiff, sharp whitish spines, and sometimes hairy. ⚘ Woods, grassland. May–July. **269**
Acanthus leaves form the design motif of many Greek sculptured scrolls and painted decorations, of which the best known is on the capitals of Corinthian columns, invented by Callimachus in 3rd century B.C. *and later developed by the Romans. The leaves were much used for gardens by both Greeks and Romans, on buildings, furniture, clothing and even cup-handles. The roots, according to Dioscorides, are good for 'ye phthisicall, and ruptures, and convulsions'.*

GESNERIACEAE – Gloxinia Family

A mostly tropical or sub-tropical family closely related to the *Scrophulariaceae*, often with rosettes of oval wrinkled and hairy leaves; flowers solitary or in few-flowered umbels.
HABERLEA. Flowers pale bluish-violet, 1–5, carried in clusters on short stalk; corolla cylindrical, 5-lobed.
RAMONDA. Flowers deep violet with golden centre, 1–6 carried on short stalk; corolla with short tube and 5 spreading lobes; leaves deeply wrinkled, coarsely toothed, greyish hairy above, reddish woolly beneath.
JANKAEA. Leaves densely woolly above; corolla bell-shaped, 4-lobed.

HABERLEA. *H. rhodopensis*. Leaves oval, softly hairy, toothed. On stems 6–10 cm. high are carried 1–5 small narrowly cup-shaped, lavender-coloured flowers. ⚘ Shady limestone rocks. Mountains of N. Greece. May–June. **511**, p. 63

RAMONDA. *R. nathaliae*. With flat rosettes of dark green, oval to roundish

131

leaves, hairy and wrinkled, and sometimes round-toothed. 10 cm. high stems carry clusters of cup-shaped dark violet-blue flowers. ❊ Shady limestone rocks. Mountains of Epirus. May–June. **512**, p. 63
R. serbica. Like *R. nathaliae* but leaves narrow-oval, distinctly and sometimes deeply toothed. Flowers blue-purple, cup-shaped. ❊ Shaded boulders and cliffs. N.W. Greece. May–July.
513, p. 63

JANKAEA. *J. heldreichii*. From rosettes of thick egg-shaped leaves, silver haired above and reddish below, rise flowering stems up to 10 cm. carrying loose clusters of thick textured rosy lavender bell-shaped flowers. ❊ Boulders and cliffs in part shade. Confined to the forest zone of Mount Olympos, from 300–1,700 m. June–Aug.
514, p. 63

OROBANCHACEAE –
Broomrape Family

Parasitic plants growing on the roots of various flowering plants. Leaves reduced to colourless scales. Flowers in dense terminal spikes, growing in the axils of bracts. Flowers symmetrical in 1 plane only. Calyx tubular with 2–5 lobes. Corolla tubular, and 2-lipped. Difficult plants to identify. *Broomrapes are often severe crop pests and can, for example, be seen decimating fields of beans and leguminous fodder crops.*

OROBANCHE. *O. alba*. THYME BROOMRAPE. With thick stems up to 30 cm. or more; the fragrant, densely packed, 15–25 mm. flowers are yellowish veined purple. ❊ On thyme and other *Labiatae*. April–Aug.
O. amethystea. A red-violet-stemmed species 10–70 cm. tall. Flowers 15–25 mm., cream tinged with violet. ❊ On various plants, including *Eryngium*. June–July. **270**
O. caryophyllacea. CLOVE-SCENTED BROOMRAPE. Stems up to 40 cm., slightly swollen at base, carrying spikes of 20–30 mm. yellowish flowers touched

with brownish-purple. ❊ On *Rubiaceae*. June–July. **271**
O. crenata. With thick stem to 50 cm. or more, slightly swollen at the base, scaly, carrying dense spikes of 20–30 mm. whitish flowers streaked with bluish-violet, which smell of carnations. ❊ Usually on beans and other leguminous crops. March–June. **272**
O. gracilis. With rather thin, 15–60 cm. stems, swollen at the base; reddish or yellowish, hairy and glandular. Flowers 15–25 mm., yellow tinged with red, blood red within. Smells of clover. ❊ On leguminous plants, occasionally *Cistus*. April–July.
O. minor. LESSER BROOMRAPE. A variable species 10–40 cm. high, with yellowish 10–20 mm. flowers veined with purple. ❊ On clovers and many other plants. April–July. **273**
O. ramosa. BRANCHED BROOMRAPE. Distinguished from other species by its flowering spike which sometimes branches below soil level. Flowers 10–20 mm., pale blue or whitish, blue-tipped. Grows to 40 cm. ❊ On many kinds of plant, including potato, tomato, and hemp. May–Sept. **274**

CAPRIFOLIACEAE –
Honeysuckle Family

Shrubs or climbers with opposite leaves, and flowers either radially symmetrical or symmetrical in 1 plane only. Calyx 4–5-lobed. Corolla fused at the base to give a tube with 4–5 spreading lobes, or sometimes 2-lipped. Fruit often fleshy.

VIBURNUM. Shrubs with toothed or lobed leaves; flowers usually in compound flat-topped heads; fruit fleshy, with hard stone.
LONICERA. Woody climbers or shrubs; corolla often with a long tube, 2-lipped, the upper lip 4-lobed, the lower lip single-lobed; some species with short tube, 5-lobed; fruit a berry.

VIBURNUM. *V. lantana*. WAYFARING TREE. A deciduous shrub to 3–4 m., with oval wrinkled leaves, smooth above but densely white-haired beneath. The white flowers are carried in large flat-topped clusters. Berries red, then black. ✤ Woods on the lower mountain slopes. May–June.

V. tinus. LAURESTINUS. An evergreen shrub to 3 m., with shiny dark green, leathery leaves, and flat heads of white or pinkish flowers, faintly scented, followed by metallic-blue berries. ✤ Woods and shady places near the sea. Feb.–June.
The berries were formerly used as a drastic purgative, and a remedy for dropsy. The pale reddish wood is very hard and fine-grained, and is used exclusively for making small, delicate objects.

LONICERA. L. etrusca. A HONEYSUCKLE climbing to 3 m., with dark green oval deciduous leaves in pairs, the uppermost pairs being fused together, encircling the stem. The creamy coloured flowers, flushed with red, are carried in long-stemmed clusters of 12 or more. ✤ Woods, thickets, hedges, on limestone. May–June.   **557**
L. implexa. A climber to 2 m. with evergreen leathery leaves, usually hairy, and with narrow translucent edges. The stemless clusters of about 6 flowers arise from cup-like encircling bracts. The flowers are cream-coloured flushed with red. ✤ Hedges, woods, rocks. April–June.   **558**
Honeysuckles were second only to acan-
thus as design inspiration for painted ornament in ancient Greece.

VALERIANACEAE –
Valerian Family

Herbs with opposite entire or lobed leaves. Flowers usually small in dense terminal clusters. Corolla funnel-shaped, with 5 sometimes unequal lobes.
FEDIA. Annual, with terminal flower clusters on much-branched stems; corolla with long tube and 5 unequal lobes; stamens 2.
CENTRANTHUS (or KENTRANTHUS). Corolla 5-lobed with narrow spurred tube; stamen 1.

FEDIA. F. cornucopiae. A hairless annual up to 30 cm., with branched hollow stems carrying terminal clusters of stalkless long-tubed rose-coloured flowers. Leaves oval and shallowly toothed. ✤ Cultivated ground and sandy places. March–June.   **275**

CENTRANTHUS. C. ruber. RED VALERIAN. A tufted perennial with smooth blue-green leaves and stout erect stems up to 80 cm. high, with flat-topped heads of many small red or sometimes white flowers. ✤ Cliffs and rocks. March–Aug.

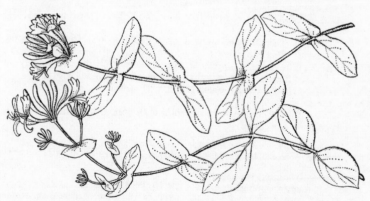

Below: 557 Lonicera etrusca. Above: 558 L. implexa. Both ×½

DIPSACACEAE – Scabious Family

Herbaceous plants with opposite or whorled leaves. Small flowers in dense heads surrounded by calyx-like bracts (involucre). Individual florets each have their own calyx. Corolla fused to form a curved tube.

KNAUTIA. Receptacle to which flowers are attached hairy, hemispherical, without bracts; calyx with 5 spreading bristles.

PTEROCEPHALUS. Receptacle with scales; calyx with 6 or more bristles having plume-like hairs.

SCABIOSA. Receptacle elongated, not hairy, with bracts; calyx with bristles or teeth.

KNAUTIA. *K. integrifolia*. An annual scabious-like plant reaching up to 50 cm. From a basal rosette of deeply cut leaves, slender branched stems carrying small, very narrow leaves, bear flat flowers of pale lilac. ✲ Fields, rocky places, hillsides. April–June.

PTEROCEPHALUS. *P. perennis*. A low-growing tufted perennial, with elliptic or spoon-shaped leaves, shallowly toothed. The rather large pinkish-purple scabious-like flower heads are carried on stems up to 25 cm. high. ✲ Rocky places and cliffs. May–June.

The closely related *P. parnassi* (sometimes technically merged into *P. perennis*) is a mountain plant, tightly tufted, and grey-woolly, with short-stemmed flowers. **276**

SCABIOSA. *S. stellata*. A rough-hairy annual, up to 40 cm. high, with toothed and deeply dissected leaves, and bluish-lilac flowering heads 2–3 cm. across. The hemispherical fruit is covered with large membranous yellow crowns. ✲ Grassy and cultivated ground. April–July.

CAMPANULACEAE – Bellflower Family

Herbs, often with milky juice. Leaves simple and alternate, without stipules. Flowers with bell-shaped or tubular corolla of 5 or more equal lobes. Calyx 5-lobed. Fruit a capsule, or fleshy.

MICHAUXIA. Leaves toothed and lobed; flowers large, reflexed, deeply lobed, on branched stems.

PETROMARULA. Flattened narrow-petalled flowers in long spikes; leaves pinnate.

CAMPANULA. Corolla bell-shaped or funnel-shaped; fruit a capsule, round or ovoid, fused to calyx.

EDRAIANTHUS. Like *Campanula* but capsule splitting irregularly at apex, not base; flowers in terminal head surrounded by leafy bracts.

SYMPHYANDRA. Like *Campanula* but with anthers joined into a tube around the style.

LEGOUSIA. Like *Campanula* but corolla with spreading petals, not bell-shaped; capsule elongated.

MICHAUXIA. *M. campanuloides*. From rosettes of basal leaves, lanceolate and lobed, arise flowering stems up to 2 m. high, branched towards the top, carrying many drooping flowers of white, tinged with purple, with 8–10 long narrow reflexed lobes and long-

projecting style. ✲ Stony and rocky places. Northern mountains. April–July. **277**

PETROMARULA. *P. pinnata*. ROCK LETTUCE. Biennial or perennial, forming basal leaf-rosettes of large oval, deeply divided leaves, with flowering stems up to 1 m. high, carrying spikes of many short-stemmed narrow-petalled blue flowers. ✤ Cliffs and rocks. Crete. May–July. **278**

CAMPANULA. *C. drabifolia.* A frail annual up to 25 cm. high, usually much less, with paired branches and oval, toothed, hairy leaves. Pale violet, bell-shaped 1 cm. flowers with white throats are carried in clusters; the calyx becomes star-like in fruit. ✤ Rocks, dry stony places. April–June. **282**
C. erinus. A softly hairy annual, much branched, making a low slender-stemmed bushy plant up to 25 cm. The oval leaves are toothed, and the 3–5 mm. tubular flowers, almost stalkless, are of a pale whitish-lilac. ✤ Dry stony and grassy places. April–May.
C. oreadum. Forms rosettes of long-spoon-shaped, softly hairy leaves and slender sprawling stems each bearing 1–3 violet-purple open bell-shaped flowers up to 2½ cm. across. ✤ Crevices of limestone rocks and cliffs at alpine levels. Mt Olympus. June–Aug.
C. rupicola is similar, with short round, toothed leaves and often only 1 flower per stem. ✤ Rocks and cliffs. Mountains of C. Greece. June–Aug.
C. patula. SPREADING BELLFLOWER. A slender, branched biennial, 25–60 cm. high, with oblong-lanceolate leaves, and spreading clusters of widely bell-shaped blue-violet flowers, 1½–2½ cm. long. ✤ Pastures, thickets. N. Greece. May–July.
C. pelviformis. A biennial, with spreading 15–30 cm. stems, oval, toothed, rough greyish leaves, and large widely open bell-shaped pale blue flowers in the leaf axils. ✤ Rocks. Crete. May–July.
C. ramosissima. A slender-stemmed annual up to 50 cm. high, with widely open deep blue flowers. Despite its name it is not always branched, but can make a small bush. Leaves hairy, toothed, oval-lanceolate. ✤ Grassy and stony places. April–May. **284**
C. rupestris (including *C. andrewsii, C. celsii, C. lyrata, C. tomentosa, C. topaliana,* etc.). A short-lived perennial. From basal rosettes of soft grey hairy leaves, egg-shaped and more or less deeply lobed, grow radiating stems up

to 30 cm. long, carrying in the leaf axils short-stalked bell-flowers, the corolla sometimes elongated, of varying shades of lavender-blue. Forms of this very variable plant have been given specific or sub-specific rank as the synonyms above suggest, but it is doubtful whether they can be considered botanically valid since so many intermediates exist. *Ssp. anchusaeflora* is noteworthy for very long, tubular, deep violet-blue flowers. ✤ Rocks, cliffs, and stony ground. March–June.
280, 281
C. spathulata. 25–50 cm. tall, with swollen root, angular stems, smooth spoon-shaped leaves, and 1–5 stalked, erect 2–3 cm. flowers of violet blue carried on rather weak flowering stems. ✤ Stony places, thickets, up to alpine levels. June–Sept. **283**
C. versicolor. With rosettes of smooth, toothed, ovate leaves, and tall un-branched flowering stems up to 1½ m. high, carrying sprays of bicoloured saucer-shaped flowers in the leaf axils, deep blue in their centre, shading to bluish-white at the edge. ✤ Rocky places, thickets, usually in shade. Lower mountain zones. N. Greece, Corfu. June–Sept. **279**

EDRAIANTHUS. *E. parnassicus.* Resembling a campanula, this small perennial forms rosettes of narrow leaves, and 10–30 cm. flowering stems carrying terminal tight clusters of small violet-blue bell-shaped flowers. ✤ Rocky slopes in the mountains. June–August.

SYMPHYANDRA. *S. cretica.* From basal tufts of smooth, deeply toothed, hairless bright green leaves, rise 50 cm. spikes of large, rather narrow white or pale blue bells. ✤ A shade-loving gorge plant. Crete. June–August.

LEGOUSIA. *L. speculum-veneris* (*Specularia speculum*). VENUS'S LOOK-ING GLASS. A slender, tightly branched annual up to 40 cm. high, with stalk-less oblong leaves, sparsely hairy and carries terminal clusters of large widely open 10–20 mm. violet-blue flowers. ✤ Cultivated ground and waste places. April–July. **286**
L. pentagonia. Like *L. speculum-veneris,*

but with larger flowers up to 3 cm. across, and with the corolla lobes spreading in star-like shape. ✤ Cornfields, waste places. April–July. **285**

COMPOSITAE – Daisy Family

A very large family, mostly of herbaceous plants, often with milky juice, and with leaves in a variety of forms. Stipules absent. Flowers in a distinctive head made up of many small flowers (florets) and surrounded by bracts (involucre), both being attached to the swollen end of the stalk. The florets may all be similar, or divided into inner disc florets with short tubular corollas, and outer ray-florets with long strap-like corollas. The calyx of each floret may be represented by scales or teeth, or by simple or feathery hairs (pappus). Fruit with or without a pappus.

TOLPIS. Involucral bracts in 1 or 2 rows, narrow and spreading; ray florets only present, strap-shaped.

CREPIS. Involucral bracts unequal, in single row; ray florets only present, strap-shaped; fruit ribbed, with or without beak; pappus white.

SCOLYMUS. Several rows of involucral bracts, the outer leaf-like and spiny-tipped; ray florets only present, strap-shaped.

CICHORIUM. Flower heads blue; ray florets only present, strap-shaped; involucral bracts in 2 rows.

TRAGOPOGON. Leaves narrow and simple with parallel veins; involucral bracts in single row and joined at base; ray florets only present, all strap-shaped; fruit with long beak surrounded by feathery pappus.

SCORZONERA. Like *Tragopogon* but with many rows of overlapping bracts. Fruit not beaked. Pappus of several rows of hairs.

ECHINOPS. Leaves and stem spiny; flower heads grouped in spherical clusters; each individual floret surrounded by spiny bracts.

CARTHAMUS. Outer involucral bracts leaf-like and spiny tipped; inner with papery edges. Disc florets only present. Pappus scaly.

CENTAUREA. Outer involucral bracts with papery edges, often fringed, or with spines; disc florets only present, outer often spreading and sterile; pappus absent or of unbranched hairs.

ONOPORDUM. Solitary large flower heads with prominent spreading or recurved spiny-tipped involucral bracts; disc florets only present.

CARDOPATIUM. Small flower heads in dense leafy flat-topped clusters; disc florets only present; involucral bracts in several rows with comb-like spiny teeth.

SILYBUM. Flower heads large and solitary; involucral bracts long, recurved and spiny tipped; disc florets only present.

TYRIMNUS. Like *Galactites* (below) but with spiny-winged stems.

ATRACTYLIS. Involucre bell-shaped or cylindrical, of several rows; the outer leaf-like and cut into spiny teeth, the inner with papery tips; disc florets only present.

GALACTITES. Disc florets only present but outer sterile florets large and spreading; pappus long and feathery; leaves white-cottony below, often mottled white above.

NOTOBASIS. Flower heads surrounded by involucre of deeply dissected spiny leaves; disc florets only present, the outer sterile; pappus of inner florets feathery, outer of hairs.

136

XERANTHEMUM. Involucral bracts papery, the inner brightly coloured; disc florets only present.
CIRSIUM. Involucral bracts many, overlapping and spiny-tipped; disc florets only present; pappus of branched feathery hairs.
CHAMAEPEUCE. Like *Cirsium*, but fruits almost as broad as long; leaves narrow, simple, dark green above, white-felted beneath.
CRUPINA. Flower heads narrow, with papery involucral bracts, not spiny; disc florets only present; leaves not spiny.
ANTHEMIS. Flower heads solitary, with both disc florets and, usually, white ray florets; leaves cut into narrow segments. Pappus absent.
OTANTHUS. Involucre of many overlapping woolly bracts; only disc florets present; corolla tube forming 2 spurs at base.
SENECIO. Involucral bracts green and leafy, usually in one row; both ray and disc florets usually present.
EVAX. Flowerheads stalkless, very small, forming a single rosette with the numerous individual bracts. Disc florets only present.
PHAGNOLON. Leaves white-woolly, with edges inrolled; flower heads usually solitary; involucral bracts papery, often brownish; disc florets only present.
HELICHRYSUM. Leaves white-woolly, with edges inrolled; involucre often coloured and papery; disc florets only present.
PALLENIS. Flower heads with both disc and ray florets present; involucre of 2–3 rows of spiny-tipped bracts.
CALENDULA. Ray florets in 2–3 rows; fruits large, often curved; pappus absent.
DORONICUM. Flower heads large; ray florets large in single row, strap-shaped; disc florets also present; fruit usually with pappus; leaves alternate.
INULA. Flower heads solitary or few in branched flat-topped clusters; both disc and ray florets present.
CHRYSANTHEMUM. Flower heads usually large, ray florets sometimes present; fruit without pappus.

TOLPIS. ***T. barbata.*** A branched annual to 40 cm., with narrow toothed and hairy leaves, and golden flowers which are often dark-centred, surrounded by long threadlike bracts. ⚘ Dry sandy places. May–July. **287**

CREPIS. ***C. incana.*** Unlike most species of this genus, which have yellow flowers, this has 3–4 cm. pink flowers, carried singly on stems to 15 cm. The plot forms low tufts of grey-hairy leaves, narrow and lobed. ⚘ Rocky places. Northern mountains. May–July. **288**
C. rubra. PINK HAWKSBEARD. Another pink-flowered species, with 4 cm. flowers carried on simple or branched stems up to 30 cm. high. Leaves long, narrow, hairy, green, and deeply toothed. ⚘ Thickets, olive groves, rocky slopes. April–June.

SCOLYMUS. ***S. hispanicus.*** SPANISH OYSTER PLANT. A thistle-like plant growing up to 80 cm., with spiny, hairy stems with discontinuous wings. The very spiny leaves are deeply cut and wavy-edged. The golden, stalkless flowers are carried in the leaf axils up the stems and are encircled by 3 spiny bracts. ⚘ Waste and sandy places. May–Aug. **289**
Cultivated since ancient times for its edible tap-root, like the Salsify, Tragopogon porrifolius. *Theophrastus says it can be eaten raw or cooked, and Dioscorides that the growth 'new come up' serves as a potherb. Of the roots he says that it 'is good for such as have the arme pits and the rest of ye body of a rank smell'. The yellow petals have been used to adulterate saffron.*
S. maculatus. Similar to *S. hispanicus*, but stem continuously winged; these

wings, like the leaf margins, have thick white borders. Flowers grouped at ends of branches. ⚘ Stony, rocky places. May–Aug.

CICHORIUM. ***C. intybus.*** CHICORY. A perennial to 1 m., with stiff green stems, lance-shaped leaves, entire or deeply lobed, and 2½–4 cm. clear bright blue flower heads. ⚘ Waste ground, roadsides, on limestone. June–Sept.
The thick roots, dried and powdered, are made into a coffee substitute, often used with real coffee in 'Continental' blends. The vegetable chicory is produced by forcing the stored roots and blanching the resulting foliage. The unblanched leaves are sometimes eaten; this is one of the 'bitter herbs' eaten with the paschal lamb. Dioscorides recommended it to comfort 'a crazie and burning stomach'. Also considered an aphrodisiac, and to be beneficial to cattle in pastures.
C. spinosum. A low-growing, much branched spiny shrub, growing to 30 cm. or less. The blue-green leaves are narrow, and the light blue flowers, carried singly, are composed of only up to 6 florets. ⚘ A sea shore plant, among shingle and on sea cliffs. May–July. **290**

TRAGOPOGON. ***T. porrifolius.*** SALSIFY, GOAT'S BEARD. An annual or biennial with narrow grass-like leaves, and stems of up to 75 cm. bearing purplish flowers backed by green bracts extending beyond the flower heads, which turn in seed into large spherical 'clocks'. ⚘ Dry waste places, field edges, and roadsides. March–May. **293**
The long tap roots are regarded as a choice vegetable. Theophrastus named it Goat's Beard in allusion to the woolly aspect of the fruiting head before it finally opens.

SCORZONERA. ***S. purpurea.*** PURPLE VIPER-GRASS. Resembles *Tragopogon*, but with the flower bracts numerous, in overlapping rows. A hairless perennial, up to 45 cm. high, with narrow-keeled leaves, and solitary pale purple flowers. ⚘ Grassy and rocky places. May–June. **292**
S. hispanica. BLACK SALSIFY. A yellow-flowered species, usually branched, growing up to 1 m. high, with oval or linear leaves. ⚘ Grassy and rocky places. May–Sept.
Long cultivated for its edible tap roots; also used medicinally.
S. lanata (including ***S. sublanata***) is similar but grey-woolly, with pale yellow flowers. **291**

ECHINOPS. ***E. graecus.*** To 1 m. tall. Leaves dark green, deeply divided into narrow segments ending in fine points, and armed with sharp spines radiating in all directions. The large rounded heads are a pale amethyst. ⚘ Stony and waste places. July–Oct. **295**
E. ritro. GLOBE THISTLE. A stiff perennial 20–100 cm. high, with deeply cut and very spiny leaves, green above and white-cottony below. The branched stems carry large terminal clusters of rounded, pale or bright blue flower heads. ⚘ Stony and rocky ground. June–Sept. **296**
E. sphaerocephalus. PALE GLOBE THISTLE. Like *E. ritro*, but leaves lanceolate, deeply lobed, and not as spiny. Usually taller, with larger flower heads of a pale whitish blue. ⚘ Stony places, waste ground. N. Greece. June–Sept.
E. viscosus. Grows up to 1½ m., with glandular-hairy stems, and large heads of pale blue flowers. ⚘ Dry stony places near the sea. W. Greece, Ionian islands, Crete. June–Sept.

CARTHAMUS. ***C. lanatus*** (***Centrophyllum lanatum***). An annual up to 60 cm. with oval, sticky, and hairy leaves, deeply lobed and spiny toothed. The golden-yellow flower heads are surrounded by very spiny bracts and cobwebby hairs. Plant rank-smelling, with reddish sap. ⚘ Dry hills, waste ground, track sides. May–Aug. **294**

CENTAUREA. ***C. cyanus.*** CORNFLOWER, BLUEBOTTLE. An annual to 30–60 cm., with narrow grey-green hairy leaves. Flowers on long stalks, solitary, with outer bright blue florets much larger than central purplish ones. ⚘ Cornfields and other cultivated ground. May–Aug.
Once a common cornfield weed in

Britain. Much cultivated in multi-coloured strains.

C. calcitrapa. STAR THISTLE. A much-branched perennial or biennial up to 50 cm., with purple flower heads surrounded by green bracts with long yellow spines. The leaves are green and deeply lobed, the upper leaves being toothed. ⚘ Waste ground and stony places. Aug.–Sept.   **559**

559 Centaurea calcitrapa × ⅔

C. mixta. A low-growing knapweed with rosettes of pinnately lobed green leaves, and several red-purple flowers almost stalkless in the centre. ⚘ Rocky places, often in the mountains. May–July.   **297**

C. solstitialis. ST BARNABY'S THISTLE. A white-hairy, slender, branched annual thistle, up to 60 cm., with the lower leaves lobed and toothed, upper leaves narrow and spiny-tipped. The solitary yellow flower heads are surrounded by bracts with long yellow spines. ⚘ Fields and waste ground. May–Aug.   **298**

ONOPORDUM. *O. acanthium.* SCOTCH THISTLE. A biennial growing to 1½–2 m., white-felted, with stout winged stems and branched flowering stems carrying solitary pale purple flowers. Leaves elliptic, spiny, and shallowly lobed. ⚘ Waste land, roadsides. June–Sept.

O. illyricum. A white-felted biennial thistle up to 1½ m. with branching, winged stems and leaves deeply cut into narrow spiny lobes; the large purple flower heads, 3–4 cm. across, are solitary, with narrow purplish bracts, ending in recurved spines. ⚘ Stony and waste places at lower levels. July–Aug.

O. myriacanthum. Very similar to *O. illyricum* but the bracts around the flower head are much larger (1½–2 cm.) and broader, so that the heads look rather like miniature globe artichokes. ⚘ Stony places, usually in the hills and mountains. July–Aug.   **299**

CARDOPATIUM. *C. corymbosum.* A branched, spreading perennial up to 20 cm., with deeply cut leaves of many spiny lobes. Blue flower heads in rounded spiny clusters, surrounded by spiny leaves. Resembles an *Echinops* at first sight. ⚘ Grassy and sandy places on the coast. July–Aug.   **300**
This was known as black chameleon (in contrast to Atractylis *gummifera) because of 'ye divers colours in ye leaves'. Dioscorides recommended a root decoction especially for toothache.*

SILYBUM. *S. marianum.* HOLY THISTLE, MILK THISTLE. A biennial ½–1½ m. high, with branched flowering stems carrying large solitary rosy purple flowers surrounded by wide, sharp-pointed tracts. The green leaves, mottled or veined with white, are deeply lobed, with spiny margins, making large overwintering rosettes the first year. ⚘ Waste ground and roadsides. June–Aug.   **301**
The young leaves, leaf midribs and young stems are often eaten as salad, or picked and eaten by the wayside, especially in Turkey and Arab countries. It was once grown as a salad plant in Britain. The English names refer to the white markings on the leaves, reputed to have been caused by drops of the Holy Virgin's milk when she was feeding Jesus.

TYRIMNUS. *T. leucographus.* A white-cottony plant with long-stemmed purplish-pink flowers, spiny-winged stems and spiny-toothed, white-spotted, lance-shaped leaves, white-cottony below. ⚘ Sandy and stony places, waste ground. May–Aug.

ATRACTYLIS. *A. cancellata.* A slender thistle up to 25 cm. high, with long, narrow, soft, hairy leaves, with long bristly hairs on the margins. The small purple flower heads are surrounded by very distinctive curved bracts cut into comb-like segments. ☘ Dry stony places, often in the hills. April–July.
560

560 Atractylis cancellata × 1

A. gummifera. PINE-THISTLE. A striking flat-growing thistle with a tight leaf rosette and solitary 3–7 cm. purplish flowerheads in the centre, surrounded by spiny bracts, the inner red-tipped. ☘ Field and track margins. July–Sept. *The root is edible but, according to Theophrastus, fatal to dogs and pigs. He calls it 'white chameleon' and 'if one wishes to discover whether a man that is sick will recover they say that he should be washed with this [a mixture in wine] for three days, and, if he survives the experience, he will recover'.*

GALACTITES. *G. tomentosa.* A slender-stemmed annual or biennial, up to 60 cm. high, with ovoid heads of pinkish flowers and narrow, deeply dissected spiny leaves, white-hairy below and green with white streaks above. ☘ Dry, uncultivated, or sandy places. April–July.
302

NOTOBASIS. *N. syriaca.* An annual thistle, with finely dissected spiny green leaves streaked with silvery-white, the stem leaves clasping the stem; the clustered heads of purple flowers, which reach a height of up to 60 cm., are surrounded by a circle of long narrow, spiny, purple-tipped bracts. ☘ Waste land, roadsides, field edges. March–May.
303
Despite its handsome colouring this plant shares with other thistles the derogatory Greek word meaning 'donkey-thistle'.

XERANTHEMUM. *X. annuum.* PINK EVERLASTING. A slender white-woolly annual up to 40 cm., with narrow leaves and smallish, solitary globular flower heads. The individual bracts are papery, the outer ones being silvery-brown, the inner longer, spreading, and of a clear pink. ☘ Rocky, stony places. June–Aug.
304
X. inapertum is similar to *X. annuum* but with cylindrical flower heads, and whitish or brownish bracts of which the inner are not spreading but erect. ☘ Dry places. June–Aug.
X. foetidum is another similar species but with the outer flower bracts hairy on the back and the inner bracts pink, erect, and hairless. ☘ Dry places. June–Aug.

CIRSIUM. *C. candelabrum.* One of the most spectacular of all thistles, growing pyramidally up to 2 m., with rather narrow, deeply lobed, and very spiny leaves, and many lateral branches carrying small yellow flower heads in branched clusters. ☘ Stony and rocky places in the mountains. May–Aug.
308
C. acarna (Picnomon acarna). A very spiny white-woolly thistle, with dense clusters of purple flowers surrounded by narrow bracts ending in slender yellow fringed spines. Stem with broad spiny wings, and leaves narrow and with strong yellow spines. ☘ Stony and rocky places. June–Aug.
309

CHAMAEPEUCE. *C. mutica.* A subshrub up to 1 m. high, with many stems carrying long narrow simple leaves, smooth and dark green above, white-woolly beneath, the edges inrolled. The rather large pinkish-purple flowers are carried in branched clusters. ☘ Cliffs and rocky hillsides. May–June.
310

Recommended by Dioscorides 'for ye griefs of ye loins'.

CRUPINA. *C. crupinastrum.* An annual, thistle-like, but soft and spineless, up to 70 cm. high, with narrow leaves, sparsely segmented, and slender branches bearing narrow cylindrical purple flowers. ⚜ Dry, uncultivated places. April–June.

ANTHEMIS. *A. chia.* GREEK CHAMOMILE. Annual, rather spreading, up to 30 cm. The deeply segmented leaves are bright green, and the white daisylike flowers are carried on littlebranched stems. ⚜ On cultivated and fallow ground, and among grass, often in immense numbers.　　　**305**
Often picked by the Greeks to dry and make into chamomile tea. Dioscorides mentions a number of soothing herbal uses.
A. cretica (A. pusilla). A branched, semi-prostrate annual with almost hairless leaves, segmented or shallowly lobed. Flower heads small, consisting of a rounded yellow disc, ray florets usually absent. ⚜ Coastal sands and shingles. Crete and the Cyclades. March–May.　　　**306**
A. tomentosa. Low-growing and densely white-woolly. The 2–3 cm. flowers have white ray florets and wide orange centre of disc florets, and are carried on 10–15 cm. high stems. ⚜ Sandy beaches, shingle, hillsides by the sea. Feb.–April.　　　**307**

OTANTHUS. *O. maritimus (Diotis maritima, D. candidissima).* A branched, spreading perennial, growing up to 40 cm., the whole plant silvery white-felted; the stalkless leaves are oblong or spoon-shaped, and the small short-stalked and rounded yellow flower heads are carried in flat-topped clusters, surrounded by oval whitefelted bracts. ⚜ Coastal sands. June–Sept.　　　**311**
Once used for treating kidney troubles, blood-spitting, and inflammations.

SENECIO. *S. cineraria (Cineraria maritima).* A shrubby perennial up to 70 cm. high, densely white-felted, with deeply segmented leaves and branched flattish heads of yellow flowers with white-woolly bracts. ⚜ Rocks and stony places. June–Aug.
A familiar garden plant.

EVAX. *E. pygmaea (Filago pygmaea).* A dwarf white-woolly annual, up to 4 cm. high but usually flat, with obovate leaves forming white rosettes around the stemless flowerheads. Flowers small, yellowish, with pointed yellow bracts. ⚜ Sandy places, grass, phrygana, near the coast. April–May.　**312**

PHAGNOLON. *P. rupestre.* A small sub-shrub up to 30 cm. high, with white-woolly stems, narrow hairy leaves, and heads about 1 cm. long of brownish-yellow rounded flowers surrounded by shiny brown papery bracts. The plant usually seen in Greece is *ssp. graecum.* ⚜ Rocky and stony places. April–June.　　　**313**

HELICHRYSUM. *H. siculum.* A white-woolly perennial with woody base and many erect stems up to 30 cm. high. The narrow leaves have inrolled margins, and the light yellow flowers are carried in tight terminal clusters. The yellow, papery bracts are 'everlasting'. ⚜ Very dry, stony places. April–Aug.　　　**314**

PALLENIS. *P. spinosa.* A branched annual, up to 50 cm., with lanceshaped leaves, and 2 cm. yellow flowers backed by long, narrow, stiff, channelled green bracts, spiny-tipped, extending star-like beyond the width of the flower. ⚜ Stony waste places, olive groves, and vineyards. March–June.　　　**315**

CALENDULA. *C. arvensis.* FIELD MARIGOLD. Annual, 10–30 cm. tall, with soft rather hairy stems. The oblong leaves are stalkless, sometimes toothed and half embracing the stem. The solitary orange flowers are 1–2 cm. across. The bristly fruit is sickle- or boat-shaped. ⚜ Fields, vineyards, olive groves, grassy places. April–Oct.　**316**

DORONICUM. *D. caucasicum.* LEOPARD'S-BANE. Perennial to 30 cm., with basal leaves smooth and kidneyshaped, and stem leaves ovate and clasping the stem. The large yellow flowers are carried singly on slender stems. ⚕ Rocky mountainsides in full sun. March–May. **317**

'Leopard's-bane' because anciently believed to kill such animals: 'it kills both Panthers and Sowes, and wolves, and all wild beasts, being put into gobbets of flesh, and given to them' (Dioscorides). Also, to quote Theophrastus, 'it is fatal to oxen sheep beasts of burden . . . and kills them the same day if the root or leaf is put on the genitals'. Because the root supposedly looked like a scorpion, it was deemed useful both against the creature itself and its sting – an early example of the doctrine of signatures.

D. columnae. Resembles *D. caucasicum* but up to 60 cm. tall, with long-stalked basal leaves of a triangular heart-shape. ⚕ Rocky places in the mountains. May–July. **318**

INULA. *I. candida.* A completely silvery, much-branched plant, 10–20 cm. with stalked spoon-shaped leaves and flat-topped sprays of small lemon-yellow flowers. ⚕ Rocky crevices, stony ground. May–July. **320**

The seeds, pounded and made into an ointment, were recommended by Dioscorides to 'keep ye face extended and without wrinkles'. Also a cough cure.

I. viscosa. A woody-based plant reaching 50–100 cm., very leafy, sticky and rank-smelling, with many stems growing to a height of about 1 m. and carrying long sprays of small yellow flowers in leafy clusters. ⚕ Very much a weed, in waste places, stony fields, and on hillsides. Sept.–Nov. **319**

The rank smell was supposed to keep away wild beasts, likewise fleas – the modern Greek name can be translated 'flea-bane'.

CHRYSANTHEMUM. *C. coronarium.* CROWN DAISY. Annual, 50–80 cm. high, with deeply-cut smooth leaves and 5–6 cm. bright yellow flowers, sometimes with a paler outer zone to the ray florets (*var. discolor*). ⚕ Waste places, by roadsides, cultivated fields, sometimes a crop weed. March–June.

322, 323

The stalks were eaten as a pot-herb in ancient times. John Goodyer adds to Dioscorides' words, 'if you take it out of ye earth before the arising of the sun, and bind it to your body and hang it about the neck, doth good, averting the women witches, and all enchantments'. Widely grown in gardens today in many colour forms.

C. segetum. CORN MARIGOLD. Annual, up to 60 cm. high, with smooth bluish leaves, the upper leaves half-circling the stem, the lower leaves stalked and coarsely toothed. The bright yellow flowers are 2½–4 cm. across. ⚕ Fields, cultivated ground, waste places. Often a serious cornfield weed. April–Aug.

321

Monocotyledons

LILIACEAE – Lily Family

Usually herbaceous plants, often with underground bulbs, corms, or rhizomes; leaves alternate, in whorls, or basal, often entire. Flowers regular with parts in threes, and with two similar petal-like whorls. Stamens 6. Ovary 3-celled, superior. Fruit a capsule or berry.

VERATRUM. Robust perennials with thick rootstock and broad-veined leaves in whorls of 3; flowers in branched terminal clusters; perianth segments spreading.

MERENDERA. Close to Colchicum (below), but perianth segments not fused below.

COLCHICUM. Petals united in tube; flowers basal; corms.

ASPHODELUS. Leaves basal; leafless flower stems simple or branched, with flowers in terminal spikes or clusters; petals all similar; roots tuberous.

ASPHODELINE. Stems leafy; flowers with lowest petal narrower than the rest, and somewhat separated; rhizomatous.

ANTHERICUM. Flowers white, petals spreading, 3–5-veined; with perennial rootstock.

GAGEA (including **LLOYDIA**). Flowers small, yellow or white, solitary or in terminal clusters; bulbs.

ALLIUM. Plants smelling of garlic; stalked flowers in clusters at end of stem; flower clusters enclosed in papery sheath while in bud; bulbs.

LILIUM. Large flowers, usually in loose clusters, with funnel-shaped perianth, sometimes recurving; style long with 3-lobed stigma; bulb formed of overlapping scales.

FRITILLARIA. Flowers often large and solitary; corolla bell-shaped and drooping, often chequered; flower stems leafy; bulbs.

TULIPA. Flowers solitary, large, erect; corolla bell-shaped; stems leafy at base; bulbs.

URGINEA. Flowers in long leafless spikes; corolla spreading; bulbs very large.

SCILLA. Flowers blue or lilac in clusters or spikes; corolla bell-shaped or spreading; petals with dark mid-vein; leaves broad; bulbs.

CHIONODOXA. Closely related to *Scilla*, distinguished by perianth segments fused at base.

ORNITHOGALUM. Flowers usually white lined with green, in clusters; leaves basal; bulbs.

HYACINTHUS. Flowers in spike; corolla funnel-shaped and fused at base, with lobes spreading and reflexed; leaves basal; bulbs.

STRANGWEIA. Like *Hyacinthus* but much smaller; anthers blue, their filaments joined into a cup around the ovary.

BELLEVALIA. Flowers in loose spike; corolla bell-shaped or tubular, not constricted at mouth, with 6 lobes; bulbs.

MUSCARI. Corolla bell-shaped or oval, constricted at mouth, with 6 short teeth; flowers in dense clusters, the upper flowers often smaller and sterile; bulbs.

ASPARAGUS. Woody or herbaceous plants, with stout rootstock, leaves reduced to scales, and branchlets needle-like, clustered, and green; flowers one-sexed with small bell-shaped corolla; fruit a berry.

143

POLYGONATUM. With leafy stems and flowers carried in leaf axils; perianth tubular with 6 short lobes; rhizomatous.

RUSCUS. Evergreen shrubs; branches flattened into leaf-like blades bearing flowers and fruits on one face; fruit a red berry.

SMILAX. Hooked woody climbing plants with heart-shaped leaves and tendrils arising from leaf bases; flowers in clusters; corolla bell-shaped with spreading segments.

VERATRUM. *V. album.* WHITE FALSE HELLEBORINE. A bold plant with large broad and deeply ridged oval leaves, and branched flowering stems up to 1½ m. carrying sprays of small greenish-yellow flowers. ⚘ Mountain pastures in the North. July–Aug.

V. nigrum is generally similar, with narrow blackish flower spikes. ⚘ Mountain woods and fields. July–Aug.

The ancient authors call veratrums 'hellebore'. V. album seems to have been the favoured species. Dioscorides has a long list of its uses, including as emetic, abortifacient, provoker of sneezes, and mouse-killer. Also, he says, 'it is made like wheat into bread'. Theophrastus writes 'The people of Mount Oeta gather it for the meetings of the Amphictyons' – which apparently included markets. He adds that at Elea it 'grows in the vineyards and makes the wine so diuretic that those who drink it become quite emaciated'.

MERENDERA. *M. attica.* The narrow-petalled star-shaped flowers are pink, and open almost flat on the ground. The leaves are narrow and appear after the flower. Related to *M. montana* of W. Europe, and may be only a geographical variant. ⚘ Stony hills; sometimes down to sea level. September.

COLCHICUM

Autumn-flowering

C. autumnale. MEADOW SAFFRON, AUTUMN CROCUS. The pale purple crocus-like flowers, 1 to 5 from one corm, have 10–25 cm. stalk-like tubes. Stigmas orange, curved; stamens attached to petals at 2 different levels. Leaves very large (20–30 cm.), glossy, appearing in spring around the 3–5 cm. seed capsule. ⚘ Damp meadows. Aug.–Sept. **324**

A very poisonous plant, which has been used in treating gout and rheumatic disorders. The ancients knew of its properties – 'it killeth by choking like to ye mushrumps', says Dioscorides. At the same time, 'it is strangely alluring to ye inexperienced for ye pleasantness', and he gives a description to avoid confusion with the favoured Bulbos or muscari. Theophrastus says that 'slaves often take meadow-saffron when greatly provoked, and then have recourse to the antidote'. The constituent colchicine has in modern times been important in plant breeding.

C. boissieri. Flowers with segments to 4 cm. long, tube 2–4 cm., of deep clear pink. Leaves appearing later, short and narrow. ⚘ Screes and stony ground in the mountains, especially Mt Taygetos, up to 1,500 m. Sept.–Oct. **325**

C. bowlesianum. Flowers very large, up to 15 cm. tall, egg-shaped, of a rosy-lilac, tessellated with purple markings. Leaves appearing later, erect, up to 30 cm. long and 3 cm. broad. ⚘ Grassy, stony hillsides, hedges. N. Greece. Oct.–Nov.

C. cupanii. Flowers small, starry, to 2 cm. long, rosy lilac with brown anthers. The paired, very narrow 2–6 cm. green leaves appear at the same time. ⚘ Rocky places in the hills and mountains, up to 1,000 m. Oct.–Nov. **326**

C. macrophyllum. Flowers funnel-shaped, with 2–3 cm. broad segments 6–7 cm. long, pale pink or lilac, lightly chequered. The leaves appear in spring, and are enormous, up to 50 cm. long and 15 cm. wide, with longitudinal pleats, reminding one of *Veratrum.* ⚘ Fields, or open glades among conifers. Crete and Rhodes. Oct.–Nov. **327, 328**

C. sibthorpii (*C. latifolium*). Rather like *C. bowlesianum.* Flowers up to 15 cm. high, segments to 6 cm. rosy lilac with darker chequering. Leaves appear late, long and broad. ❧ Stony places in the low mountains. Oct. **329**

C. variegatum. Distinguished by its strongly tessellated, flattish flowers of pinkish-purple up to 8 cm. across, its pointed petals, and its short, broad, bluish-green, prostrate, wavy-edged leaves which appear in the spring. ❧ Rocks, dry banks, and among scrub. E. Aegean islands. Sept.–Nov. **331**

Spring-flowering

C. catacuzenium (**C. triphyllum**). With clusters of small globular rosy lilac 2–3 cm. flowers with black anthers. The 3 narrow, channelled leaves appear with the flowers. ❧ Stony places as the snow melts. Mountains of C. and S. Greece. March–April. **330**
The colchicums known as C. ancyrense, C. biebersteinii, *and* C. bulbocodioides *are now considered the same as* C. catacuzenium, *a species with a very wide range and hence described separately several times.*

ASPHODELUS. *A. albus.* WHITE ASPHODEL. A strong-growing perennial up to 1 m., with clumps of rush-like keeled leaves, and leafless, usually unbranched flowering stems carrying stout terminal spikes of white flowers with brownish stripes. Bracts brown. ❧ Stony open hill and mountain slopes in N. Greece. April–August.
332
Although often indicating overgrazed land, because not usually eaten by animals, the asphodel is rich in starch and, as Theophrastus writes, 'provides many things useful for food: the stalk is edible when fried, the seed when roasted, and above all the root when cut up with figs'. Atchley records that this ancient use was remembered during the First World War. Asphodel was sometimes planted around graves because the roots were thought to nourish the spirits of the dead. Dioscorides gives a varied list of medicinal uses.
A. fistulosus. A delicate plant only reaching about 50 cm. It has narrow hollowed leaves, and simple or branched heads of small pinkish flowers with darker veins. ❧ Sandy and stony places. March–June. **333**
This is probably the Asphodel of the Elysian Fields – the home of the dead in Greek mythology. The Common Asphodel seems too coarse for this locality!
A. microcarpus. COMMON ASPHODEL. A stout plant with long, narrow swordlike leaves, and much-branched stem reaching up to 1½ m., each branch bearing a pyramidal head of brownveined white flowers. ❧ Dry, rocky places. March–June. **334**

ASPHODELINE. *A. lutea.* YELLOW ASPHODEL. Differs from *Asphodelus* in having the 1 m. high unbranched stem densely clothed with leaves. The golden-yellow flowers are carried in a densely packed terminal spike on 1 m. stems. ❧ Stony and rocky places, often in the hills and mountains. April–May. **335**
A. liburnica. Like *A. lutea*, but with the flowering stem bearing very narrow leaves for only the lower two-thirds of the flowering spike; also generally more slender. ❧ Bushy places, hillsides. May–June.

ANTHERICUM. *A. liliago.* ST BERNARD'S LILY. A graceful lily-like plant carrying pure white flowers on slender stems of up to 50 cm. The narrow leaves arise from a basal rosette. ❧ Sunny dry mountain slopes in the North. May–June.

GAGEA. *G. fistulosa.* Leaves basal, bright green, rush-like, channelled and hollow. Flowers in clusters of 1–5, golden tinged with green on the petal reverse. Stems 3–10 cm. ❧ Rocky slopes of hills and mountains. Jan.–April. **342**
G. graeca (**Lloydia graeca**). Like a miniature lily 4–15 cm. tall, with drooping clusters of 2–6 bell-shaped flowers, 10–15 mm. long, white streaked finely with purple. Leaves narrow and grass-like. ❧ Stony, dry places, rock crevices. March–April.
343
G. lutea. YELLOW STAR OF BETHLEHEM. Loose terminal clusters of 1–7 bright yellow starry flowers, striped with green on the petal reverse, grow on stems up to 25 cm. high. Leaves flat, narrow, ribbed, and hairless. ❧ Grassy and shady places. April–May.
G. arvensis is like *G. lutea*, but with

145

the bracts of the flower heads longer and very hairy. Flowers 1–12. Basal leaves 2, flat and grooved. ✲ Fields, olive groves, and vineyards. Feb.– April. **341**

ALLIUM. *A. ampeloprasum.* WILD LEEK, GREAT ROUND-HEADED GARLIC. With stout stem to 1 m. high, leafy up to half its height, and carrying 7–10 cm. globular heads of pinkish-lilac flowers. Leaves flattish, 1–3½ cm. wide, with rough edges and keeled midrib. ✲ Dry places, banks, and hedges. June–July. **355**

A. neapolitanum. NAPLES GARLIC. Strong 60 cm. stems, triangular in section, carry heads of 20–40 pure white cup-shaped flowers with rounded petals. Leaves basal, 2–3, flat, 1–3 cm. broad. ✲ Stony places, fields, and olive groves. March–May.

A. roseum. ROSE GARLIC. Rounded flower heads on stems up to 50 cm. carry up to 20 flowers of a pale rose colour; miniature bulbs sometimes among the flowers. Leaves basal, 4–10 mm. broad, finely toothed at the margins. ✲ Grassy places, roadsides, vineyards. April–June. **357**

A. sphaerocephalon. ROUND-HEADED LEEK. With 2–2½ cm. globular dark purple flower heads carried on stems up to 1 m. high. ✲ Dry, sandy, and rocky places. May–July. **358**

A. subhirsutum. Not unlike *S. neapolitanum,* up to 50 cm. high, with spreading heads of white starry flowers with pink anthers. Leaves 2–3, soft and broad, hairy at the margins, carried on the stems. ✲ Stony and rocky places, woods. March–May. **356**

Garlics of various kinds have been used for flavouring, medicinally, and for eating since ancient times. In principle they were believed to encourage good health.

LILIUM. *L. albanicum.* A graceful lily up to 75 cm. high, carrying 1–4 recurved 'turk's-cap' flowers of unspotted amber-yellow with reddish anthers. ✲ Open woods, rocky slopes. Hills of Epirus and Macedonia. May–June.

L. candidum. MADONNA LILY. Leafy 1 m. stems carry a few large funnel-shaped flowers of pure white. ✲ Dry stony slopes, thickets, in Epirus,

Peloponnese, and the Eastern Aegean islands. A true native of Greece. May–July. **336**

The Madonna lily is the most frequent floral motif of Minoan art. It symbolised grace and purity from early days, and both Greeks and Romans placed wreaths of lilies and corn on the heads of those being married at the appropriate season, as emblems of virginity and fertility, just as today lilies are often carried by brides. Later on, of course, the white lily became a symbol of religious purity to the Christians. In Crete the lily was sacred to Britomartis, the 'sweet virgin'. Pursued by Minos, she leapt into the sea, where she was saved from drowning in a fisherman's nets and afterwards became both Dictynna, 'mother of the nets', and the Mother Goddess. To later Greeks the lily was the flower of Hera, who was among other things goddess of marriage and childbirth, as was Juno to the Romans. This sanctity gave the flower a positive magical power against witches and evil: Judith wore a wreath of lilies when she killed the Assyrian general Holofernes.

The juice, or an ointment made from the pounded bulb, was early recognised as soothing for skin ailments and, beaten up with honey as a face-pack, to remove wrinkles.

L. chalcedonicum. A brilliant scarlet lily with up to 10 flowers on stems up to 1 m.; the narrow leaves have silvery edges and grow on the lower part of the stems. ✲ Woodland clearings on mountains. June–Aug. **338**

Another floral motif of Minoan art.

L. heldreichii is probably only a form of *L. chalcedonicum,* very vigorous, the flowers tomato-red with broad wavy petals. ✲ Woodland. Mt Olympos and mountains of C. Greece and Peloponnese. **339**

L. martagon. Martagon Lily. Leaves lance-shaped in whorls on stems to 1 m. carrying loose clusters of 3–10 pinkish-purple flowers with recurred segments. ✲ Woods and forests. C. and N. mountains. June–July. **337**

FRITILLARIA. *F. bithynica (F. pineticola).* With single yellow bell-shaped flowers to 2 cm. long, on stems up to 15 cm. Style varying from 3-parted to entire. Upper leaves projecting markedly above the flowers. ⚘ Pine forests. Samos. March–April.   **352**

F. sibthorpiana is similar, with bright yellow flowers and always 3-parted style. ⚘ Scrub, open pinewoods. Euboaea and E. Aegean Islands. March–April.

F. pinardii is again similar, but the flowers are more conical, yellowish to brownish-red or green edged purple, with entire style. Upper leaves barely projecting above flowers. ⚘ Scrub, open pinewoods. Samos and other E. Aegean Islands. March–April.   **353**

F. conica. Up to 12 cm. high, with opposite blue-green lanceolate leaves and 1 or 2 funnel-shaped yellow flowers, marked with green. ⚘ Spiny scrub on limestone hills near the sea. S.W. Peloponnese. Feb.–March.

F. ehrhartii. 6–20 cm. tall, with 1 or 2 dark red-brown or purplish bells, gold and green within. ⚘ Grows in schist, often among scrub. Islands, notably Andros, Syros, Petalia, and Euboea. March–April.

F. graeca. Usually 10–20 cm. tall, with narrow pale green leaves, and 1–2 wide, bell-shaped flowers, 1½–3 cm. long, purple and brown streaked or lightly chequered with green on the exterior, or sometimes entirely chestnut brown. *Var. gussichiae* is very distinctive, with grey leaves and large pale green, lightly brown-shaded flowers. *Ssp. thessala* has 3 leaflets projecting above the flower, which has strong green stripes. ⚘ Rocky slopes of hills and mountains, up to 3,000 m. March–April.   **349, 350**

F. messanensis. A slender plant up to 30 cm. high with 7–12 bluish-green, narrow lanceolate leaves carried on the stem, the topmost projecting above the 1–3 bell-shaped flowers, 3½ cm. long, which are greenish with brown stripes or chequering, yellow within the bell. ⚘ Stony places in scrub or pinewoods, to over 2,000 m. Feb.–April.   **351**

F. obliqua. A variable plant sometimes exceeding 30 cm., with twisted blue-green leaves, the two at the base often opposite, the upper stem-leaves bract-like with a flower in each axil. Flowers 1–3 or more, conical, of a dark mahogany colour with a silvery-sheen. Scented. ⚘ Rocky ground, on low

mountains especially in Attica. April–May.   **354**

F. tuntasia resembles *F. obliqua,* but is more robust, with 1–4 flowers; style is entire instead of trifid. ⚘ On mica schist. Kythnos. April–May.

F. pontica. 15–35 cm. tall with broad blue-green leaves, the top 3 projecting beyond the 1–3 bell-shaped flowers, generally of green touched with brown at the tips. ⚘ In semi-shade, in scrub and thickets. Hills up to 1,000 m. April–May.

F. rhodokanakis. 10–15 cm. tall with narrow leaves and single, widely flared bell-shaped maroon and yellow flowers. ⚘ Rocky slopes on limestone. Hydra. March–April.

TULIPA. *T. australis.* A slender tulip, usually with 2 narrow leaves, and flowering stems up to 30 cm. carrying the solitary flowers with narrow pointed segments, golden-yellow within and sometimes reddish without. ⚘ Rocky and grassy places, low scrub, often in mountains. April–June.   **347**

T. boeotica. Perhaps the finest of the Greek tulips, growing up to 40 cm.; the large bell-shaped flowers of deepest crimson open widely to show a narrow zone of yellow at the base of the cup, surrounding a small central black area. The bluish-green leaves have wavy edges. ⚘ Cultivated land, often among growing crops. C. Greece and Peloponnese. March–April.   **5, 345**

T. orphanidea. A slender tulip, with stems up to 30 cm. high and narrow green leaves. The outer segments of the slightly drooping flowers, up to 9 cm. across, are of a brownish-orange or bronze touched with green and purple, the inner surface is usually of a more uniform orange with green centre. ⚘ Fields, rocky grass hillsides. April–May.

T. hageri is closely related to *T. orphanidea;* these may be forms of the same species. A little more robust, it differs somewhat in colouring, having more definite green markings bordered with scarlet on the outer segments, and a yellow centre. ⚘ Fields, rocky grassy hillsides. March–April.   **348**

T. rhodopaea. Up to 50 cm., with wide, pointed blue-green leaves, and usually solitary flowers of a dull purple, cup-shaped, becoming star-shaped when open, with dark central blotch. ✽ Fields in the hills. N. Greece. March–April.

T. suaveolens. Up to 15 cm. with 3–6 broadly lanceolate leaves, and solitary cup-shaped flowers of a bright crimson-scarlet, with yellow basal blotch. ✽ Fields, N. Greece. March–April.

Cretan Tulips

Apart from T. australis (*described above*) *the tulips of Crete are endemic and quite distinctive. However, they have given rise to much confusion, and the status of* T. saxatilis *and what is now considered its smaller variety* bakeri *need further investigation.*

T. cretica. A slender plant 8–15 cm. tall. Leaves 2–3, nearly flat, 1–2 cm. wide. Flowers opening star-like with segments 15–32 mm. long, almost entirely white, green-tinged on back, with pinkish tips and yellow centre. ✽ Fields in rich soil; mainly in the mountains, but also at lower altitudes. Throughout Crete. March–April.

T. saxatilis (including **T. bakeri**). Bulb producing long stolons (underground runners). 10–15 cm. tall. Leaves 2–4, 15–20 cm. long, to 4½ cm. wide but often less, flat or slightly waved, shining green. Flowers 1–3 or sometimes more on a stem, the green buds drooping; flowers erect, opening into a wide cup, with segments 3–5½ cm. long; clear pale-pink, lilac, or purplish-pink, shading into white with a sharply defined golden basal blotch. ✽ Often in rock crevices but also in stony ground and fields. From sea-level to 1,500 m. Mainly in W. Crete. March–May.

344, 346

Botanists studying herbarium specimens suggest that what were originally named T. saxatilis *and* T. bakeri *grade into each other and cannot be separated. However, there are undoubtedly distinct differences in the field, notably that* 'T. saxatilis', *as its name suggests, lives mainly in rock crevices, whereas* 'T. bakeri' *grows in open ground, as on the Omalos plateau. One botanist claims to have seen gradations between* T. saxatilis *and* T. cretica *in the Akrotiri area, and others claim that the form with wavy leaves is a distinct species. They are certainly all rather similar and presum-*

ably originated from a common ancestor.

URGINEA. *U.* **maritima.** SEA SQUILL. From the very large bulbs, often projecting above ground, there arise long unbranched flowering stems 1–1½ m. high, carrying dense heads of small, spirally arranged white flowers. The 3–6 cm. broad, pointed leaves appear after the flowers and persist into summer. ✽ Dry rocky hillsides, often on or near the coast. Aug.–Oct. **340**
The large bulbs have been used medicinally since ancient times, for cough mixtures, treatment of heart disease, chapped feet, and so on. Virgil mentions it as an ingredient of sheep-wash. Red squill rat poison is made from a North African sub-species. Theophrastus remarks on the length of time the dry bulb will survive – it will put out leaves in season for a number of years. This made it a fertility symbol hung up outside a house (the Greeks still sometimes do this at New Year). It was also believed to ward off evil. Theophrastus adds 'it is even able to keep other things that are stored, for instance the pomegranate, if the stalk of the fruit is set in it, and some cuttings strike more rapidly if set in it'. Bulbs unearthed in ploughing are sometimes used to mark field boundaries.

SCILLA. *S.* **autumnalis.** AUTUMN SQUILL. The slender flowering stems, 10–20 cm. high, carry up to 20 small pale lilac or sometimes blue flowers in a terminal cluster. The very narrow (1–2 mm.) leaves appear after the flowers. ✽ Dry stony places, vineyards, olive groves. Aug.–Oct.

S. **bifolia.** Usually with 2 leaves, 2–6 mm. wide, keeled, glossy green. The brilliant dark blue flowers, up to 8 in number, are carried in loose clusters on 5–20 cm. stems and have blue or violet anthers. ✽ Among shrubs or rocks. Mountains. March–May. **366**
'Being smeared on with white wine upon boyes is thought to keep them impuberes,' remarks Dioscorides.

S. **hyacinthoides.** A stout plant to 100 cm., with a large bulb, narrowly lanceolate leaves hairy on the edges, and long conical spikes of very numerous blue-violet flowers. ✽ Stony fields, hills, hedges. April–Ma **367**

S. messeniaca. With 15–20 cm. stems carrying 7–14 starry pale blue 1 cm. flowers in fairly dense, cylindrical spikes. Leaves numerous. ⚘ Stony and rocky places. S. Greece, especially Taygetos Mountains. March–May.

CHIONODOXA. ***C. nana.*** A very small plant, with 2 grass-like leaves, and a 5–10 cm. stem carrying 1–2 scilla-like flowers with 10–13 mm. segments, bicoloured in white and pale blue. ⚘ Rocks and stony places. Mountains of Crete, from 2,000–2,500 m. May–June. **510**, p. 63

C. cretica resembles *C. nana* (which may only be a high-altitude form) but is larger, with blue flower segments 15–17 mm. long. ⚘ Rocky and stony places. Crete from 1,300–1,700 m.; Rhodes.

ORNITHOGALUM. ***O. montanum.*** A variable plant up to 10 cm. high but sometimes almost stemless, with 2–4 leaves 5–10 mm. wide, and spreading heads of 3–20 white flowers to 3 cm. across, the backs of the petals bearing central wide green bands. Some forms have wider petals and leaves than others, and two spp. may well be included here. ⚘ Grassy and rocky places. Feb.–April. **360, 362**

O. nanum. A low-growing STAR OF BETHLEHEM with 2–5 cm. flowering stems arising from a tuft of narrow dark green leaves, and carrying dense clusters of 1·5 cm. flowers with long, rather narrow pure white petals striped with green beneath. ⚘ Stony hillsides and sandy places. March–April. **363**

O. narbonense (O. pyramidale). Pyramidal heads of many starry white, green-striped flowers are carried on stout upright stems up to 60 cm. high. Leaves blue-grey, channelled. ⚘ Grassy places and fields. March–May. **364**

O. nutans. DROOPING STAR OF BETHLEHEM. On stems up to 50 cm. high are carried one-sided clusters of drooping white 2–2½ cm. flowers broadly banded with grey-green on the outside. The long narrow leaves are soft, with a broad whitish band. ⚘ Fields, vineyards, and olive groves. April–May. **361**

O. tenuifolium. With very narrow (1–2 mm.) hairless leaves and flattish flower heads on 12 cm. high stems, of 5 or more star-shaped white flowers backed with green on the petal reverse. Petals 11–14 mm. long. ⚘ Dry rocky places, often in the hills. April–June.

O. umbellatum. STAR OF BETHLEHEM. 20–30 cm. high, with narrow 2–8 mm. leaves, grooved and with white median line. The 10–20 white flowers, backed with green, are carried in spreading heads; the flower stalks about 8 cm. long. Petals 15–20 mm. long. The bulb produces many bulbils (unlike *O. tenuifolium*). ⚘ Cultivated ground, stony places, olive groves, and orchards. April–June.

HYACINTHUS. ***H. orientalis.*** HYACINTH. With broad (1–2 cm.) leaves, the flower stems growing to 25 cm., carrying very sweetly scented flowers of a light blue. ⚘ Hillsides, edges of olive groves and fields. Eastern Aegean Islands. March–April. **365**

In mythology, Hyacinthos was a handsome youth who preferred Apollo to Zephyrus, god of the winds. During a game, Zephyrus deflected one of Apollo's quoits so that it struck Hyacinthos and killed him. In his sorrow Apollo caused the lovely hyacinth flower to grow from the boy's blood. H. orientalis *is the parent of our modern garden hyacinths.*

STRANGWEIA. ***S. spicata (Hyacinthus spicatus).*** An inconspicuous plant, 5–10 cm. high, with hyacinth-like 7 mm. light blue flowers, pointing more or less upward in a loose spike. The bulb is black and the small leaves very narrow. ⚘ Stony and grassy places on lower mountain slopes. March–April. **359**

BELLEVALIA. ***B. ciliata.*** From a large bulb rise 4–6 large leaves, 1½–2 cm. wide, 15–20 cm. long, and the flowering stem up to 50 cm., bearing numerous bell-shaped drooping long-stalked flowers of a pale purplish-brown. ⚘ Cultivated and waste ground. March–April. **368**

B. romana resembles *B. ciliata*, but with narrower leaves and more slender stem carrying whitish flowers, violet at the base.

B. trifoliata is a tall species with 3 finely hairy leaves, and dingy violet flowers.

B. dubia (which has been referred to as *Muscari trojanum*) has blue flowers of striking cobalt-blue. **369**

MUSCARI. *M. comosum (Leopoldia comosum).* TASSEL HYACINTH. With flower stems up to 60 cm. high, bearing an upper group of violet-blue sterile flowers on long stalks, and a lower group of more widely spaced brownish fertile flowers. Leaves narrow and erect. The weird **var. plumosum (var. monstrosum)**, in which the flower heads are transformed into an oval mass of sterile, contorted filaments, is occasionally seen wild. ✲ Fields and uncultivated ground; coastal sands. March–May. **374, 375**

The Greeks called this Bulbos; Theophrastus' translator renders it 'purse-tassels', referring to the cluster of fertile flowers. The bulbs have been prized for food since ancient times, and (with other species of muscari) are still collected for market and eaten, especially picked during Lent. 'In some places,' writes Theophrastus, 'they are so sweet as to be eaten raw.' Dioscorides lists many uses, including as ointments 'for luxations, bruises, splinters, and for griefes of the jointes, and for gangraenes and gowtes . . . for ye bitings of doggs . . . and they take away the Piles also, being roasted in hott embers, and with ye burnt heads of ye fishes called Maenae, and so applied'.

M. commutatum. DARK GRAPE HYACINTH. With densely crowded heads of fragrant indigo-blue flowers without a white rim, on 10–15 cm. high stems. Leaves grass-like, longer than flower-spikes. Grassy slopes, cliffs, stony hillsides. March–April. **370**

M. macrocarpum. A yellow-flowered muscari with stems 15–20 cm. high, carrying large bright yellow flowers tipped with brown. The uppermost flowers are a blue-purple. Leaves rather wide, strap-shaped. ✲ Thickets. Samos, Lesbos, and other East Aegean islands. March–April.

M. moschatum, with which *M. macrocarpum* is sometimes confused, has musk-scented purplish flowers which become yellow. An Asian plant,

possibly only found cultivated in the Greek Islands.

M. neglectum (M. atlanticum, M. racemosum). 10–20 cm. tall, with many very narrow leaves. Flowers dark blue with white outcurved lobes. ✲ Cultivated land, vineyards, olive groves. March–May. **371**

M. parviflorum. A frail Grape Hyacinth with 10–15 cm. stems bearing small heads of china-blue flowers. ✲ Among rocks, stony hillsides. Sept.–Oct. **372**

M. pulchellum. Up to 15 cm. high with dark indigo-blue flowers with white teeth; the upper, sterile flowers bright blue. Leaves very narrow, grooved. ✲ Grassy hills, rocky places, pine woods. April–May.

ASPARAGUS. *A. acutifolius.* A scrambling or low growing woody-stemmed perennial, in which leaves are replaced by scales or branchlets; scales on the main stems develop into spines, and the star-shaped clusters of 4–12 branchlets are narrow, smooth, and sharp pointed. The single or paired small bell-shaped flowers are greenish-yellow, followed by black fruit. ✲ Dry places, hedges, on limestone. July–Dec. **378**

A. aphyllus is similar, lower growing and much branched, with angular stems and 2–6 branchlets in a cluster. ✲ Stony, sandy places. July–Oct.

A. stipularis (A. horridus) has stiff solitary branchlets, sharp-pointed and radiating. Habitat similar, but flowers March–April.

The Greeks sometimes collect soft young shoots of these and eat them as we do cultivated asparagus. They are bitter and indigestible. Apart from various medicinal uses, Dioscorides remarks, 'And some have related that if one having beaten rammes hornes in pieces do bury them, Asparagus commes up, which yet is incredible to me.' Further, 'it makes one barren, and not fitt for generation'.

POLYGONATUM. *P. odoratum (P. officinale).* SWEET-SCENTED SOLOMON'S SEAL. From fleshy rhizomes arise leafy stems up to 50 cm. high carrying alternate stalkless oval leaves, with the drooping greenish-white sweet-scented flowers borne singly or in pairs in the leaf axils. ⚜ Damp shady woods and rocky places in the hills and mountains. May–June. **373**

P. multiflorum, SOLOMON'S SEAL, resembles *P. officinale,* but reaches 1 m. and has smaller unscented flowers carried 2–5 in the leaf axils. ⚜ Shady woods. May–June.

P. latifolium is smaller, but with broadly elliptic and shortly stalked leaves which are finely downy above. ⚜ Woods. N. Greece. May–June.

P. pruinosum has white powdery leaves and single flowers in the leaf axils. ⚜ Rocky places in the Northern mountains. April–May.

RUSCUS. R. aculeatus. BUTCHER'S BROOM. An evergreen shrub, 25–80 cm. tall, spiny and much branched. True leaves are replaced by flattened, hard, prickly expanded branches bearing small greenish flowers followed by round scarlet 1 cm. fruits. ⚜ Woods and thickets on the hills. Jan.–April. **379**

R. hypoglossum. Like *R. aculeatus,* but with larger and softer false leaves, elliptic and without spines. ⚜ Woods and thickets. Jan.–April.

In ancient times the new shoots were eaten like asparagus. Also believed useful to drive out bladder-stones.

SMILAX. S. aspera. A climbing or scrambling shrub, spiny and with tendrils. The alternate leaves are leathery and heart-shaped, and the pale yellow, sometimes pinkish fragrant flowers are carried in clusters, followed by the red berries. ⚜ Dry stony places, stone walls, hedges. Aug.–Oct. **376, 377**

The young shoots are eaten like asparagus although, as Dioscorides remarks, 'it moves urine, and is a causer of troublesome dreams'. However, it was considered an antidote to poison, and if the berries were crushed into a drink and given to a new-born child, 'he shall be hurt by no poisonous medicine'. In more recent times it was considered as 'poor man's sarsaparilla', useful as a tonic and general-purpose remedy.

AGAVACEAE – Agave Family

Differs from *Liliaceae* in the thick flowering stems and fleshy spiny-edged leaves in basal rosettes. Flowers numerous in clusters.

AGAVE. A. americana. CENTURY PLANT. From very large rosettes, 2–4 m. in diameter, formed of thick and spiny spear-shaped leaves, there arise, after several years, thick and woody flower stems, 8–10 m. high, which carry sprays of yellowish-green flowers. This is followed by the death of the parent rosette. ⚜ On cliffs, among rocks, and on waste ground. June–Aug. **425**

The Century Plant was introduced into the Mediterranean area from Mexico over two centuries ago. It is sometimes used for hedging, forming an impenetrable barrier. In Mexico the national drink, pulque, is made by fermenting the large quantities of sap exuded if an incipient flower spike is cut off. The dry flower stems are sometimes used as razor straps.

AMARYLLIDACEAE – Daffodil Family

Usually herbaceous plants with bulbs. Leaves basal and narrow. Flowers solitary or in umbels, enclosed before flowering in papery bracts. Flowers with parts in threes, with two whorls of petal-like segments, and sometimes with an additional inner ring (corona) in the throat of the corolla tube. Stamens 6. Fruit a capsule.

LEUCOJUM. Corolla bell-shaped, 6-petalled; flowers single or a few, carried terminally on stem, with 1–2 enclosing bracts.

GALANTHUS. Flowers solitary, the outer 3 perianth segments form a spreading bell, the inner 3 segments broader and not spreading, forming a tube; leaves 2.

STERNBERGIA. Corolla funnel-shaped and 6-petalled; flowers erect, crocus-like.

NARCISSUS. Flowers solitary or clustered; corolla with funnel-shaped tube below, 6 spreading or reflexed segments above, and a cup-like or ring-like corona, or a more elongated trumpet, in the centre.

PANCRATIUM. Corolla long and funnel-shaped, widening above, with 6 long narrow petals and a 12-toothed corona; flowers in long-stemmed umbel above 2 spathes.

LEUCOJUM. *L. aestivum.* SUMMER SNOWFLAKE. Up to 70 cm. high, with strap-shaped, light green basal leaves. A stout stem carries terminal clusters of 2–8 bell-shaped flowers, white with green tips. ✾ Low-lying fields, damp places, river banks. April–June.

L. autumnale. AUTUMN SNOWFLAKE. With 1–3 bell-shaped flowers, 8–12 mm. long, white touched with pink, carried on slender stems 10–25 cm. high. The very narrow leaves appear after the flowers. ✾ Stony and rocky hillsides. Crete and Cephalonia. Sept.

GALANTHUS. *G. elwesii.* With broad (2 cm.), flattish, bluish-green leaves which are wrapped round each other as they develop, and have a hooded tip. Flower segments 2 cm. long, inner marked with green at base and apex. A form called *var. maximus* has broad, twisted leaves, and may be intermediate between *G. elwesii* and *G. graecus*, or conceivably a hybrid between them. ✾ Open woods. N. Greece; E. Aegean islands. Feb.–April.

G. graecus. With narrow, twisted grey leaves. Outer flower segments pure white, inner green-marked at base and apex. ✾ Woods. N. Greece, E. Islands. Jan.–Feb.

G. ikariae. With leaves ½–1½ cm. broad, deep green, the outer wrapped around the inner. Flowers with large claw-shaped outer segments, 2–2½ cm. long; inner segments with large green mark on apical half. ✾ Scrub. Ikaria, Andros, Skiros. Feb.–March.   **380**

G. nivalis. SNOWDROP. With narrow blue-green leaves appearing with the flowers, which are widely bell-shaped with pure white segments. The species itself, flowering in early spring, is dubiously recorded from Greece (possibly N. Thrace, Athos); the form

normally seen is *ssp. reginae-olgae* (*G. corcyrensis, G. rachelae*), which produces its flowers in autumn, before or with the flowers; inner segments usually with green markings near apex. ✾ Rocky places, thickets, sometimes in the mountains. Oct.–Dec.   **381**

STERNBERGIA. *S. colchiciflora.* With 3 cm. pale yellow, short-lived flowers, segments narrow, not overlapping, perianth tube long. Leaves 1–2 mm. broad, twisted, appearing after the flowers. ✾ Stony and rocky places in hills and mountains. Sept.–Oct.

S. lutea. Like a large golden-yellow crocus, with flowers up to 7 cm. long, rather globular and with blunt-tipped petals. Leaves strap-shaped, ½–2 cm. broad, dark green, appearing with the flowers. ✾ Fields, thickets, hillsides. Sept.–Oct.   **382**

S. sicula. Similar to *S. lutea* but smaller, flowers 3–4 cm. long, leaves 3–5 mm. broad, with grey central band, appearing with the flowers. ✾ Stony hillsides. Sept.–Nov.   **384**

NARCISSUS. *N. papyraceus.* PAPER-WHITE NARCISSUS. Carrying 2–6 fragrant pure white 3 cm. wide flowers on 20–30 cm. stems. ✾ Damp meadows. N. Greece, Corfu.

N. poeticus. PHEASANT'S EYE NARCISSUS. The pure white, flat, 4–6 cm. fragrant flowers have a shallow yellow, red-edged corona and are carried singly on 40–60 cm. stems. The form of this familiar garden flower usually seen in Greece is *var. hellenicus* which has rather smaller flowers with more rounded segments than the species. ✾ Damp mountain meadows. N. Greece, Epirus. May–June.   **385**

The legend of Narcissus is so well known that it has provided the word for self-admiration, *narcissism. The hand-some youth Narcissos fell in love with his own reflection in a pool, with the result that he wasted away (the nymph Echo, who loved him, did likewise). One legend has it that Hera punished him for this conceit and turned him into the narcissus flower; another that when the nymphs came to give him funeral rites his body had vanished, and a narcissus bloomed there instead.*

In fact the word is derived from the Greek narkau, meaning to grow stiff, because the plant is narcotic: it became associated with death and also madness. Pluto used it to dull Proserpine's senses before carrying her off to the underworld. The Furies and Fates wore garlands of narcissi, and the Greeks placed wreaths of them in the hands of the dead. Theophrastus mentions its cultivation, from seed as well as bulbs.

N. serotinus. A small autumn-flowering narcissus with narrow white starry perianth segments 9–12 mm. long, and very small golden corona. Stems to 20 cm. tall. The narrow leaves usually appear after the flower. ✲ Rocky, sandy, and hilly places, usually near the sea. Sept.–Dec. **387**

N. tazetta. BUNCH-FLOWERED NARCIS-SUS. Carries 3–18 flowers in a cluster on 20–50 cm. stems. The flowers are normally 2–4 cm. across, with white perianth and golden corona, and are very fragrant. ✲ Fields, damp places. Dec.–March. **386**
From this and its colour forms found elsewhere in Europe and N. Africa are derived the horticultural varieties of bunch-flowered or polyanthus narcissi.

PANCRATIUM. *P. maritimum.* SEA DAFFODIL. From a large bulb arise thick blunt-tipped narcissus-like leaves 8–15 mm. broad, and stout flower stalks up to 40 cm. high, bearing clusters of 3–12 sweetly scented flowers, 6–8 cm. across, with funnel-shaped crown, white striped with green on the outside of the petals and long tube. ✲ Coastal sands. July–Sept. **383**
The Greek words making up the name mean 'all' and 'strength', referring to the supposed tonic properties of the plant. Dioscorides says it is 'good for ye same griefs' as Urginea. The bulb is edible like Muscari, according to Theophrastus, and the woolly layer between its outer skin and interior provides fibre from which were woven felt shoes and other items of clothing.

IRIDACEAE – Iris Family

Herbaceous plants with rhizomes, corms, or bulbs, and often with sword-shaped leaves sheathing the stem. Flowers large with parts in threes. Petals usually fused at the base into a tube. Stamens 3. Style 3-lobed and sometimes petal-like and coloured.

CROCUS. Leaves narrow, with white mid-rib; flowers at first stalkless, with ovary below ground; corolla a long tube with 6 segments; stigmas often deeply cut. The appearance of the fibrous-coated corm is sometimes the only accurate means of identification.

ROMULEA. Like *Crocus*, but with short-tubed corolla; flowers long-stalked on simple or branched stem; leaves very narrow. Corm lop-sided, with thick tunic.

IRIS. Rhizomatous or bulbous plants; flowers large, with 2 whorls of petals, the outer 3 (falls) often bearded, the inner 3 (standards) narrower and erect; style with 3 broad petal-like arms.

HERMODACTYLUS. Like *Iris*, but roots tuberous; flowers solitary with outer perianth segments bearded; leaves narrow, 4-angled.

GYNANDRIRIS. Like *Iris*, but bulbous; the ovary forming a distinct 'beak' when the flowers wither.

GLADIOLUS. Flowers in long one-sided spike, horizontal with short curved corolla tube; bracts on flowering stem often leafy; corm with fibrous scales.

CROCUS. The fibrous covering, or tunic, of the corm referred to in the descriptions may consist of a uniform membrane, a fine or coarse network (reticulation), a series of annular rings, triangular scales which may divide into narrow parallel fibres, or a smooth, hard covering.

The corms of crocuses are edible and several species, notably C. cancellatus, are roasted and eaten like chestnuts; the peasant name, indeed, is kastanea. *Oil of crocus, according to Dioscorides, 'hath a warming soporiferous facultie' and is valuable for boils and the like. There are various legends about the origin of the crocus. One makes it arise from the warmth of Jove and Hera disporting themselves on a grassy bank on Mt Ida. In another, somewhat botanical tale, a youth called Krokos died of unrequited love for the shepherdess Smilax, and the flowers arose from his grave.*

Autumn-flowering
(September–December)
Colour white, or white combined with lilac or mauve

C. boryi. Flowers creamy-white with striking scarlet stigmas and white anthers. The strongly white-striped leaves appear with the flowers. Corms shining, hard. ❋ Rocky hillsides. Oct.–Nov. **391**

C. cancellatus. Flowers white or pale lilac, touched with yellow in the throat, with yellow anthers. Leaves usually appearing after flowers. Corm coarsely netted. ❋ Rocky hillsides. Sept.–Nov. **392**

C. hadriaticus. A Saffron Crocus relation (see *C. cartwrightianus* below), with smallish white, lavender or sometimes cream flowers, with red-purple veins or blue shading at the base outside. Stigmas scarlet, prominent, but shorter than stamens. Throat often yellow. Leaves with the flowers. Corm silky, finely netted. ❋ Stony hillsides. Mainly in C. and S. Greece. Sept.–Oct.

C. laevigatus (including **C. cretensis**). Flowers white to lilac, veined with mauve and sometimes marked with pale yellow; throat yellow; stigmas orange, thread-like; anthers white. Flowers and leaves appearing together. Corm hard and smooth. ❋ Rocky hills and mountainsides. Oct.–Dec. **395**

C. niveus. Flowers medium-sized, pure white with yellow throat; distinguished from *C. boryi* by its yellow anthers and much-divided orange stigmas. Leaves with the flowers. Corm netted. ❋ Hills and mountains. S. Peloponnese. Nov.–Dec.

Autumn-flowering; colour lilac to purple

C. cartwrightianus. GREEK SAFFRON CROCUS. Often considered a variety of the cultivated Saffron Crocus, *C. sativus*, which is however only known in cultivation. Flowers small, of varying shades of lilac and purple with darker veining, and large scarlet stigmas. Leaves with the flowers. Corm netted. ❋ Stony hillsides. Oct.–Nov.

The long stigmas of the Saffron Crocuses were – and are – used to produce the famous yellow saffron dye so highly prized in eastern Asia, to colour and flavour food and, in India, as a constituent of perfumes. It had various soothing medicinal uses; as late as 1921 'saffron tea' flavoured with brandy was used in England to relieve measles and similar diseases.

C. goulimyi. A distinctive crocus with very slender 10–12 cm. flower tube and globular lavender flowers with white throat; stigmas and anthers yellow. Leaves appear about the same time as flowers. Corm hard and smooth. ❋ Stony places, in heavy clay, by rocks and walls. Mani, S. Peloponnese. Nov.–Dec. **394**

C. pulchellus. Flowers large, pale lavender, only slightly veined, yellow in the throat; stigmas yellow. Corm small and annulate. Related to *C. speciosus* (which does not occur in Greece but is often grown in gardens). ❋ Meadows, woods. N. Greece. Sept.–Oct.

C. pallasii. Another Saffron Crocus relation, like *C. hadriaticus* but its rather small flowers varying from rosy lilac to white, with yellow throat; stigmas large, drooping, but shorter than stamens. Corm silky, finely netted. ✤ Stony places in the hills. Oct.

C. tournefortii. Flowers large, pale rosy-lilac with yellow throat, orange-scarlet stigmas and white anthers. The leaves appear with the flowers. Corm large with membranous tunic. ✤ Stony places. Cyclades, Rhodes. Oct.–Nov. **400**

Spring-flowering (January–May)
Colour white or pale lilac

C. biflorus. Flowers medium-sized, of varying shades of lilac feathered or striped purple, with yellow throat and yellow anthers. Leaves appear with the flowers. Corm with annulate tunic. ✤ Stony hillsides. Feb.–March.

C. crewei. Flowers small, white feathered purple, with black anthers. Corm annulate. Closely related to the more widely distributed *C. biflorus.* ✤ Stony places. S. Peloponnese and islands. Flowers Dec.–Jan., thus linking the autumn and spring flowering species.

C. nubigenus. Another of the *C. biflorus* group, similar to *C. crewei* but lilac with darker markings. ✤ Stony mountain slopes. E. Aegean Islands. Feb.–March. **397**

C. fleischeri. Flowers small, starry with very narrow segments, white touched with basal purple striping; stigmas scarlet. Corm yellow, tunic densely netted. ✤ Stony slopes. Rhodes. Jan.–Feb.

C. sieberi var. sieberi (var. heterochromus). A Cretan form of the variable *C. sieberi* (see below): flowers large, white to pale lilac, with variable darker feathering or banding on the outer segments, and a golden throat. ✤ Mountain slopes. Crete. Jan.–Feb.

Spring-flowering; colour purple

C. sieberi. A very variable crocus with yellow anthers, stigmas orange to red, frilled; leaves produced with or just after the flowers; corm coarsely netted. Besides *var. sieberi* described above, two other varieties have been named.

Var. atticus. The medium to large flowers are usually soft purple with

orange throat; the segments sometimes have darker tips. ✤ Moist woods, high meadows, mountain slopes. Mountains of mainland Greece. Feb.–April. **398**

Var. tricolor. Large flowers with purple, white, and yellow bands. ✤ High meadows, mountain slopes. Mountains of N. Peloponnese. Feb.–April. **399**

C. veluchensis. Flowers lavender to purple; stigmas orange, frilled. Distinguished from *C. sieberi* by the white, not yellow throat, and by its more slender appearance due to the greater length and narrowness of the segments. Leaves with the flowers or shortly after. Corm small, netted. ✤ Alpine turf from 1,500–2,500 m. N. Greek mountains. March–May. **401**

Spring-flowering; colour yellow

C. chrysanthus. Flowers golden, somewhat globular, 1–3 together, produced at the same time as the narrow grassy leaves. Stigmas yellow to red, anthers yellow, sometimes blackish at base. Corm with annulate tunic. ✤ Grassy and stony places. Jan.–Feb.

C. flavus (C. aureus). A large crocus, deep golden to orange, sometimes with brown markings; stigmas yellow to orange. The narrow erect leaves appear with the flowers. Corm tunic membranous. ✤ Grassy or stony hillsides, light woodland. N. Greece. Jan.–Feb. **393**

C. olivieri. With rather small, globular, golden to deep orange flowers; stigmas orange-yellow. Corm tunic smooth and membranous, splitting lengthwise. ✤ Dry stony hillsides, scrub. Feb. **396**

C. balansae is probably best considered a ssp. of *C. olivieri*, differing in the brown markings sometimes on the outside and the much-cut stigmas. ✤ Dry stony places, scrub. Mountains of Samos. Jan.–Feb.

ROMULEA. *R. bulbocodium.* With narrow rush-like leaves and stems up to 4 cm. carrying 1–5 funnel-shaped flowers up to 3 cm. across, usually purple or yellowish-violet outside, with yellow throat. Variations which have been named include *var. pygmaea*, a small form from various islands including Crete; *var. leichtliniana*, white or creamy with violet exterior markings; and *var. subpalustris*, violet throughout. ✲ Sandy places, often by the sea, but also high up. Feb.–April. **388, 389**

R. linaresii. Only 3–5 cm. tall, with very narrow dark green leaves and flowers 1–2 cm. across, bright violet. The Greek plant is *ssp. graeca*. ✲ Stony places, short turf. Jan.–April. **390**

R. ramiflora. Up to 6 cm. tall with 1–4 starry flowers 1½ cm. across, lilac streaked with yellow. Leaves grass-like but up to 30 cm. long. ✲ Sandy and grassy places by the coast. Feb.–April.

Two further tiny Romuleas are *R. columnae*, whitish-lilac streaked purple, and its *ssp. rollii*, lilac striped purple, yellow within. ✲ Sandy coastal spots. Feb.–March.

IRIS. *I. florentina*. This large white, blue-veined, fragrant 'flag' iris reached 40–60 cm. with branched stem bearing many flowers, and shorter, sword-shaped leaves. ✲ Usually cultivated but naturalised in rocky places. March–April. **403**
The Mohamedan flower of the dead, often planted in their cemeteries; and the original of the Fleur-de-lys of heraldry. The main source of orris root, used in perfumery and pot-pourri. Of this, and tuberous-rooted irises in general, Dioscorides says 'in generall they are of very much use', and lists many attributes.

I. ochroleuca (*I. spuria ssp. ochroleuca*, *I. orientalis*). A large plant up to 2 m. high with sword-shaped leaves, bearing white or pale yellow flowers. ✲ Swamps, edges of lagoons. Thrace, Crete, E. Aegean Islands. April–June. **405**

I. pseudacorus, the YELLOW FLAG, is another iris of swampy places with 1–1½ m. stems carrying terminal and lateral clusters of large clear, yellow flowers. April–June.

I. pumila. A dwarf bearded iris with rhizomes, 8–12 cm. rather sickle-shaped leaves and flowering stems to 15 cm., carrying single, fragrant flowers varying from palest yellow to light blue and deep purple, sometimes bi-coloured. The typical Greek form is

ssp. attica. ✲ Dry stony places. Feb.–April. **406, 407, 408**
I. sintenisii. Up to 30 cm. high, with 1–3 blue-violet flowers carried on rounded stems. The very narrow leaves are up to 50 cm. long. ✲ Thickets, hillsides. May–June.

I. graminea resembles *I. sintenisii*, but grows up to 50 cm. high, with blue-violet flowers which are sweet-scented. ✲ Woods, thickets. Corfu. May–June. **404**

I. unguicularis ssp. cretensis (*ssp. graeca*; *I. cretica*). This dwarf form of the Algerian Iris familiar in gardens has a creeping rhizome forming clumps of narrow (1–3 mm.) leaves 15–20 cm. long, often longer than the flower stems. The solitary flowers are relatively large, on a long tube, bluish-lilac with yellow markings. The mainland forms are often more uniformly blue, though considered botanically the same. ✲ Among bushes, in hedges, field edges. Feb.–April. **409, 410**

HERMODACTYLUS. *H. tuberosus*. SNAKE'S HEAD or WIDOW IRIS. A tuberous rooted iris, with narrow rush-like leaves, and solitary rather conical flowers of a light yellowish-green, the reflexed petals being of an almost black purple. Occasionally yellow and brown forms occur. A slender green spathe forms a hood which rises above the flowers, bringing the height to 20–25 cm. ✲ Stony places, hillsides, among bushes. March–April. **411**

GYNANDRIRIS. *G. sisyrinchium* (*Iris sisyrinchium*). BARBARY NUT. An iris with a small nut-like bulb enclosed in fibrous scales. Usually dwarf but up to 40 cm. Flowers bright blue with white centres and sometimes yellow markings, several in the axils of thin papery bracts, usually opening only in the afternoon. ✲ Dry places, stony hillsides. Feb.–April. **402**
The root is nut-like in flavour as well as appearance.

GLADIOLUS. *G. segetum* (*G. italicum*). FIELD GLADIOLUS. The 6–16 rosy purple to light pink flowers, 4–5 cm. long, are carried in 1-sided spikes 50–100 cm. high, with leafy bracts; lower bracts as long as flowers, 3 upper petals unequal. Anthers longer than their stalks. ✲ Cornfields and other cultivated ground. April–June. **6, 414**

G. communis resembles *G. segetum* closely, but the 10–20 flowers, 3–4½ cm. long, have petals nearly equal in size, bracts are shorter than flowers, and anthers shorter than their stalks. The lower flower segments are often blotched or streaked. ✲ Cornfields, grassy places. N. Greece. May–June. **413**

G. byzantinus is distinguished by its 6–20 large flowers of a striking magenta colour, with petals almost touching, not separated as in *G. segetum*. ✲ Fields and uncultivated ground. Possibly only naturalised. N. Greece. May–June. **412**

G. illyricus. A smaller, more slender plant than *G. segetum*, growing to 25–60 cm. with 3–10 smaller purple flowers (2–4 cm), the 3 upper petals unequal. Leaves less than 1 cm. broad. ✲ Damp fields, macchie. May–June.

To various medicinal virtues of wild gladioli Dioscorides adds that the 'upper root' (the new corm) 'being drank with wine doth provoke venery, but that ye undermost doth make them lustless'. He also adds, rather unclearly, 'that ye upper root is profitably given to children that are broken'. Theophrastus recommends cooking the corm and mixing the pounded result with flour to make bread sweet and wholesome, adding that the corms are often found in mole runs because these animals collect them.

GRAMINEAE –
Grass Family

A very large family of herbaceous plants with narrow alternate leaves with sheathing base. Flowers clustered in spikelets, either stalked in loose clusters, or stalkless in a spike. Only three of the most noticeable are described here.

A family found all over the world, especially in areas of low rainfall. Very important to the human race, it includes all cereal crops, sugar cane, the bamboos of so many uses; most of our fermented drinks and much animal fodder is derived from it also.

ARUNDO. *A. donax.* GIANT REED. Resembling a bamboo, with underground rhizomes from which arise long leaves, 2–5 cm. across, and thick stems up to 5 m., carrying plumes of whitish flowers. ✲ Damp places, stream edges. Aug.–Dec. **415**
The largest grass in Europe. Probably an Asiatic plant but long cultivated and fully naturalised in the Mediterranean. Often planted as a windbreak or boundary fence. Used for making walking sticks, fishing rods, and baskets.

BRIZA. *B. maxima.* QUAKING GRASS. An annual up to 50 cm. high, with large ovoid silvery drooping flower heads carried on very slender branches. ✲ Dry sandy places. April–June. **416**
Much grown as an ornamental, both fresh and dried.

LAGURUS. *L. ovatus.* HARE'S-TAIL GRASS. An annual, 5–50 cm. tall, soft, and greyish-green, with dense ovoid flowering heads, whitish and softly hairy. ✲ Dry places, often on the coast. April–July. **417**
Grown for ornament, especially dried.

ARACEAE – Arum Family

Herbaceous plants with fleshy rhizomes. Flowers small, on a club-like stem (spadix) encircled by a leaf-like sheath (spathe), the whole forming the 'flower'. Individual flowers usually 1-sexed, male flowers above, female below.
ARUM. Spathe constricted below middle; spadix shorter and club-like; fruit a berry; leaves arrow-shaped.
DRACUNCULUS. Spathe very large, with a spadix almost as long; leaves deeply segmented.

157

BIARUM. Spathe arising directly from the ground, narrow and somewhat cylindrical; spadix often as long or longer than spathe; leaves long, narrow and entire, appearing after the flowers.

ARISARUM. Spathe partly forming a tube; spadix often longer than spathe, and curved forward; leaves arrow-shaped.

ARUM. *A. creticum.* Like a miniature 'arum lily' up to 30 cm. tall, with short rather tubby spathe, pale yellow to cream, spadix deeper yellow; fragrant. Forms from higher altitude may have whitish spathes and purple spadix. ❈ Rocky and stony places. Crete, Karpathos, Samos. April–May. **418**

A. dioscoridis. Spathe almost stemless, variable in colour but typically yellowish-green with black spotting, the spots sometimes merging into a blackish or dull red zone at the base (Asiatic specimens are often entirely red). Spadix blackish-red. ❈ Grassy places, tracksides. E. Aegean Islands, Rhodes. April–May. **419**

A milder tasting version of A. italicum *(see below); the leaves, preserved in salt, were eaten, and 'the roote being applyed with bullocks dunge' was good for gout.*

A. italicum. Spathe broad but elongated, usually pale yellow, but sometimes reddish or red-margined; spadix yellow, ⅓ length of spathe. The leaves are often white-marked, strongly so in *var. pictum* or *marmoratum.* ❈ Woods, thickets, tracksides. April–May. **420**

A. maculatum, our native LORDS AND LADIES, is common in Greece, differing from *A. italicum* in its narrower, paler spathe.

These Lords and Ladies were sometimes apparently eaten in ancient times, though they are very acrid. They were considered generally health-giving, apart from a number of specific uses including provoking abortion; while 'if anyone doe rubbe his hands with ye roote, he remains unbiteable of the viper' (Dioscorides).

A. orientale. Resembling *A. italicum* but spathe and spadix more often blackish-purple; spadix ½–¾ as long as boat-shaped spathe. Leaves with pointed lobes. ❈ Woods, thickets. N. Greece. April–May. **421**

DRACUNCULUS. *D. vulgaris.* DRAGON ARUM, GREAT DRAGON. A coarse-growing arum up to 1 m. high, with long stalked leaves deeply cut into 11–15 narrow leaflets. Leaf sheaths and ribs white-spotted. The flowers consist of a dark chocolate-purple spathe up to 60 cm. long, and a thick spadix almost as long of the same colour. The flower has a powerful and disgusting odour. *Var. creticus* has more prominent white markings on the leaves, and purple-blotched stems. A white-flowered form has been recorded in Crete. ❈ Waste ground, often near villages. April–June. **424**

The qualities ascribed to the Dragon Arum were similar to those of Arums, but it was only used medicinally, not eaten. 'Being drank with wine, it stirs up the vehement desires to coniunction' (Dioscorides). Besides drakontia, the Greeks also call it pheidochorto, *or snake-plant, referring to the white snakeskin-like markings on the stems – echoed in the English name Adderwort (anciently Edderwort).*

BIARUM. *B. tenuifolium.* With tongue-shaped purple spathe 5–10 cm. long and narrow cylindrical spadix, longer than the spathe. Rudimentary male flowers present above the fertile ones. Flowers stalkless, usually appearing after the short-stemmed spoon-shaped leaves. ❈ Rocky places. June–July or Sept.–Dec. **422**

B. spruneri is similar to *B. tenuifolium,* but with narrow leaves and narrow purple and green spathe; no rudimentary male flowers present. ❈ Fields, stony places. Epirus. June–July.

ARISARUM. *A. vulgare.* FRIAR'S COWL. A well-named little plant, with shiny green leaves shaped like an arrow-head, and flowers only 5–15 cm. high. The upright cylindrical spathe, striped green and dull purple, is curved forward and downward at the tip to form a hood, under which the greenish spadix protrudes. ❈ Grassy and stony places. Nov.–March. **423**

ORCHIDACEAE – Orchid Family

One of the largest and most curious plant families, including many decorative species and ranging from the equator to the Arctic circle. Unlike their exotic relations, the Greek species, many of which are found elsewhere around the Mediterranean, are entirely terrestrial. The description which follows refers specifically to the Mediterranean genera.

Roots mostly rounded tubers, sometimes rhizomes or vertical rootstocks. Leaves entire, sometimes reduced to scales. Flowers usually in spikes, often with leafy bracts among them. Flowers zygomorphic, that is symmetrical if divided vertically, with six segments. There are three outer segments, referred to as sepals in the descriptions, one being vertical and the other two lateral. Two of the inner segments, or petals, are placed between the sepals, while the third, or lip, is the lowest, usually much larger than the others. A nectar-producing spur is sometimes produced at the back of the lip.

Stamens and stigmas are combined into a unique central structure, the column; one stigma is often converted into a beak-like organ called the rostellum. Ovary below the flower, twisted, resulting in a dry capsule with very numerous, tiny seeds.

Many of these flowers are named for their resemblance to insects, animals, or humans; we have therefore used anthropomorphic descriptions where applicable as they are so often apt.

The Greeks, French, and Spaniards all use the Arabian word salep *for orchids, which means the paste from orchid tubers ground up as food. This probably continues today; certainly the inhabitants of Corfu were making 'bulb tea' from the tubers of* Orchis laxiflora *only a few years ago. Alice Coats has written how in the eighteenth century 'a thin, hot gruel made from the dried and powdered roots was sold under the name "saloop" at the street-stalls and coffee-shops of London. It was believed to be exceptionally wholesome and nutritious . . .'*

Dioscorides says that orchid roots were eaten boiled, and if the larger of the habitual pair of tubers is eaten by men it would make them beget males, while the smaller, eaten by women, led them to beget females. The testicle-like appearance of many orchid tubers led them to be considered aphrodisiacs.

CEPHALANTHERA. With creeping rhizomes and leafy stem. Flowers large, white or pink, with pointed segments. Lip bearing small toothed crests; no spur.

LIMODORUM. With long, deep root, tall cane-like purple stem, leafless but with scales; flowers very large, violet, long-spurred.

OPHRYS. Tuberous. Leaves fairly broad, more or less pointed, at base and on lower part of stem. Flowers in loose spikes, usually 3 to 9, unmistakable with a large convex lip, which often resembles an insect, and usually has shiny reflective areas. Lip usually with distinct side lobes or shoulder-like humps; often with a small protuberance at apex. Sepals outspread; petals usually small; no spur.

BARLIA. Similar to *Loroglossum* and sometimes included in that genus. Spike thick and massive; lip large but central lobe not greatly elongated.

LOROGLOSSUM. Tuberous. Stem tall, stout, leafy. Flowers large, in spike with bracts. Lip extended into 3 strap-like lobes, the centre one especially long and narrow. Spur very short.

ORCHIS. Tuberous. Leaves basal in rosette and sheathing the stem. Flowers in spike with membranous bracts. Upper segments often combined into a 'hood' or 'helmet' over the column. Lip usually 3-lobed; spur prominent.

DACTYLORHIZA. Like *Orchis*, but tubers lobed or divided, not round, and basal leaves not in a rosette at flowering time. Bracts on flower spike leaf-like. Segments never forming a hood.

ANACAMPTIS. Tuberous. Stem leafy. Flowers small, in dense cone-shaped spike; bracts very small. Segments outspread; lip 3-lobed, with 2 small vertical guides which direct the probosces of insects into the long, thin spur.

SERAPIAS. Tuberous. Stem leafy, with bluish leaves. Flowers unmistakable with a large pointed 3-lobed lip at right angles to an elongated hood composed of the other segments in which sepals are joined and petals concealed within them. Flowers in a spike, among very leafy bracts. No spur.

Besides the genera and species here described, the following British species may be seen in Greece: *Cypripedium calceolus*, the Lady's Slipper (in the N. only); *Epipogium aphyllum*, the Ghost Orchid (N. only); *Epipactis helleborine*, the Broad Helleborine; *Spiranthes aestivalis and S. spiralis*, the Summer and Autumn Lady's Tresses; *Platanthera bifolia and P. chlorantha*, the white Butterfly Orchids; *Listera ovata*; and *Aceras anthropophorum*, the Man Orchid. Also to be seen is the insignificant whitish *Neotinea intacta*, an Irish native.

CEPHALANTHERA. *C. rubra.* RED HELLEBORINE. 20–60 cm. tall, rather slender; leaves few, long, narrow, pointed, widely spaced. Flowers carmine-pink, 3 cm. across, with pointed, wide-based segments of almost equal size, among long bracts. ⚘ Dry woods and clearings, often among pines. April–July. **426**

The white *C. longifolia*, the Sword-leaved Helleborine, and *C. damasonium*, the White Helleborine, also occur in Greek woods and scrub.

LIMODORUM. *L. abortivum.* LIMODORE. 20–80 cm. tall, with thick cane-like stem, green overlaid with violet; leaves reduced to stem-clasping scales. Flowers violet with yellowish shadings, up to 4 cm. across, with wide horizontal sepals, long narrow petals, large triangular lip, and long down-pointing spur. Usually considered a saprophyte (living on decaying matter) though some authors suggest it is a parasite on tree roots. ⚘ Dry open woods and clearings. April–July. **427**

OPHRYS. In the descriptions below, the 'base' of the lip is visually its

highest point, and the 'apex' its lowest. The leaves are not described as they are very similar in all species and often withering at flowering time. Some authorities regard the sub-species described here as individual species. ⚘ All these 'insect orchids' grow in similar habitats, usually in grass, sometimes in stony places, in the open or in light woodland, normally on limestone soils.

O. apifera. BEE ORCHID. 15–45 cm. tall. Sepals large, blunt, pink with green line; petals very small, green. Lip 9–12 mm. long, oblong, rounded at apex, with large hairy pointed side lobes; protuberance green, backward-pointing. Lip deep brownish-red with yellow pattern enclosing a pale red patch near the base; often with 2 yellow spots or lines near apex. ⚘ April–May. **432**
O. argolica. 10–25 cm. tall. Sepals broad, pointed, pink with green line; petals smaller, triangular, deep pink. Lip round to squarish, 15 mm. long; sometimes with hairy side lobes and large basal protuberance, sometimes with flared hairy edge and small protuberance. Colour rich reddish-orange to brown with a white pattern, usually of small rectangular 'eyes' around blue

patches. ❧ C. and S. Greece, Crete, Karpathos. March–April.   **434, 435**

O. bombyliflora. BUMBLEBEE ORCHID. Seldom over 10 cm. tall, with few flowers. Sepals broad, rounded, green; petals ⅓ length of sepals, green. Lip 9–10 mm. long, squarish, dull brown with vague bluish central area. Side lobes forming large hairy humps, with a rearward point behind the lip. ❧ March–April.   **433**

O. cretica. 20–30 cm. tall. Sepals greenish, with pink shading; petals narrow, reddish. Lip around 16 mm. long, pear-shaped, with short hairy side lobes and prominent protuberance. Colour blackish or maroon with a white, roughly H-shaped pattern, sometimes with a second horizontal bar, sometimes reduced to white blotching. ❧ Crete, Syros, Naxos, Karpathos, Aegean only. March–April.   **438**

O. ferrum-equinum. HORSESHOE ORCHID. 15–30 cm. tall. Rather variable but usually with a blue horseshoe pattern on the dark purple or purple-brown lip, though this is sometimes reduced to two short vertical strokes, or becomes a square. Sepals whitish to pink with green central line, broad, blunt-pointed; petals pink to carmine, almost as long as petals, narrow-triangular. Lip 14–18 mm. long, with small pointed protuberance; usually squat and rounded at the apex but sometimes relatively long and narrow, side lobes typically minimal but sometimes extended into narrow drooping 'arms'. ❧ More frequent in the islands, especially to the E. March–May.   **447**

O. fuciflora (O. arachnites). LATE SPIDER ORCHID. 15–40 cm. tall. Very variable but lip usually squarish, with prominent shoulder-like humps and large forward-pointing protuberance. Sepals broad, usually roundish, drooping, white to pink, with green line. Petals much smaller, triangular, of same colour. Lip tending to flare at sides and apex, usually around 15 mm. long, dark brown, with a variable white pattern enclosing a blue area. *Forma maxima* has much larger flowers, with lip to 2½ cm. ❧ Largely restricted to S. Peloponnese, Crete, Rhodes, and the E. Aegean islands. March–May.   **437**

Ssp. candica has almost square lip 13 mm. long, large whitish pattern of white and red-brown; petals very small. ❧ Crete, Rhodes only.

O. bornmuelleri is similar to *O. fuciflora* with green petals and minute petals, large protuberance, and whitish humps. ❧ Rhodes only.   **436**

O. fusca. 10–25 cm. tall. Sepals broad, green, pointed, often incurving; petals smaller, strap-shaped, yellowish-green. Lip long, indented at apex, dark brown to black, with oblong bluish 'eye' patches, and wide flattish side lobes. Three distinct sub-species exist:

Ssp. fusca: Lip 11–15 mm. long, often with narrow yellow or greenish margin. ❧ Feb.–May.   **439**

Ssp. iricolor: Lip up to 23 mm. long widening at apex, with very large blue patch; petals often reddish; few-flowered. ❧ Feb.–April.   **440**

Ssp. omegaifera: Lip around 15 mm. long, usually broad and rounded, with rounded hairy side lobes, and a large blue or brown shiny patch, above a yellow or whitish W-shaped band. ❧ Crete and Rhodes only. Jan.–March.   **441**

O. lutea. 10–15 cm. tall. Sepals broad, green, pointed, upper hooded; petals smaller, strap-shaped, green to yellow. Lip oblong, with marked side lobes and broad terminal lobe, with wide yellow margin around a brown central area with oval bluish 'eyes'. Lip oblong to round, with broad flat 'flange' partly formed by side lobes, resulting in deep side notches near apex, and with a central notch also. *Var. lutea* has 12–18 mm. lip and flange of pure yellow around a brown central area with oval bluish 'eyes'; *var. minor* has a wider, reddish central area forming an inverted V at the apex. ❧ March–April.   **442, 443**

O. reinholdii. 20–40 cm. tall. Sepals broad, triangular, pink tinged green, with central green line. Petals triangular, reddish. Lip 11–15 mm. long, pear-shaped, very deep at apex, with prominent protuberance and large, hairy, arm-like side lobes. Colour deep purple with strong white pattern, like a horseshoe but extended sideways at top, or reduced to two vertical lines. ❧ Peloponnese, Corfu, Ionic Islands. March–May.   **454**

O. scolopax. WOODCOCK ORCHID. 8–35 cm. tall, usually with many flowers. A variable plant with several ssp., but the rotund 9–15 mm. lip, ovoid to almost oblong in outline, with projecting side lobes and forward-pointing protuberance, is characteristic. It is brown or reddish-brown with a more or less complex pattern of lines and circles in white or yellow, sometimes with a small blue central patch. ✤ March–May.

Ssp. attica: Sepals and petals green. Lip lobes short, triangular; pattern tending to be in circles. (Sometimes regarded as a distinct sp.) **445**

Ssp. cornuta. Unmistakable with the forward-pointing lip lobes horn-like, up to 1 cm. long. **446**

Ssp. heldreichii. Sepals pale pink to dark red; petals reddish. Lip lobes short, pointed. Pattern often a simple X shape. (This ssp. replaces *ssp. scolopax* from the W. Mediterranean in Greece. They are almost indistinguishable.) **494**

O. speculum. MIRROR ORCHID, MIRROR-OF-VENUS. 10–25 cm. tall. Sepals narrow, green, maroon-striped, the upper hooded; petals very small, maroon. Lip 15–18 mm. long, pear-shaped, with broad strap-shaped side lobes; centre forming a large reflective blue patch, surrounded by a thick fringe of dark red or blackish hairs. ✤ March–April. **448**

Var. regis-ferdinandi-coburgi is similar but smaller, the lip narrow and almost oblong, strongly resembling a blue-bottle. ✤ Rhodes only. March–April. **449**

O. sphegodes (or *O. sphecodes*) (*O. aranifera*). EARLY SPIDER ORCHID. A very variable plant 15–60 cm. tall. The petals are usually $\frac{2}{3}$ to $\frac{3}{4}$ length of sepals, and the rich brown lip is almost always patterned, the typical marking being a bluish H with the bar near the top and sometimes another bar below; this may be reduced to 2 vertical lines, or is sometimes X-shaped.

The Greek sub-species are as follows: all flower February–April depending on altitude. Sub-species *mammosa* and *spruneri* appear to grade into each other and two such forms, with flattened, flange-like side lobes, are illustrated as nos. **453** and **454**.

Ssp. aesculapii. Sepals green, slightly drooping; petals green, strap-shaped, waved. Lip 9–11 mm. long, almost round, with large well-defined marking and a border of greenish-yellow; humps very small. ✤ Mainland and Crete. **456**

Ssp. mammosa. Sepals usually green, sometimes lower pair partly red, drooping; petals green or reddish, narrow or triangular, often waved. Lip 13–18 mm. long, round to oblong; marking usually H-shaped, or 2 parallel bars; lobes typically large projecting humps near top of lip. ✤ Mainland and Crete. **450, 451**

Ssp. helenae is virtually the same with no lip markings. ✤ Corfu, possibly N. mainland. **452**

Ssp. sphegodes. Sepals green, rather long and narrow; petals green or reddish, strap-shaped, sometimes waved. Lip 10–12 mm. long, rounded; marking often X-shaped; side lobes usually reduced to tiny humps, markedly hairy. ✤ N. Greece.

Ssp. spruneri. Sepals pink, or bi-coloured green above and pink below, drooping; petals pale pink, about half as long. Lip 15 mm. long, rounded, with strong H-shaped pattern; lobes large, rounded, at sides of lip, very hairy. ✤ S. Greece, Crete. **455**

O. tenthredinifera. SAWFLY ORCHID. 10–30 cm. tall. A showy plant with sepals very broad, rounded, bright pink with green line; petals small, triangular, pink. Lip 16–20 mm. long, squarish with rounded humps; apex with rounded lobes and central protuberance; very hairy, yellow to greenish with central red-brown area and a small white-edged blue pattern in centre. ✤ Feb.–May. **458**

BARLIA. *B. robertiana* (*Himantoglossum longibracteatum*, *Loroglossum longibracteatum*). GIANT ORCHID. A stout plant with 2 cm. thick, 30–50 cm. flower stem. Leaves large, glossy, narrow-oval. Flowers densely packed in a spike up to 23 cm. long with narrow bracts longer than the flowers. Upper flower segments short and slightly incurving; outer sepals erect, reddish-violet. Lip 15 mm. long, 3-lobed, the central lobe itself divided, and entirely wavy-edged; spur short, conical, down-pointing. Colour greenish, reddish-violet, or purplish; flowers often fragrant. ❧ Grass, dry bushy places; Feb.–April. **430, 431**

LOROGLOSSUM. *L. hircinum (Himantoglossum hircinum).* LIZARD ORCHID. A stout plant to 20–40 cm. or more, with large unspotted leaves and 10–25 cm. spike of numerous flowers, greenish and purple-spotted except for the very long, wavy lip which is whitish and lightly spotted. Flowers with distinct odour of goat. The species has a 4 mm. spur; the form usually seen in Greece is *ssp. caprinum* with 12 mm. spur. ❧ Mountains of N. Greece. May–July. **429**

ORCHIS

Both sepals and petals joined into a tight hood

O. coriophora ssp. fragrans. A vanilla-scented form of the unpleasant-smelling species, the Bug Orchid (which only just enters N. Greece). A slender 20–40 cm. plant with long narrow pointed leaves and a narrow flower spike with 1 cm. bracts. The 15–20 mm. flowers have a pointed hood, brown-purple with green streaks, and purple or pink lip, often greenish in the centre. In profile the flowers look like thin-beaked birds. Lip 3-lobed, with slightly waved side lobes, and short, down-arching spur. ❧ Grassy, sometimes marshy places. April–June. **467**

O. sancta, the HOLY ORCHID, is similar to *O. coriophora* and sometimes considered a ssp., but distinctive with much larger (20 mm.) flowers, pinkish-red, the lower lip lobe being divided into several long, narrow teeth. ❧ Sandy and grassy places. Aegean Islands, Rhodes. April. **468**

O. italica (O. longicruris). A stout plant 20–60 cm. tall, with a rosette of long, narrow, wavy-edged leaves, sometimes spotted. The 20 mm. flowers are packed into a dense ovoid head and resemble little men with a narrow striped hood and long narrow lip, pale pink with darker spots, bearing 2 very thin arm-like upper lobes and a lower lobe divided into two long, thin, pointed 'legs'. Spur short, narrow, down-pointing. ❧ Grassy and stony places. March–May. **459**

O. papilionacea. PINK BUTTERFLY ORCHID. 10–30 cm. tall, with 3–10 flowers in a loose spike with large pinkish bracts. Flower segments forming a loose hood; lip very large, fan-shaped and wavy-edged, with deeper coloured lines on white or pink background. Spur a narrow cone, shorter than the ovary, usually down-pointing. A variation with pale lip 25 mm. wide and deep from Crete has been named *forma grandiflora.* ❧ Dry, sunny places, in grass or near shrubs. March–May. **463, 464**

O. purpurea. LADY ORCHID. A stout orchid 20–40 cm. tall or sometimes much more, with a dense many-flowered spike, the bracts very small. Leaves large and wide, markedly shining. Flowers about 20 mm. long, variable, with large, roughly triangular lip, the side lobes broad and arm-like, almost as long as the central one, expanding like a flat 'skirt', slightly divided by a central notch, and frilly at the lower edge. Flowers almost black in bud; hood dark red-purple, lip whitish, mauve, flushed, covered with purple tufts. ❧ Woodland, dry grassy hillsides. April–May. N. Greece. **460**

O. simia. MONKEY ORCHID. 20–50 cm. tall, with oval-oblong to lance-shaped leaves. The 20–25 mm. flowers are packed into an egg-shaped head. Each flower indeed resembles a little monkey with a rounded hood for head, and strap-shaped lobes for arms and legs. The hood is silvery pink, the lip whitish, and the lobes dark red. The upward-curling lobes are blunt-ended in distinction to *O. italica* where they are pointed. Spur short, swollen, down-pointing. ❧ Dry, grassy places, scrub, under trees. March–June. **462**

O. tridentata (O. commutata). A variable plant, 15–40 cm. tall, with bluish, strap-shaped leaves, the upper ones stem-clasping. The 10–15 mm. flowers are tightly packed into a rounded head, with small papery bracts. The small hood has long points; the lip is strongly 3-lobed, the central lobe usually divided into two and toothed along its lower edge. The cylindrical spur as long as the ovary is down-pointing. The fragrant flowers vary from red to pink, lilac and violet, or white; The hood is streaked with darker lines and the lip usually speckled in pink or purple. ⚘ Grassy places, scrub. April–May. **470**

O. lactea (O. acuminata) is related to *O. tridentata* and is sometimes considered a ssp. It is a smaller plant with white or pale pink flowers in which the hood segments produce long whiskery points. ⚘ March–April. **471**

Other orchids of this group occasionally found in Greece are *O. militaris*, the Military Orchid (in the N.), and *O. morio*, the Green-Winged Orchid.

Sepals spreading; petals joined to form a 'peak'; flowers pink or red

O. anatolica. ANATOLIAN ORCHID. A slender plant not usually exceeding 25 cm., with 5–8 flowers in loose spike, and oblong to lance-shaped leaves. Flowers 20 mm. long, rosy purple, with white patch on long 3-lobed lip; distinguished by the very long thin spur, more or less horizontal, which is much longer than the ovary. ⚘ Grassy and stony places. Cyclades and Aegean Islands. March–April. **465**

O. collina (O. saccata). A robust but short plant, not exceeding 20 cm., with broad, deep green, often spotted leaves, the upper ones stem-clasping. Flowers 3–18, 15–20 mm. long, the lateral sepals erect and ear-like, with a large undivided wavy-edged lip, usually broader at the apex than the base. Flowers purplish-red, lip paler than the rest; spur short, broadly conical, down-pointing. ⚘ Dry grassy places. Mainland, Crete, Rhodes. Feb.–April. **466**

O. laxiflora. LOOSE-FLOWERED ORCHID. An orchid of 30–60 cm., exceptionally to 1 m. tall, with long, narrow, keeled, erect leaves, glossy above, bluish below. 6–20 flowers, 15–20 mm. long, are carried in a long thin spike. The side petals are held outwards, the top sepal arching over the forward-pointing petals; the lip is roundish, the sides folded back, wavy-edged, slightly 3-lobed, the centre lobe shorter than the others. Spur long, tubular, blunt-ended. Flowers usually rich red or violet-red. ⚘ Damp meadows, marshes. March–June. **469**

🌿 *O. palustris* is very similar to *O. laxiflora* and often grows in the same places. The lip is not folded at the sides until the flowers begin to fade; it is more definitely 3-lobed and the central lobe is longer than the side ones. The colour is more often magenta, with a white central area marked in purple.

O. quadripunctata. FOUR-SPOTTED ORCHID. A slender plant 15–25 cm. tall with a usually loose spike of 8–25 smallish flowers, and small, narrow leaves. The squarish lip is 3-lobed. The spur very long, thin, down pointing. Colour pink, lip white-centred, with 2, 4, or more small purple spots. ⚘ Stony hillsides. April–May. **461**

Other orchids in this group occasionally found in Greece include *O. mascula*, the Early Purple, *O. patens* (in Crete), and *O. spitzelii*.

Flowers usually yellow

O. pallens. 20–40 cm. tall, with up to 15 flowers in a dense spike; leaves thick, shining, broad in relation to length, forming an erect rosette. Flowers 20 mm. long, pale yellow or cream, the lip deeper yellow with light brown spotting; lip deeply 3-lobed, spur as long as ovary, cylindrical, strongly upturned, often kinked. ⚘ Mountain meadows and light woodland, often in large colonies. May–June. **473**

O. provincialis. PROVENCE ORCHID. Usually 10–20 cm. tall, rarely up to 40 cm., with up to 14 flowers in a loose spike. Leaves bluish, usually purple-spotted, narrow, pointed. Flowers 18–20 mm. long, cream to pale yellow, with light purple spots on lip, faintly scented; lip with three lobes, often frilled at the edge. Spur thick, cylindrical, swollen at the end, and curving upwards. **474**

Ssp. pauciflora (sometimes considered a distinct species), is more robust, with leaves usually unspotted, and up to 8 flowers of deep yellow, orange in the centre with small brown spots. **475**

⚘ Woods, thickets, in grass. April–June.

DACTYLORHIZA. *D. romana.* A stout plant 15–35 cm. tall with long narrow spreading leaves and a long loose spike of many flowers, and large erect bracts. Sepals erect; petals pointing forwards and touching. Lip oblong or widening towards rounded apex, 3-lobed, the centre lobe largest. Spur as long as ovary, cylindrical, usually curving upwards, even vertically. Colour either yellow to cream, or in pink, violet, carmine range. ⚘ Rocky or sandy places, sometimes in scree. March–May. **472, 476**

D. sambucina resembles *D. romana* but has a down-pointing spur. It may also be yellow or red. Typically a mountain orchid.

D. iberica may also be found occasionally in subalpine areas: it is white flushed pink, with violet markings, the 3-lobed lip being very narrow at the base under the hood made by the upper segments, and widening abruptly.

ANACAMPTIS. *A. pyramidalis.*
PYRAMIDAL ORCHID. A slender 20–50 cm. plant, with long, narrow, pointed, keeled leaves. Flower head conical, often expanding to an oblong, very densely packed with the 12 mm. pink flowers which conceal the small bracts. Side sepals outspread; centre sepal and petals forming a loose hood. Lip of 3 nearly equal strap-shaped lobes; spur very thin, long, down-pointing. *Ssp. brachystachys* is commoner in Greece than the species; it is smaller, with rounded flower head and paler pink flowers. ⚘ Dry meadows, waste ground, sometimes on sand dunes. March–July. **428**

SERAPIAS.
This group of orchids is variable and the species often seem to grade into each other. The descriptions below have therefore been arranged in approximate order of lip size.

The lip has two lower sections, the epichile or apical (lower) end, and the hypochile or upper part. The proportions of these may assist in identification. Humps or ridges occur at the base of the lip; all species have two except *S. lingua*, which has one. The side lip lobes are usually concealed in the hood formed by the other segments.

S. parviflora (*S. occultata*). Lip 15–18 mm. long. A plant seldom over 20 cm. tall, with narrow leaves, slightly wavy. Flowers 3–8. Bracts as long as flowers, red, purple-striped. Hood greenish-red.

Epichile about as long as hypochile; lip narrowly triangular, rusty red, often pointing back towards stem, hairy in throat; side lobes partly hidden, with parallel humps in the throat. The *ssp. laxiflora* is sometimes treated as distinct, with lip up to 20 mm. long. ⚘ Grassy, stony, or sandy places, usually by coast. March–June. **477, 478**

S. lingua. TONGUE ORCHID. Lip 25–30 mm. long. Slender, 10–25 cm. tall, with narrow, channelled leaves, bending outwards. Stem with 2–9 flowers, distinctive because upper part of flower is roughly horizontal and lip projects vertically. Bracts as long as flowers, greenish-red to violet. Hood flesh-pink to violet, often green or purple-striped. Lip widening slightly below hood, varying from very pale to deep pink, red, or violet, occasionally yellowish, not hairy. Side lobes deep purple, partly concealed; one large blackish lump in throat, sometimes grooved. ⚘ Damp grassy and sandy places, marshes, scrub, open woods. March–June. **479**

Dioscorides' remarks have an unwonted touch about them in his description of the 'flowers like little hats, in fashion like to Comical Persons gaping'.

S. vomeracea (*S. pseudocordigera*). PLOUGHSHARE ORCHID. Distinctly variable. Lip around 35 mm. long. Often quite tall, 10–50 cm., with narrow, channelled leaves bending outwards. 4–10 flowers on stem; bracts longer, of similar colouring. Hood pale or silvery red with darker veins. Epichile much longer than hypochile; lip broadly triangular, not or very slightly widening below hood (*vomeracea* means like a ploughshare), brick-red to reddish-brown; hairy in throat and less markedly so on lip. Side lobes hidden; throat with two ridge-like humps. ⚘ Scrub, damp grass, marshy land. April–June. **480**

S. neglecta. Lip 30–40 mm. long. 10–20 cm. tall, with narrow, channelled leaves. 2–8 flowers in compact spike; bracts heart-shaped, shorter than flowers, greenish-red, never spotted. Hood silvery-red, darker striped. Epichile as broad as hypochile, with marked constriction between; lip very broad in relation to length, pale clear red or purplish, yellowish in centre, lightly hairy. Side lobes partly hidden; two parallel humps in throat. The Greek plant is *ssp. ionica*. ⚘ Dry places, scrub, near the sea. Corfu and Ionian Islands. **481**

S. orientalis. Lip 30–40 mm. long. Similar to *S. neglecta* but side lobes not projecting beyond hood, and lip colouring yellow to reddish-buff; side lobes dark red. ⚘ Dry places, scrub, near the sea. S. Greece and islands. March–April. **482**

S. cordigera. Lip usually 35–40 mm. long, sometimes shorter. 15–50 cm.

tall, leaves narrow, channelled, arching inwards, spotted near the base. 3–10 flowers on stem reddish near the top; bracts shorter than flowers, reddish to silvery. Hood reddish-violet to wine-red, or silvery. Epichile heart-shaped, merging with little constriction into equally broad hypochile; lip very broad, widening immediately below hood, and flared towards pointed apex, dark red or blackish-purple. Side lobes partly hidden; two blackish, diverging humps in throat. ⚘ Meadow, and sandy places in heaths and open woods. March–May. **483**

INDEX

In this index to the descriptive text, entries in small capitals are to families and genera, and the remainder to species, except those in italics which are Latin synonyms or English names.

The bold italic numerals refer to the illustrations (numbers 1 to 483 in colour, numbers 484 to 514 the line drawings on pages 59 to 63, and numbers 515 to 560 the line drawings in the text); the other numerals refer to the text pages.

169

171

174

176

SOME GREEK PLANT NAMES

Acacia Akakía
Agave americana Athánatos
Anchusa hybrida Voidóglossa
Anemone Agriopaparoúna, Anémoni
Arbutus Koumariá, Lagomiliá
Arisarum vulgare Lýchnos, Lychnaráki
Asphodeline liburnica Peridromóchorto
Asparagus Asparangiá, Spharangiá
Asphodelus Asphedeliá, Asphendyliá, Spherdoúkla
Ballota acetabulosa Loumínia
Calicotome Aspálatos, Sphálaktro
Capparis spinosa Káppari
Centaurea Asprangáthi
Ceratonia siliqua Kharoupiá, Xylokeratiá
Cercis siliquastrum Koutsoukiá, Koutsoupiá
Chrysanthemum Agriomantilída, Mandilída
Cichorium intybus Radíki
Cistus Angíssaros, Kounoúkla, Ladaniá
Citrus limon (lemon) Lemoniá
Citrus nobilis (mandarin) Mantariniá
Citrus sinensis (orange) Portokaliá
Clematis cirrhosa Perikokláda
Clematis flammula Pordalás
Colutea arborescens Agriosinamikó, Phouská
Convolvulus althaeoides Chonáki, Foustanáki
Corydalis Chionístra
Crepis rubra Starídha
Crocus Crócos, Krináki
Crocus cartwrightianus Zaphorá
Cupressus Kyparíssi
Cyclamen Choirópsomo, Cyclamiá, Cyclámino, Triklamiá

Dracunculus vulgaris Drakontiá, Pheidóchorto
Ecballium elaterium Agriangouriá, Pikrangouriá
Echinops Kephalangáthi
Echium plantagineum Voudóglosson, Voúglosson
Erica Eríki, Ríki, Richiá
Eriobotrya japonica Meskouliá, Mousmouliá
Eruca vesicaria Azoúmata, Róka
Euphorbia acanthothamnos Hippopheous (anc.)
Euphorbia myrsinites Galatsída
Euphorbia sibthorpii Phlómos
Ficus carica Fíkos
Gladiolus Maïs, Spathóhorto
Gynandriris Agriókrinos, Vourlítis, Vroúla
Helichrysum Amáranto
Hermodactylus tuberosus Agriókrinos
Hyoscyamus Discýamo, Gérontas
Hypericum empetrifolium Agoúthanos
Inula viscosa Konýza, Psyllíthra
Iris Agriókrinos, Krínakia
Iris cretensis also Máza, Nevrída
Juniperus Ágriokyparissi, Kédro
Laurus nobilis Dáphni, Vaïá
Lavandula Levánta, Livanáki, Sindóni
Leontice leontopetalum Pordalás
Linum Agriolínaro, Linári
Lonicera Agrióklimon, Hagióklima
Lupinus Loupinári, Loúpino
Mandragora officinarum Mandragóras, Mandragoúda
Matthiola Agrióvioletta, Violétta
Medicago arborea Évenos
Muscari Bolbós, Bulbós, Voirós
Myrtus communis Myrtiá, Smirtiá
Narcissus Manousáki, Zambáki

179

Nerium oleander Pikrodáphne, Rhododáphne
Notobasis syriaca Gaidourángathos
Olea europea Eliá
Opuntia Fragosykiá
Orchis Salépi, Sernikovótano
Orobanche Liýkos
Paliurus spina-christi Palioúri
Pallenis spinosa Astrátegos, Stavrángathos
Pancratium maritimum Krínos tis thálassas
Papaver Koutsounáda, Paparoúna
Phlomis Alisphakiá, Aspháka, Spháka
Pinus Pévko
Pistacia lentiscus Mastichiá, Skínos, Skinári
Pistacia terebinthus Kokkorevithiá
Platanus orientalis Plátanos
Prunus dulcis Amygdaliá
Psoralea bituminosa Kalosýki, Vromóchorto
Punica granatum Rodiá, Roïdiá
Quercus coccifera Pournári, Prinári, Prinós
Romulea Kátsa
Ruta chalepensis Apíganos

Salvia Alisphakiá, Faskomeló, Faskomiliá
Sarcopoterium spinosum Aphána, Astívi, Stivída
Satureia thymbra Throúmbi
Scolymus Asprágatho, Skólymvros
Scorzonera lanata Stoumbíl
Serapias Glossári
Smilax aspera Arkoudóvatos, Arkóvatos
Spartium junceum Spárto
Styrax officinalis Astýrakas, Lagomiliá, Stourakiá
Teucrium polium Lagokimithiá, Panayóchorto
Thymelaea hirsuta Phinokaliá, Therókalo
Thymelaea tartonraira Kolophoúsa
Thymus Thymári
Tragopogon Lagóhorto, Pigounítis
Urginea maritima Askillitoúra, Skyllokrómmyda
Verbascum Phlómos
Vinca Agriolíza
Vitex agnus-castus Alygaría, Lygariá
Vitis vinifera Ampéli
Zizyphus jujuba Tjtjifiá